PRESENTING DIFFICULT PASTS THROUGH ARCHITECTURE

Architectural design can play a role in helping make the past present in meaningful ways when applied to preexisting buildings and places that carry notable and troubling pasts. In this comparative analysis, Rumiko Handa establishes the critical role architectural designs play in presenting difficult pasts by examining documentation centers on National Socialism in Germany.

Presenting Difficult Pasts Through Architecture analyzes four centers – Cologne, Nuremberg, Berlin, and Munich – from the point of view of their shared intent to make the past present at National Socialists' perpetrator sites. Applying original frameworks, Handa considers what more architectural design could do toward meaningful representations and interpretations of difficult pasts.

This book is a must-read for students, practitioners, and academics interested in how architectural design can participate in presenting the difficult pasts of historical places in meaningful ways.

Rumiko Handa is Professor of Architecture at the University of Nebraska-Lincoln, USA. She holds a PhD in architectural theory from the University of Pennsylvania and a BArch from the University of Tokyo, Japan. Her writings have appeared in: *Montreal Architecture Review*; *Interiors: Design, Architecture, Culture*; *The Journal of the Society of Architectural Historians*; *Preservation Education & Research*; *Design Studies*; and so on. She co-edited *Conjuring the Real: The Role of Architecture in Eighteenth- and Nineteenth-Century Fiction*. She is also the author of *Allure of the Incomplete, Imperfect, and Impermanent*.

PRESENTING DIFFICULT PASTS THROUGH ARCHITECTURE

Converting National Socialist Sites to Documentation Centers

Rumiko Handa

LONDON AND NEW YORK

First published 2021
by Routledge
2 Park Square, Milton Park, Abingdon, Oxon OX14 4RN

and by Routledge
52 Vanderbilt Avenue, New York, NY 10017

Routledge is an imprint of the Taylor & Francis Group, an informa business

© 2021 Rumiko Handa

The right of Rumiko Handa to be identified as author of this work has
been asserted by her in accordance with sections 77 and 78 of the Copyright,
Designs and Patents Act 1988.

All rights reserved. No part of this book may be reprinted or reproduced or utilised
in any form or by any electronic, mechanical, or other means, now known or
hereafter invented, including photocopying and recording, or in any information
storage or retrieval system, without permission in writing from the publishers.

Trademark notice: Product or corporate names may be trademarks or registered trademarks,
and are used only for identification and explanation without intent to infringe.

British Library Cataloguing-in-Publication Data
A catalogue record for this book is available from the British Library

Library of Congress Cataloging-in-Publication Data
A catalog record has been requested for this book

ISBN: 978-0-367-21761-7 (hbk)
ISBN: 978-0-367-21762-4 (pbk)
ISBN: 978-0-429-26589-1 (ebk)

Typeset in Bembo
by Newgen Publishing UK

CONTENTS

List of Figures	*vi*
Acknowledgments	*x*
Introduction	1
1 Postwar Rebuilding and Coping with the Past	10
2 Four Documentation Centers – Histories	39
3 In the Shadow of Propaganda Architecture	68
4 Presenting Pasts through Architecture – Intellectual Framework	80
5 Formal Characteristics	92
6 Physical Traces	128
7 Designation	149
8 Memento	174
Conclusion	194
Bibliography	*195*
Index	*207*

FIGURES

1.1	Königsplatz, Munich. November, 1936. Looking west through Brienner Straße	13
1.2	Führerbau, Munich. The blank wall above one of the entrances	14
1.3	Führerbau, Munich. The ceiling over one of the entrance porticos	15
1.4	Führerbau, Munich. Looking over the main stairwell toward the former office of the Führer, presently "Room 105"	16
1.5	Führerbau, Munich. Outside of the former office of the Führer, presently "Room 105"	17
1.6	Zeppelin Grandstand, Nuremberg	19
1.7	Aviation Ministry Building, Berlin. Window motif	20
1.8	Aviation Ministry Building, Berlin. Socialist mural, installed in 1953	21
1.9	Aviation Ministry Building, Berlin. Memorial for the 1953 Uprising	22
1.10	Dürer House, Nuremberg. 1930	26
1.11	Dürer House, Nuremberg. 1944	26
1.12	Dürer House, Nuremberg. 1971	27
1.13	Dürer House, Nuremberg. Present	27
1.14	Kaiser Wilhelm Memorial Church, Berlin	29
1.15	Alte Pinakothek, Munich. South façade	32
1.16	Alte Pinakothek, Munich. South façade detail	33
1.17	Kolumba, Cologne	35
2.1	Documentation Center, Cologne. Present	40
2.2	EL-DE House, Cologne. In the National Socialist newspaper *Westdeutscher Beobachter*, December 5, 1934	41
2.3	Documentation Center, Nuremberg. The space intended for the main auditorium of the Congress Hall	47

2.4	Documentation Center, Nuremberg.	51
2.5	Documentation Center, Berlin	53
2.6	Prinz-Albrecht-Straße, Berlin. 1933	54
2.7	Documentation Center, Berlin. In its context, looking west	55
2.8	Documentation Center, Munich	60
2.9	Brown House, Munich. 1930	61
5.1	Documentation Center, Cologne. Proposed Appelhofplatz elevation, not executed	96
5.2	Documentation Center, Cologne. Proposed floor plans, not executed	98
5.3	Documentation Center, Cologne. Drainpipe on Elisenstraße façade	99
5.4	Documentation Center, Nuremberg. Insertion of new elements	101
5.5	Office of Günther Domenig, detail drawing for the Documentation Center, Nuremberg	102
5.6	Documentation Center, Nuremberg. Floor and wall joint detail	103
5.7	Documentation Center, Berlin. Ground cover	106
5.8	Documentation Center, Berlin. View of the entrance	106
5.9	Documentation Center, Munich. Ground surface	108
5.10	Documentation Center, Cologne. Proposal for exhibition panels, not executed	110
5.11	Documentation Center, Cologne. Chronological timeline on the floor	113
5.12	Documentation Center, Nuremberg. Model	114
5.13	Documentation Center, Nuremberg. The Insertion of the "*Pfahl*"	115
5.14	Documentation Center, Nuremberg. Balcony at the end of the "*Pfahl*"	116
5.15	Documentation Center, Munich, and Führerbau	118
5.16	Documentation Center, Munich. Expansion joint	119
5.17	Documentation Center, Cologne. New openings	121
5.18	Documentation Center, Munich. View out to Führerbau	124
6.1	Documentation Center, Cologne. Stained floor and walls	131
6.2	Documentation Center, Berlin. Basement walls of the buildings along Niederkirchnerstraße	133
6.3	Documentation Center, Berlin. Segments of building foundations exposed on the ground surface, along Wilhelmstraße	134
6.4	Documentation Center, Berlin. Wartime trench	135
6.5	Documentation Center, Berlin. Excavated kitchen celler	136
6.6	Documentation Center, Berlin. Prison cells, covered and turned into a memorial for the victims	137
6.7	Documentation Center, Berlin. The Berlin Wall	140
6.8	Documentation Center, Berlin. Commemoration of the Active Museum of Fascism and Resistance	141

viii Figures

6.9	Documentation Center, Berlin. Remains and commemoration of Peter Zumthor's building	142
6.10	Documentation Center, Nuremberg. The circular saw used to cut the preexisting brick and stone walls	144
6.11	Documentation Center, Nuremberg. Traces of the circular saw	145
7.1	Documentation Center, Cologne. Sign post on sidewalk	156
7.2	Documentation Center, Cologne. Letters EL DE on the glass over the entrance door	157
7.3	Documentation Center, Cologne. Poster of the temporary exhibit	158
7.4	Documentation Center, Cologne. Stumbling stones	159
7.5	Documentation Center, Nuremberg. Sign post	160
7.6	Documentation Center, Nuremberg. Exhibition panels	161
7.7	Documentation Center, Nuremberg. Large stone blocks	162
7.8	Documentation Center, Nuremberg. Tram and bus stop in front of the center	163
7.9	Documentation Center, Berlin. Sign post for the Berlin Wall memorial	165
7.10	Documentation Center, Berlin. Sign post with basic visitor information	166
7.11	Documentation Center, Berlin. Sign post on the content of exhibitions	167
7.12	Documentation Center, Berlin. Institutional name on the building	168
7.13	Documentation Center, Munich. Sign post on the sidewalk	169
7.14	Documentation Center, Munich. Sign post in the center forecourt	170
7.15	Documentation Center, Munich. Institutional name and its exhibitions, on the surface of the building	171
7.16	Documentation Center, Munich. Art installation, "Brienner 45"	172
8.1	Documentation Center, Cologne. Large photograph looking northward on Appelhofplatz	177
8.2	Documentation Center, Nuremberg. Large photograph of Hitler ascending steps	178
8.3	Documentation Center, Cologne. Entrance	182
8.4	Documentation Center, Cologne. Limited view out	183
8.5	Documentation Center, Nuremberg. View out to the unfinished assembly hall	185
8.6	Documentation Center, Munich. View from the gallery on 1933–39 to Führerbau	186
8.7	Documentation Center, Munich. View from the gallery on after 1945 to Führerbau	187
8.8	Documentation Center, Berlin. View of the former Aviation Ministry building	188

8.9	Documentation Center, Berlin. Benches along the east-facing glass wall	189
8.10	The former Congress Hall, Nuremberg, interior. Photograph provided by the Nuremberg City Museums at the time of the competition, 1998, taken in 1997	190
8.11	Documentation Center, Nuremberg. Large photograph hidden in the alcove	191
8.12	Wannsee Station, Berlin	192

ACKNOWLEDGMENTS

I have many individuals and institutions to thank, without whose help I could not have come to this point.

I would like to thank the four documentation centers that feature in this book, as well as their staff members and librarians. Among them, I would like to send special thanks to Ulrich Tempel of Topography of Terror Foundation, who on a number of occasions pointed me to relevant materials of which I was previously unaware. I also extend my gratitude to the architects and their collaborators who designed the centers and who allowed me to examine architectural drawings, competition documents, and newspaper clippings. Gerd Fleischmann kindly accepted my request for an interview, and Bettina Georg and Simon Wetzel of Büro Georg Scheel Wetzel, and Edzard Schultz of Heinle Wischer Architekten allowed me to visit their offices to review their collections of related documents. Among architectural archives, thank you also to Yorck Förster of Deutsche Architecturmuseum in Frankfurt for showing me the design proposal booklet by Peter Kulka. I send much gratitude to Christoph Freyer of Architekturzentrum Wien who, while working at the Zentrum's remote warehouse, allowed me to go through documentation center materials among what would eventually become the Domenig collection.

I would like to thank two universities. The University of Nebraska–Lincoln granted me one semester of faculty developmental leave to focus on this project. At the College of Architecture, I received financial support from Scott Killinger Funds. And a number of graduate and undergraduate research assistants worked on this project. Leibniz University in Hannover allowed me in as a visiting scholar over two summers. I am very much grateful to Markus Jager, who hosted me on both occasions, including me on lunch conversations and field trips with his students.

I also thank the organizers of the following academic conferences for providing me with the opportunities to share my ideas: Atmosphere conference at the University of Manitoba; Association of Collegiate Schools of Architecture; International Association for the Study of Traditional Environments; Architecture Culture Spirituality Forum; and the Aesthetics and Ethics of Imperfection Symposium.

Last, but not least, love you always, my daughters Maya and Ami. Maya was with me in Nuremberg when this project got started in my head, and Ami, who works at a history museum, gives me things I need to think about. The two of them cheered me on in many different ways through the process.

INTRODUCTION

This study deals with the question of how architectural design, when applied to historical places, can assist in bringing an extremely difficult – notable and troubling – past to the present in meaningful ways. In particular, it examines postwar architectural designs that converted National Socialist perpetrators' places into documentation centers on National Socialism whose explicit purpose is, above all, to present and discuss the community's involvement in the National Socialist ideology and actions.

Although the cases I have selected for close study vary stylistically and in many other ways, these centers have a number of common attributes that make the comparison valid. First and foremost, they not only exhibit the history of National Socialist operations but also deal specifically with the themes of the city's and its citizens' involvements in the movement and regime. Second, they are authentic sites, being located at historical places where National Socialist operations actually took place. Third, they were the perpetrators', as opposed to the victims', places. Fourth, they are in a city, which makes them part of everyday life for many. Because they shared these conditions, the selected centers faced the same set of challenges: how to make present the history of National Socialism and the community's involvement as its agents, corroborators, or bystanders in an authentic perpetrators' place, where evil deeds were conceived, but in a place that also had a prior history of peace and is now part of people's everyday life.

In all of Germany, four centers exist, which satisfy all the criteria above. They are, in chronological order of their opening, in Cologne, Nuremberg, Berlin, and Munich. NS Documentation Center of the city of Cologne, opened on June 17, 1997, occupies the majority of the building that was used as the Gestapo regional headquarters, and features a permanent exhibition on the history of the city during the National Socialist regime.[1] The task of designing the conversion was commissioned to Peter Kulka, an architect and professor based in Cologne, and Gerd Fleichmann, a typography and exhibition designer. Later, in 2009–2010, Konstantin Pichler, who assisted Kulka in

2 Introduction

the 1997 design, collaborated again with Fleichmann to expand the space the center occupies in the building and installed a number of media stations throughout the exhibit. Documentation Center Nazi Party Rally Grounds in Nuremberg, opened on November 4, 2001, is housed in a portion of the building intended as a congress hall but which was still under construction at the end of the war, and allocates 1,300 m² for the permanent exhibition, titled "Fascination and Terror," on the causes, connections, and consequences of the National Socialist tyranny.[2] The center building is the result of an international invitational competition held in 1998. Peter Kulka, mentioned above, was among those invited. The winner was Günther Domenig (d. 2012), an architect and professor from Graz, Austria. Gerhard Wallner from his office assisted Domenig in developing the design and supervising the construction. Topography of Terror Documentation Center, Berlin, which opened on May 6, 2010, occupies the majority of a large city block where a number of buildings that housed Gestapo and SS headquarters had stood but which were demolished after the war. It offers three distinct areas of exhibits: The first is inside the newly constructed center building, which holds a permanent exhibit titled "Topography of Terror: Gestapo, SS and Reich Security Main Office on Wilhelm- and Prinz-Albrecht-Straße," as well as a changing exhibit;[3] the second is the exterior gallery in the excavated area along the frontal street; and the third is composed of 15 stations scattered throughout the site and threaded by the route of a self-guided tour, titled "Topography of Terror," which covers the history of each historical building whose physical remains are visible.[4] The center design was won in an open international two-stage competition whose result was announced in January 2006. The winner was the team of Ursula Wilms, an architect associated with the Heinle Wischer und Partner in Berlin, and Heinz W. Hallmann, a landscape architect and professor from Aachen.[5] And NS Documentation Center Munich, which opened on May 1, 2015, is a brand-new building on the former site of the so-called Brown House that housed Hitler's office at one time. It devotes 1,000 m² to the permanent exhibition, titled "Munich and National Socialism," which examines the topics of the origins and rise of National Socialism in Munich, the special role of the city in the terror system of the dictatorship, and the difficult process of coming to terms with the past since 1945.[6] The center is housed in a building designed by Büro Georg Scheel Wetzel Architekten, based in Berlin, who won the two-stage open international competition in 2009.

Before we go any further, I need to explain what I mean by "National Socialist perpetrators' places" that were converted to "documentation centers on National Socialism." And to do so, we need, first, to distinguish them from those places that deal with the history of National Socialism and the Holocaust, but which are located in a site that did not host the operations of the Third Reich. Examples of the latter include internationally renowned institutions, such as the Jewish Museum designed by Daniel Libeskind and the Memorial to the Murdered Jews of Europe by Peter Eisenman, both in Berlin, and, outside Germany, the United States Holocaust Memorial Museum by James Ingo Freed, of Pei Cobb Freed & Partners. The distinction between the two groups is important as it helps to highlight some significant opportunities and challenges that these four documentation centers have

Introduction **3**

in common. The authentic location has the potential of making the content of the exhibit more immediate to the visitor, which becomes both an opportunity and a challenge to the architects and designers to generate a design that bridges the difficult past and the present that critically examines that past.

Second, "perpetrators' places" present a set of opportunities and challenges different from those that "victims' places" do. Here, victims' places would include concentration camps or forced labor camps, while perpetrators' sites are "places where the crimes were conceived but not necessarily perpetrated."[7] The distinction between these two groups may seem insignificant, if not fairly obscure, at first. Perpetration was committed also in victims' places, and victims were consequences of perpetrators' operations, even if the former did not occupy the latter's offices. However, the distinction between the two, *Täterorte* and *Opferorte* in German, is important in the context of postwar German memory culture and politics as special difficulties and challenges have existed in memorializing the perpetrators' places. Winfried Nerdinger, a well-known and respected architectural historian and the inaugural director of the NS Documentation Center Munich at the time of its opening, articulated the concepts, and drew attention to the distinction.[8]

In the postwar history of memory culture in Germany, it generally is the case that the commemoration of victims and resistances came a long time before people began turning the perpetrators' buildings into memorial sites. This is understandable. At victims' places, the visitors' focus is first and foremost on the victims, and the reflections on the perpetrators come as a result. Take, for example, the former Bergen Belsen concentration camp, which now functions as a memorial site. The exhibition focuses on how the victims were treated, the grounds provide a number of memorials for specific individuals or groups of people, and the whole site is a somber place of contemplation. In comparison, at perpetrators' places, we not only are reminded of the genocide as we are at a victims' place but also must put ourselves in the shoes of perpetrators in the context of National Socialism and the Holocaust and perhaps reflect on how we are to refrain from turning into perpetrators ourselves in any settings. Additionally, each city and its citizens likely are associated with perpetrators, or at least with corroborators or bystanders. This is an extremely difficult experience, while the recalling of an experience in which one was the victim is also extremely painful but in a different way. It therefore is understandable, if not defensible, that the commemoration of *Täterorte* generally came later than the memorialization of *Opferorte* in Germany. But at the same time, it is highly meaningful to offer *Täterorte* as a lesson for the future. At *Täterorte*, it is especially important to present the critical stance of the present-day society.

The small number of these centers and the relatively (and in some cases, extremely) recent dates at which they opened demonstrate how difficult and complex German *Vergangenheitsbewältigung*, coping with or dealing with the past, has been. Willful forgetfulness, self-victimization, and fear that preserving perpetrator sites as historical relics inadvertently would promote neo-Nazi sentiments predominated. As a result, many perpetrator buildings that were not destroyed by Allied bombing were demolished or converted for mundane purposes after the war.

4 Introduction

And at those that were converted to other purposes, clear and overt identification of the National Socialist–era usage of the building is not commonplace.

While the four documentation centers shared the above challenges and opportunities, their responses varied depending on different factors. These cities had played different roles in the National Socialist regime. The pre- and postwar histories of the four sites also are different. Germany's postwar memory culture and politics as well as the ways German communities dealt with the past shifted in time. Experience with designing such sites also accumulated through time. The four buildings present varied conditions as places of memory. In two cases (Berlin and Munich), the building already had existed on the site while the third (Cologne) was under construction as a private citizen's residential and commercial property when the National Socialists adopted it for their purpose, and the fourth (Nuremberg) was designed anew by them. In three cases (Cologne, Berlin, and Munich), the building was fully in use by the National Socialists, while in the third (Nuremberg), it was still under construction. In two cases (Berlin and Munich), the historical buildings, heavily damaged by the Allied air raids, were destroyed after the war, while in the two other cases (Cologne and Nuremberg), they survived fairly unscathed and were used for new, mundane purposes. And finally, in two cases (Berlin and Munich) a completely new building was constructed on the site, while in one case (Cologne) the interior of the historical building was altered to house the center with the exterior fairly unchanged, and in the fourth case (Nuremberg) the old and the new are presented simultaneously.

Next, what do I mean for an architectural design, when applied to historical places, to assist in presenting an extremely difficult past in meaningful ways? As a matter of fact, some would say that, while historical places have a way of referring to the past, what helps them do so is something other than the architectural design whose task simply is to convert them into documentation centers. Winfried Nerdinger stated that, while there is no denying that "the stone turned into history" ("Stein gewordenen Geschichte") is the "strongest form of visual memory" ("die stärkste Form der optischen Erinnerung"), it "must, however, be made intelligible by appropriate instructions" ("allerdings durch entsprechende Hinweise ablesbar gemacht werden muß"). The statement appeared in his 1988 piece titled "Umgang mit NS Architektur – Das schlechte Beispiel München" ("Dealing with NS architecture – The bad example of Munich"), which then was further developed and presented, under the title "Umgang mit den Spuren der NS-Vergangenheit – Indizien zu einer Geschichte der Verdrängung und zum Ende der Trauerarbeit" ("Dealing with the traces of the Nazi past – evidence of a history of repression and the end of mourning work"), at the Karl Hoper Symposium, held at the Hochschule der Künste Berlin on November 12–17, 1990. He stated:[9]

> Aber die stärkste Form der optischen Erinnerung in einer Stadt an ein geschichtliches Ereignis ist die ständige Konfrontation der Öffentlichkeit mit der Stein gewordenen Geschichte, mit der Architektur einer Epoche, die allerdings durch entsprechende Hinweise auch für die Nachgeborenen ablesbar gemacht werden muß.[10]

(But the strongest form of visual memory in a city of a historical event is the constant confrontation of the public with the history of stone, with the architecture of an epoch, which, however, must be made intelligible to the subsequent generations by appropriate references.)

Making the "the stone turned into history" "intelligible" is, then, is the way to accomplish the challenging task of, on the one hand denying the National Socialist propaganda the building carried and, on the other, promoting critical reflection on the history. The question should be asked: How do we provide the "appropriate instructions"? Nerdinger answered this question elsewhere:

> *Saxa loquuntur* – die Steine sprechen, diese römische Sentenz sollte ergänzt werden, denn sie sprechen nur zu dem, der ihre Geschichte kennt. Zu den Aufgaben eines Architekturhistorikers zählt es, Bauten zum Sprechen zu bringen, damit sie ihre Geschichte erzählen und helfen, historische Zusammenhänge zu verstehen. Wenn Gebäude, Plätze oder Städte in einen Dialog mit dem Betrachter treten, vermögen sie, als authentische Zeugen historische Erinnerung zu bewahren oder zu erzeugen. Architektur gibt der Erinnerung einen Ort und verankert sie damit stärker als Schrift oder Wort im Gedächtnis von Individuen und Völkern: ...[11]

> (*Saxa loquuntur* – the stones speak, this Roman sentence should be supplemented, because they only speak to the one who knows their story. One of the tasks of an architectural historian is to make buildings speak so they can tell their stories and help [the audience] understand historical contexts. When buildings, squares, or cities enter into a dialogue with the viewer, they are able, as authentic witnesses, to preserve or create historical memory. Architecture gives memory a place and thus anchors it more than writing or word in the memory of individuals and peoples. ...)

As Nerdinger suggested, the task of making readable the history of a place typically is assigned to historians, and, in the case of history museums, to the exhibits, and not to architectural designs that are applied to historical buildings. Instead, people, including the architects themselves, expect architectural designs to fulfill the role of providing a container to hold the exhibit or of supplying a visual attraction that draws people to the exhibits. While I do not take lightly the roles of exhibits, I believe architectural design has much to offer in assisting in presenting the past in meaningful ways. This study will demonstrate this position by observing the four documentation center designs and analyzing the effects of certain aspects of these designs, some of which may have been intended by architects and designers and others have not.

In the above context, it is important to consider the possibilities of presenting the past not in any ways but in meaningful ways. As will be discussed in Chapter 3,

6 Introduction

when Hitler desired to emulate Roman architecture with his own buildings, he was seeing the ruined Roman buildings presenting the empire's power and reach even nearly two thousand years later. It would be greatly problematic if the contemporary population – visitors or inhabitants – saw National Socialist buildings and saw, just as Hitler desired, their power and reach. In this sense, the strategy that the community adopted toward many National Socialist buildings, namely, normalization, that is, making the meanings of those buildings banal by giving them a mundane usage, did make sense. However, when it came to using the perpetrator places for documentation centers, we may want to use these places to their fullest extent. The question therefore is how, if at all, architectural design can help them present not only the past but also the contemporary stances against the past.

The book is divided into eight chapters. Chapter 1 will focus on the postwar treatments of physical environment. In order to provide a context within which to situate the four building projects of the documentation centers, I will discuss two small groups of cases, selecting them from the four cities in which these centers in question are located, namely, Cologne, Nuremberg, Berlin, and Munich. And the two groups are: first, National Socialist *Täterorte*, to discuss denazification and normalization; and second, buildings that were not used for National Socialist operations but were damaged during the war and required substantial rebuilding, to discuss the various design strategies of rebuilding.

Chapter 2 will outline the history of each documentation center site. While they share many similarities, especially on the conceptual level, the particulars are of course different, which will be important when we try to identify and examine notable design strategies that have been effective in assisting in meaningful presentation of the past. For each site, I will illustrate each place's situations before, during, and after the Third Reich. The regime adopted preexisting buildings to their purposes in Berlin and Munich, took over a building still under construction in Cologne, and designed a new building in Nuremberg. The buildings in Berlin and Munich were damaged during the war and, although they were not irrecoverable, were torn down. A citizen's movement demanded excavation, and some remaining underground structures were unearthed in Berlin. In Cologne and Nuremberg, the buildings survived the war fairly unscathed, and subsequently were adopted to new mundane purposes before the documentation center projects.

Complex issues surround the question of how, if at all, the architectural design converting historical *Täterorte* into documentation centers on National Socialism can contribute toward the meaningful presentation of the past. The issues have to do with what we expect from today's architectural design in general as well as what roles architecture played in the National Socialist era in particular, which resonate in historical buildings. Chapter 3 will review the expectations toward historical buildings as well as toward architectural design, and in particular, Hitler's view of architecture, which inevitably accompanies historical perpetrator buildings, and the resistance to architectural design that seems to be laden with the architect-artist's self-expression as it was exemplified in the criticism against the winning scheme by

Peter Zumthor for the 1993 competition for the Topography of Terror documentation center in Berlin.

Chapter 4 presents the intellectual frameworks which will be used in Chapters 5–8 so that we will have a systematic understanding of various mechanisms that are at work when architectural designs assist in presenting the past in meaningful ways. The framework has been developed by looking at architectural design from the points of view of representation (a piece of architecture as an artifact that represents ideas) and interpretation (the viewers take certain meanings out of their experiences), and in reference to philosophical works in semiotics and hermeneutics, particularly those of Charles Sanders Peirce and Hans Georg Gadamer. My framework identifies four distinct mechanisms: First, a building may refer to the time of its origin by way of its *formal characteristics*. Second, a building may recall an otherwise neglected past by bearing *physical traces*. Third, a building may commemorate a particular event or individual by being *designated* to do so. Fourth, as a *memento*, a building is a reminder of a past simply because an event took place there, even when there is no deliberate designation, formal characteristics, or material trace.

For the consideration of architectural designs taking advantage of the historical building's formal characteristics, in Chapter 5, I will observe a number of strategies at work on the site. They are:

1. physically isolating the National Socialist–era building from the postwar additions;
2. contrasting between the new and the old by way of form, including style, geometry, and materials; and
3. creating a place from which to view the historical.

In discussing what physical traces were left on the historical building or place and how architectural design can incorporate them as a reminder of the past, in Chapter 6, I have classified those actions by their agents. They are:

1. the National Socialist regime during 1933–1945, who constructed and/or used the building;
2. the Allied forces, who damaged and/or used the building during the war or postwar occupation;
3. the postwar German communities, who used, altered, or even destroyed the building; and
4. the architect, who converted the place into a documentation center.

We can observe how each architectural design harnessed some of the above, depending mostly on the availability at their site.

Chapter 7 expands the possibilities of buildings' presentation of the past by way of designation. While "to be designated" means to be given "a specified status or name," the documentation centers' designation requires an additional layer, that is, one that acknowledges the places' pasts. We will observe how the designation

8 Introduction

both about the present and the past is physically pronounced at the documentation centers, on the immediate front of the building, to the street, and beyond. Granted, architects may not take the design of such pronouncements – signposts, poster cases, and so on – as a significant part of their contributions, or these tasks may not be included in their scope of work. And when it comes to the question of naming the institution, it often is the case that community leaders or stakeholders are in charge of that decision. However, by examining the variety of pronouncements and their effectiveness, this chapter tries to draw the attention of architects and their design collaborators to what they could do to enhance their design work in this area.

Expanding the concept of memento, which requires the person to have personally experienced the past being recalled, to quasi-memento, especially for the younger generations and the international audience, Chapter 8 will discuss how the physical environment allows the visitor to gain memento-like experiences, that is, to put themselves in the shoes of those who actually experienced the past events. Some of this is accomplished by the exhibitions, but there are instances in which architectural designs do so on their own or by enhancing the exhibitions. Highlighted strategies include:

1. incorporation of oral history;
2. large-scale photographs that are as big as the architectural space allows;
3. incorporation of the spatial experiences that could have happened in the past into the current exhibition route; and
4. creation of new spatial experiences that put the visitor at unease.

When I began working on this topic, the typical question I received from the audience at conferences in the United States, Canada, or Japan, was why I had become interested in it. I am neither a Jew nor a German. The question therefore has implications, which I need to address here. That is, what credentials I could possibly bring to the topic when I am an outsider? I fully admit that the lack of cultural background certainly is a disadvantage, and I apologize in advance if any part of my assumptions or summations are out of place or even erroneous from a cultural point of view. However, that same lack of background may allow me to cast a fresh eye on the topic. At the very least, my considerations could possibly represent the centers' international audience.

With my last book, *Allure of the Incomplete, Imperfect, and Impermanent: Designing and Appreciating Architecture as Culture* (2015), I argued that it is a fallacy that a piece of architecture is complete when construction is finished, and advised that the architects, when designing a building, should take into consideration the afterlife of their buildings. I offer this point of view to the designs of documentation centers, which inevitably had to take into consideration the afterlife of the National Socialist buildings and places.

Lastly, I need to mention that this study employs careful on-site observations of the buildings as well as of the visitors including myself, supplemented by a study of documents, both published and unpublished, and both in text and image. This work should not be taken as a report on the center architect's design intentions but rather, as a search for architectural design's potential contribution to the meaning of life.

Notes

1 Barbara Becker-Jákli and NS-Dokumentationszentrum (Historisches Archiv der Stadt Köln), *Cologne during National Socialism: A Short Guide through the EL-DE House* (Köln: NS Documentation Centre of the City of Cologne: Emons, 2011). See also the Center's official website for 360-degree tour, information about the building's history, permanent and temporary exhibits, and more at https://museenkoeln.de/ns-dokumentationszentrum/default.aspx?s=314. The website also includes the information about the Gestapo prison memorial, located in the building's basement, which had been used as a Gestapo prison during the Third Reich, and was opened for the public as a memorial since December 4, 1981.

2 Hans-Christian Täubrich et al., *Fascination and Terror: Documentation Centre Party Rally Grounds: The Exhibition* (Nürnberg: Museen der Stadt Nürnberg, 2001).

3 Andreas Nachama, *Topography of Terror Gestapo, SS and Reich Security Main Office on Wilhelm-and Prinz-Albrecht-Strasse* (Berlin: Stiftung Topographie des Terrors, 2010).

4 Erika Bucholtz et al., *Site Tour "Topography of Terror" History of the Site*, 2016.

5 Erika Bucholtz et al., *Realisierungswettbewerb Topographie des Terrors, Berlin: 309 Entwürfe – Katalog zur Ausstellung der Wettbewerbsarbeiten* (Berlin: Bundesamt für Bauwesen und Raumordnung: Stiftung Topographie des Terrors, 2006).

6 Winfried Nerdinger, *Erinnerung gegründet auf Wissen / Remembrance Based on Knowledge. Das NS-Dokumentationszentrum München / The Munich Documentation Centre for the History of National Socialism* (Berlin: Metropol Verlag, 2018). See also NS-Dokumentationszentrum München et al., *Munich and National Socialism: Catalogue of the Munich Documentation Centre for the History of National Socialism* (München: Beck, 2015).

7 Timothy W. Ryback and Florian M. Beierl, "Opinion | A Damnation of Memory." *The New York Times*, February 12, 2010, sec. Opinion, www.nytimes.com/2010/02/13/opinion/13iht-edryback.html.

8 Winfried Nerdinger, "Umgang mit den Spuren der NS-Vergangenheit – Indizien zu einer Geschichte der Verdrängung und zum Ende der Trauerarbeit," Wolfgang Ruppert, Hochschule der Künste Berlin, and Karl-Hofer-Symposion, *"Deutschland, bleiche Mutter" oder eine neue Lust an der nationalen Identität? Texte des Karl Hofer Symposions, 12. – 17.11.1990,* ed. Wolfgang Ruppert (Berlin: Hochschule der Künste, 1992), 51–60.

9 Nerdinger, "Umgang," 1992. Also: Winfried Nerdinger, "Umgang mit NS Architektur – Das schlechte Beispiel München." *Werk und Zeit,* no. 3 (1988): 22–6. This was also stated in the preface of his collected papers *Architekur Macht Erinnerung Stellungnahmen 1984 bis 2004* (2004).

10 Nerdinger, "Umgang," 1992. Also: Nerdinger, "Umgang," 1998. This was also stated in the preface of his collected papers *Architekur Macht Erinnerung Stellungnahmen 1984 bis 2004* (2004).

11 Winfried Nerdinger, *Architektur – Macht – Erinnerung: Stellungnahmen 1984–2004,* ed. Christoph Hölz and Regina Prinz (München: Prestel Verlag, 2004), 9.

1

POSTWAR REBUILDING AND COPING WITH THE PAST

Building documentation centers on National Socialism is part of Germany's *Vergangenheitsbewältigung*, coping with or coming to terms with that past. The postwar history of memory culture and politics, however, is far too multifarious and multifaceted to be explored comprehensively here.[1] For this reason, I will focus on the postwar treatments of physical environment, and, in doing so, I will also include those by the occupying American forces or during the time of divided Germany. These treatments have been varied: they have been different by the agents or have changed through time, ranging, in general, from denazification to normalization, and from restoration to demolition.

The purpose of studying the postwar rebuilding of Germany's physical environment, for the current study, is not to survey them comprehensively, a method that characterized the scholarship on German postwar reconstruction since the 1980s, as Michael S. Falser has pointed out, in a chapter in the book *Rekonstruction in Deutschland*:

> Während aber die deutschen Wiederaufbaustrategien der Nachkriegszeit seit den 1980er Jahren im Zentrum der Forschung stehen, wird einer Typologie des Wiederaufbaus teilzerstörter Baudenkmäler als Denkmalkategorie sui generis – über Bemühungen einer Gesamtbilanzierung und Inventarisierung hinaus – nur selten Aufmerksamkeit geschenkt.[2]

> (But while German post-war reconstruction strategies have been at the center of research since the 1980s, a typology of the reconstruction of partially destroyed monuments as a sui generis category has been rarely paid attention beyond efforts for overall balance sheet and inventory.)

Instead, the purpose here is to provide a context within which to situate the four building projects of the documentation centers. With this in mind, I have further narrowed down my study by selecting cases from the four cities in which these centers in question are located, namely, Cologne, Nuremberg, Berlin, and Munich.

In selecting cases, I have two groups of buildings in mind. The first group consists of a small set of National Socialist *Täterorte*, and they are Zeppelin Grandstand in Nuremberg, Führerbau and Honor Temples in Munich, and Aviation Ministry building in Berlin, all of which are immediate neighbors of the documentation centers. With the first group, I intend to relate the postwar actions taken on the buildings to two main approaches of dealing with the past, namely, denazification and normalization. The second group consists of buildings that were not used for National Socialist operations but damaged during the war and required substantial rebuilding. With the second, I intend to compare different design strategies. For this group I have selected: Dürer House in Nuremberg, as a case of restoring the historical building to its prewar state; Kaiser Wilhelm Memorial Church in Berlin, as an example of a new construction that is detached from and contrasted with the remains of the historical; Alte Pinakothek in Munich, which has inserted a modern interpretation of the old using new materials and methods; and Kolumba in Cologne, which exemplifies a new construction capping the ruins as if to encase a display. They represent four different ways of either forgetting or memorializing the Second World War and the damage caused by it. This overview will provide a foundation for our understanding so that we will be able to appreciate the opportunities and challenges that the four cities have faced as they arrived at the decision of establishing a documentation center on National Socialism by converting the authentic places into memory places, which will be discussed in Chapter 2.

Denazification and Normalization

We will first focus our attention on *Täterorte*, or perpetrators' places, which accommodated National Socialist operatives. The postwar dealings with these buildings and places varied, from merely taking down the National Socialist emblems to destroying the building altogether, and from repurposing the building for a totally unrelated function to turning it into a commemorative place.

Immediately after the war, the Allied Forces went about denazifying Germany.[3] In May 1945, the Allied authority issued a directive to remove German military and National Socialist monuments by a deadline of January 1, 1947, calling for the

> removal and/or defacing of all "monuments, mementos, statues, buildings, plaques, emblems, street and road signs, … which might serve to keep the tradition of the German military alive, to revive militarism or to preserve memory of the National Socialist Party or its Führer."[4]

In 1946 the responsibility of denazification within the US-, UK-, and French-occupied areas was transferred to German-run legal tribunals. Denazification of physical environments was a part of more general scheme of dissolving the National Socialist Party and punishing prominent National Socialist leaders and removing

12 Postwar Rebuilding and Coping with the Past

them from key posts in politics and business. In specific terms, this ranged from removing National Socialist emblems from a building to destroying the building altogether.

There also were attempts at normalizing *Täterorte*, adapting them to other mundane purposes unrelated to National Socialism. Sometimes the conversion to mundane purposes is explained in that there were pragmatic and economic reasons for doing so. However, an additional, if not stronger, motivation than the purely pragmatic must have existed for the community, that is, to forget or detach their involvement in the National Socialist perpetration. Normalization happened not only to buildings constructed by the National Socialist regime but also to those that had been adopted by the Third Reich. In fact, two of the four documentation centers to be examined in the following chapters were normalized prior to the documentation center projects. In case of the building, EL-DE Haus, which would later turn into the Cologne center, it was being constructed for residential and commercial purposes by a private citizen when it was adopted by the Gestapo, and after the war it was returned to the original owner and was rented by the city to house its various departments of everyday purposes. The Nuremberg building, designed as the Party's Congress Hall and standing incomplete at the end of the war, became the property of the city and was used as storage, exhibition hall, and music venue.

Concerning normalization of *Täterorte*, the notion that trivial use would suppress the monumental power of National Socialist buildings has some parallel to the philosophical observation made by Hannah Arendt in her "Report on the Banality of Evil," originally published in a series of five installments in *The New Yorker* in 1963.[5] The piece was written as a report from the trial held in Jerusalem in 1961 of Adolf Eichmann. In it, Arendt observed how Eichmann, one of the key perpetrators of the Final Solution, presented himself as a mere follower of orders given by others who dictated the policy. Hermann Glaser, the influential cultural historian based in Nuremberg, promoted a profanation of National Socialist buildings during 1970s and 1980s.

Führerbau and Honor Temples in Munich, Zeppelin Grandstand in Nuremberg, and Aviation Ministry building in Berlin are just a few examples of denazification and normalization.

Führerbau, Munich

Führerbau, or Führer Building, was a part of the National Socialist German Workers' Party (NSDAP, Nationalsozialistische Deutsche Arbeiterpartei) center complex, designed by Paul Ludwig Troost (1878–1934) and completed after his death, in 1937. The center was an extension of the T Königsplatz, and Brienner Straße is the axis of the bilateral symmetry, the line connecting the Propyläen to the west and the Residenz to the east. In addition to Führerbau, there were the Administration Building (Verwaltungsbau der NSDAP), the mirror image to the

FIGURE 1.1 Königsplatz, Munich. November, 1936. Looking west through Brienner Straße. Members of SA, SS, and Standarten. Included in view are: Führerbau to north; Administration Building to south; Honor Temples; Brown House beyond the northern Honor Temple. The obelisk marks Karolinenplatz. The photograph was taken at the occasion of the anniversary of the Beer Hall Putsch, honoring the dead. Photograph: Heinrich Hoffmann. Source: Bayerische Staatsbibliothek München/ Bildarchiv, hoff-14387.

Führerbau in the exterior appearance but different in the floor plan, and the two Honor Temples, all of which were designed by Troost (Figure 1.1). Early on, Hitler adopted the preexisting Palais Barlow for his office, located on the north side of Brienner Straße, immediately east of the northern Honor Temple, but moved into Führerbau once it was completed. The most significant historical event that took place in the Führerbau is the signing of the Munich Agreement. On September 29 and 30, 1938, the leaders of Great Britain, France, and Italy – Neville Chamberlain, Eduard Daladier, and Benito Mussolini – met with Hitler to discuss and agree on the annexation of part (Sudetenland) of Czechoslovakia, without representation from Czechoslovakia. A propaganda photograph from this occasion shows the French and British flags displayed on the building with the National Socialist emblem on the building dominating over them, as if to pronounce the power of the Third Reich.[6] The emblem consisted of an eagle holding swastika in its claws and was placed prominently on the blank wall above the pillared portico of the two entrances.[7]

14 Postwar Rebuilding and Coping with the Past

FIGURE 1.2 Führerbau, Munich. The blank wall above one of the entrances. Mounting holds are visible. Photo by author.

When the 7th U.S. Army entered Munich's city center on April 30, 1945, they found the Führerbau and the Administration Building barely damaged. They took down the National Socialist emblems from each building as a way of denazification. The mounting holes of these emblems are still visible on the façades of the two buildings today (Figure 1.2). In the interior, the reliefs with propagandistic

FIGURE 1.3 Führerbau, Munich. The ceiling over one of the entrance porticos. The tile mosaic is in a pattern in reference to National Socialist swastika. Photo by author.

content also were removed.[8] Other architectural components, however, remained on the building despite their strong visual association to National Socialism. The fluted pillars and the windows with their frames protruding from the surface of the building's façade are clear references to typical National Socialist architecture.[9] The mosaic ceilings over the entrance porticos are in a pattern that has an inescapable reference to a swastika but were kept without scraping (Figure 1.3).

With these visual references to National Socialism still remaining on the building, the occupying forces proceeded to normalize the building for their own purposes. Their actions must have been for pragmatic reasons; there was a scarcity of usable buildings at that time. According to Ulrike Grammbitter,

> From the very outset, the American Army in the Bavarian capital, whose centre was heavily destroyed, used the confiscated NSDAP buildings for its own purposes. Taking this necessary step apparently did not pose any ideological difficulties for the American military authorities.[10]

In May/June in 1945, the former Führerbau and Administration Building were turned into the Central Art Collection Point, for the purpose of gathering art works that had been looted by the National Socialists. The former also housed, in addition to the art depository, the departments of the Bavarian State Library, which operated

16 Postwar Rebuilding and Coping with the Past

FIGURE 1.4 Führerbau, Munich. Looking over the main stairwell toward the former office of the Führer, presently "Room 105." Photo by author.

there till 1952. In 1948, the occupying forces set up the newly founded Amerika Haus in the southern half of the former Führerbau, placing their own national eagle on the spot the National Socialist emblem used to occupy over the corresponding, southern entrance. The Amerika Haus was intended by the American military authorities for democratic "re-education" of the German people through promotion of an international ethos of cultural exchange, and operated from there till it moved in 1957 into a newly constructed building at Karolinenplatz.

Normalization of the former Führerbau extended further, in the hands of German community. Today, Hochschule für Musik und Theater occupies the former Führerbau.[11] Its Great Hall was remodeled into a concert hall in the 1960s. The former office of the Führer, the room prominently located, on the second floor overlooking the street, is now identified as mundanely as "Room 105" and is a place for music instruction, with the schedule of classes listed in front (Figure 1.4 and 1.5).

Honor Temples, Munich

Honor Temples (Ehrentempel) were built for the purpose of commemorating the 16 National Socialist Party members who died in the putsch on November 9, 1923, with their sarcophagi installed here. Once the Honor Temples were completed and inaugurated on November 9, 1935, the annual November 9 propaganda march was expanded to include, at the end, Königsplatz, at which the 16 names were read out loud, and those marching would answer to those calls, by which action they were understood to be identifying themselves with those fallen.[12]

FIGURE 1.5 Führerbau, Munich. Outside of the former office of the Führer, presently "Room 105." Photo by author.

Immediately after the war, General Eisenhower sent a telegram to the Office of Military Government for Bavaria, ordering that the National Socialist monuments be immediately removed and that the sarcophagi be melted.[13] A number of proposals were made for the site, including setting up cafes or beer gardens, turning them into sites of atonement and peace, by Mayor Karl Scharnagl, or establishing a Catholic and a Protestant chapel, by Cardinal Michael von Faulhaber. Each time, however, public controversies and political crises resulted. And in January 1947, the pillars and the architraves of the Honor Temples were blown up without damage to Führerbau or Administration Building. Stairs also were removed from the base of the temples.[14]

The use of vegetation needs to be mentioned here. When removal of the party emblems or demolition of buildings were prompted to reject the National Socialist ideology, vegetations also worked for similar purposes, which have a way of taking over the built objects, just as happens at ruin sites. Trees were planted along the eastern edge of the Königsplatz, which conceal the views of the Führerbau and the Administration Building from Königsplatz. And planting atop the bases of the Honor Temples was developed to hide them, which remained at the site after the demolition of the upper portion of the buildings, in preparation for Munich's 800th anniversary of 1956.[15]

Zeppelin Grandstand, Nuremberg

Denazification and normalization took place also at the Zeppelin Grandstand (Zeppelintribüne). Here, as was the case at Führerbau in Munich, the American army

18 Postwar Rebuilding and Coping with the Past

was the agent of denazification, who continued on to normalize the place, which then was carried over by the German community. Well aware of its significance for the Third Reich, the American army, immediately after the capture of Nuremberg in April 1945, held a victory parade in the Zeppelin field, and afterward blasted the large National Socialist symbol, in the design of the swastika surrounded by laurel wreath, which had been positioned centrally atop the Zeppelin Grandstand.[16] The film recording of this destruction was shown all over the world as a demonstration of the power taken away from the regime. The Americans then took over the area, identifying it "Soldiers' Field" by the large letters on the wall that supports the central portion of the grandstand. A photograph from the 1960s is shown at the Nuremberg documentation center of an American baseball team lined up with the grandstand in the background, as if to demonstrate the conversion of military oppression to sporting entertainment.[17] The American army was stationed in Nuremberg until 1992, after the dissolution of the Soviet Union and the end of the Cold War.

In addition to the large symbol, there were other destructions that reduced the menacing power of the grandstand, although they were not so much for the purpose of denazification, unlike at Honor Temples in Munich, as for pragmatic reasons. And, unlike at Honors Temple, the agent of destruction was not the occupying forces but German community. By the decision of Nuremberg's Municipal Building Committee, in 1967, the colonnade on the grandstand was blown up. The colonnade that had extended for the entire width of the grandstand on both sides of the central raised block, had decayed to the extent that the maintenance was impractical. Subsequently, in 1973, the pylons that prominently had stood at the two ends of the grandstand, as tall as the colonnade, were removed to the level of the grandstand's top steps (Figure 1.6).[18] Since the same year, however, the buildings on the Party Rally Grounds including the grandstand has been protected by the Historical Monuments Law.

The Zeppelin Field and its grandstand have been the site of many events, totally unrelated to the National Socialist past. Two major events are the rock concert and the car race, both of which are held annually, which continue to this day. The American army helped establish a motorsport club in Nuremberg, and racing events began with motorcycles in 1947, and adding cars in the following year. On those days the grandstand becomes the central part of Norisring circuit.[19] The annual rock festival called "Rock im Park" started in 1977. More than 75,000 tickets are sold for the three-day event, and the audience not only fill the field but also use other areas of the Party Ground for camping in their tents.[20] Around those days, the Nuremberg documentation center's entrance stairs carry a large poster promoting the festival.

The event related the former grandstand to the National Socialist past was the exhibition titled "*Faszination und Gewalt*," which was held inside the building every summer since 1985.[21] It addressed the role the city played in relation to National Socialism, including its role in Party Rally and the postwar Nuremberg Trials. Here, just like at entrance portico of the Führerbau in Munich, the

FIGURE 1.6 Zeppelin Grandstand, Nuremberg. It is missing the large symbol featuring the swastika wreath, colonnade spanning the entire width of the grandstand, and (not in view) the top half of the end pylons. Photo by author.

ceiling's mosaic of the grandstand building's golden hall recalling the National Socialist swastika was conserved rather than defaced. The good reception of the exhibit and a large number of audience led to a demand for a permanent venue and paved the way to the establishment of documentation center in the former Congress Hall.

Aviation Ministry

In Berlin, across the street from the site of Topography of Terror documentation center to the north is the massive building that housed the Reich's Aviation Ministry (Reichsluftfahrtministerium), headed by Hermann Göring.[22] It was designed by Ernst Sagebiel (1892–1970), who worked in the office of Erich Mendelsohn till 1932. Constructed in 1935–36, the building showcases formal characteristics common to National Socialist architecture (Figure 1.7). It occupies the entire length of the large city block facing Wilhelmstrazße, the important address for National Socialist government with its offices lining up. The main entrance of the New Reich Chancellery was to face this street, designed by Albert Speer and officially dedicated in January 1939.

Having suffered little damage from the air raids during 1944–45, the building, in the occupying Soviet sector, was used to house the Soviet Military Administration.

20 Postwar Rebuilding and Coping with the Past

FIGURE 1.7 Aviation Ministry Building, Berlin. Window motif. Signature forms common to National Socialist architecture include the window motif, with pronounced frame and much protruding windowsill supported by two large members. Photo by author.

In 1949 the official ceremony to establish the German Democratic Republic was held here, and the building became to be known as House of Ministries. East Germany had its own ways of dealing with the National Socialist past, and in particular, communist resistance was celebrated as a way to put down National

Socialism. In 1951 East Berlin renamed Prinz Albrecht Straße, which divided East and West Berlin and separated the site of the former Aviation Ministry and that of the future documentation center, to Niederkirchnerstraße, after a communist resistance. On the entire surface of the large wall behind the colonnade of the main entrance to the building, a Socialist mural was installed in 1953, replacing the National Socialist soldier's relief in 1953 (Figure 1.8).

The building, along its extended time of existence, may pick up a new significance. The former Aviation Ministry building, or Houses of Ministries during the German Democratic Republic period, became one of the important sites of the 1953 Uprising, in which about one million people are said to have participated throughout East Germany in protest against the communist government. Soviet and East German military was engaged and suppressed the protest. In 2000 a memorial was installed in the forecourt of the main entrance of now the Federal Ministry and Finance building, at the corner of Wilhelmstraße and Leipziger Straße. The memorial is made of glass, horizontally laid slightly sunken from the ground level of the square, and on it are printed enlarged, rasterized photograph of the protesters (Figure 1.9). The forecourt was named Platz des Volksaufstandes von 1953, and its history is prominently displayed with much information provided by additional boards.

FIGURE 1.8 Aviation Ministry Building, Berlin. Socialist mural, installed in 1953. Photo by author.

22 Postwar Rebuilding and Coping with the Past

FIGURE 1.9 Aviation Ministry Building, Berlin. Memorial for the 1953 Uprising. Photo by author.

The above examples are *Täterorte* that have gone through denazification or normalization, or both. In the early days of postwar period, any acknowledgment of the National Socialist past typically was limited to victims' places or sites related to resistance. In the background of the lack of acknowledgment were the desire to forget the unbearable past or the desire to suppress the evil or shameful past. There desires went together with the fear of inadvertently celebrating the past via commemoration and thereby supporting National Socialism. During the 1970s with Holocaust denial gaining force, commemoration of perpetrator sites met with the fear that preserving the sites as historical relics inadvertently would promote neo-Nazi sentiments.

The fact that it had taken a long time for the German communities to openly and publicly acknowledge National Socialist perpetrators' sites as such, much longer than it took to acknowledge victims' sites as the Holocaust-related ones is a proof of this difficulty. The four documentation centers are special because they have been converted to memory places, that is, institutions whose purpose explicitly is to engage visitors in reflection upon the past. Of course, it is not always appropriate to turn a perpetrators' building to a memory place. Also, not all authentic perpetrator sites can be turned into memorial sites. There were pragmatic demands and economic reasons for using buildings. These make these documentation center projects even more special.

Forgetfulness and Memorialization

Undeniably, after the war the citizens and leaders of German communities went through a number of phases of dealing with the National Socialist past. In close relationships were, on the one hand, the people's ideological, political, or moral stances and, on the other, their treatment of the physical environments that either were associated with the Third Reich's operation or otherwise were damaged by the war. The former sometimes was reflected in the latter and other times was shaped by it. The rebuilding of course was influenced by other forces, too, including the economic and other pragmatic factors affecting the particular site. In Germany, Michael S. Falser summarized the scholarship on the postwar reconstruction, especially that from after the 1980s, in the book chapter mentioned above. In the United States, Gavriel Rosenfeld offered a way to categorize diverse postwar reconstructions in his comprehensive study of postwar building projects in Munich.[23]

Both studies identify two extremes of the reconstruction strategies, with returning a war-damaged building to its prewar state on one end, and demolishing a building and constructing a new one in its place on the other, with a variety of other approaches in between. The two extreme types of rebuilding – demolition of the historical building and new construction on the same site and reconstruction of the historical building to the postwar appearance – seem completely opposite of each other and result in totally different outcomes. However, they nonetheless reflect the same mental attitude toward the difficult past, willful forgetfulness. Rosenfeld in his comprehensive study on the rebuilding of Munich explained willful forgetfulness as one aspect of *Vergangenheitsbewältigung*.[24] And this attitude toward the difficult past predominated during the 1950s and 1960s, especially in West Germany. It was this attitude that the Frankfurt School thinker Theodor W. Adorno was against when, on November 9, 1959, he gave a lecture in Wiesbaden addressing a group of schoolteachers. Adorno rejected the contemporary catchphrase "working through the past" as misleading, observing that "its intention is to close the books on the past and, if possible, even remove it from memory." He argued that "the attitude that everything should be forgotten and forgiven" would be appropriate "for those who suffered injustice" but is a problem when it was "practiced by those party supporters who committed the injustice."[25] Adorno instead promoted the kind of critical self-reflection that Freudian theory called for in order to come to terms with the past.[26]

Willful forgetfulness, which often went hand in hand with self-victimization, is understandable, if not justified, as a natural human reaction to such a difficult past. Once the evil force is eliminated, both the city authorities and citizens desire, on the one hand, to return the district to its distant past, restoring the peaceful setting for leisurely activities that citizens enjoyed before the site was taken over by a political force that used it for hostile purposes. Restoration of buildings to their prewar state is the result. Demolition of a building to make way for completely new construction both at the scales of an individual building and of the city, also is a way to distance oneself from the difficult past. It also reflected an opportunistic attitude in

24 Postwar Rebuilding and Coping with the Past

many cases to implement modernist architectural design or to modernize the city's zoning or traffic patterns. Some also understood modernization as a departure from history, especially the immediate past of National Socialism. In both directions, there was little consideration regarding the possibility of tasking the building to carry the difficult memory of the immediate past so that it provides lessons for the present and future.

Dutiful Reconstruction: Dürer House, Nuremberg

The sentiment that supported the restoration of buildings to the prewar state may have included self-victimization, a tendency in the immediate postwar era to see National Socialism as having come from outside and the city as a casualty of Allied bombing, as Sharon MacDonald suggested in her study on postwar dealings with perpetrator sites in Nuremberg.[27] Accordingly, the city's medieval and Renaissance pasts were promoted, perhaps as a means to suppress one past by elevating another. Nuremberg's old city, largely destroyed by air raids by the British and American forces, was an example of the latter.[28] In 1947 a competition was held for ideas for urban planning, and the Kuratorium für den Wideraufbau Nürnbergs (Board of Trustees for the Reconstruction of Nuremberg) advised the city administration.[29] Not only the old city wall and the castle but also many other buildings within the city wall were rebuilt, including the house that Albrecht Dürer once had occupied near the castle or the Mauthalle on Königstraße. The newly reconstructed Dürer House was considered the exemplary built heritage. Mauthalle, constructed in 1498–1502 as Germany's largest granary, which also housed the city's municipal scales and customs office (Mauthalle = toll hall), was reconstructed in 1953 and now houses a number of commercial entities including a restaurant and a Nuremberg newspaper, *Nürnberger Nachrichter.*

Dürer House in Nuremberg is an early example of complete restoration to the prewar time and reflects the citizens' devotion and pride toward the built heritage and the cultural treasure the building represented. Already in the nineteenth century the building was open to the public as a place to exhibit Dürer's work. The city of Nuremberg took a great part in restoring the building.

Albrecht Dürer (1471–1528) has long been the pride of the citizens of Nuremberg, the artist having been born and died there, and the house he purchased in 1509 and resided in until his death had long been city property and a museum dedicated to the artist.[30] The building had prominence in the old city, owing to its location across a small urban square from the Nuremberg Castle, situated on top of the hill at the north end of the medieval city wall. It has the appearance of medieval architecture with the heavy timber of the upper stories visible on its façades. Already in the nineteenth century, demand was such that the city purchased it from the contemporary owner, had the building repaired, and opened it to the general public. The Albrecht Dürer Association took care of the exhibition. In the 1870s the Albrecht Dürer Foundation was established, for the purpose of keeping the building in good repair and restoring its interior. The city and the Foundation

Postwar Rebuilding and Coping with the Past 25

collaborated in expanding the collection and restoring the interior. In 1927 under a fresh agreement the city took over all maintenance.

The house suffered considerable damage during the Second World War (Figures 1.10, 1.11, and 1.12).[31] The city undertook the restoration, and the building was reopened on August 31, 1949. All of the building's contents, which had been stored elsewhere for safekeeping, were brought back. Today, the Dürer House is a top tourist attraction of Nuremberg, prominently presented in the City's Tourism Bureau's brochures and pamphlets. Many tourists likely assume that Dürer lived and worked in the spaces presented without being aware of the reconstruction process (Figure 1.13). In this encounter, Germany's recent pasts – the domination of the Third Reich in the city fabric, the war damage to the building and the city, or the postwar reconstructions – are outside the visitors' imagination. The following criticism that Falser quoted from Norbert Mühlen's "Das Land der Großen Mitte, Notizen aus dem Neon-Biedermeier" (1953) about the Goethe House in Frankfurt applies to Nuremberg's Dürer House reconstruction, that it failed "to confront the reality of traumatic loss experience through the repression strategy of full reconstruction":[32]

> Hinter dem aus Fleiß, Behagen und Betrieb gewebten Vorhang des Lärms verbirgt sich die Stille, die über Westdeutschland liegt [...] es vermischen sich das Alte und das Neue bis zur Unkenntlichkeit [...] haargenau wurden die vernichteten Bauten restauriert, bis sie wieder dastanden – abgesehen von den sie allseits umgebenden Ruinen – 'als ob nichts gewesen wäre'. Mit einiger Phantasie – oder genau genommen, ohne Phantasie –könnte man glauben, der junge Johann Wolfgang habe auf diesen Fußböden gespielt und die deutschen Kaiser seien durch diese Portale zur Krönung geschritten. Den Sinn der Katastrophe, die zur Vernichtung des Alten geführt hatte, haben nur wenige zu begreifen gesucht [...] Ruinen sind das Riesenmahnmal eines Alpdrucks, der noch nicht einmal ganz Vergangenheit ist und den man schon vergessen möchte; sie erinnern an vieles, was das Gefühl der Sicherheit bedroht und was man deshalb nicht wahrhaben will. Das Trauma wird, weder geklärt noch geheilt, da sein Ursprung ja nicht bewusst geworden ist, in das Unterbewusste abgedrängt [...] Ruinen helfen wenigstens noch der Erinnerung nach, wie alles ausschaute bevor sie Ruinen waren; die Neubauten aber löschen alles Erinnern aus, die Formen eine fremde Stadt.[33]

> (Behind the curtain of noise woven from diligence, comfort and operation lies the silence that lies over West Germany [...] the old and the new are mixed beyond recognition. [...] the destroyed buildings were restored exactly to the point where they stood again apart from the ruins surrounding them, "as if nothing had happened". With some imagination – or, more precisely, without imagination – one could believe that the young Johann Wolfgang had played on these floors and that the German emperors stepped through these portals to the coronation. Only a few have sought to understand the

FIGURE 1.10 Dürer House, Nuremberg. 1930. Source: Stadtarchiv Nürnberg. A 38 Nr. D-18-1.

FIGURE 1.11 Dürer House, Nuremberg. 1944. Source: Stadtarchiv Nürnberg. A 41/II Nr. LR-729-32a.

FIGURE 1.12 Dürer House, Nuremberg. 1971. Source: Stadtarchiv Nürnberg. A 39/II Nr. Fi-A-1188.

FIGURE 1.13 Dürer House, Nuremberg. Present. Photo by author.

meaning of the catastrophe that had led to the destruction of the old [...] ruins are the giant reminder of a nightmare that is not even quite a past and that one already wants to forget; they are reminiscent of many things that threaten the feeling of security and therefore do not want to admit it. The trauma is neither cleared nor healed, since its origin has not become conscious, pushed into the subconscious [...] Ruins help at least in the memory of how everything looked before they were ruins; but the new buildings erase all memory, the forms a strange city.)

Incorporating Damaged Historical Buildings

In comparison to the Dürer House restoration, in which the new construction becomes unrecognizable as new, Kaiser Wilhelm Memorial Church, Kolumba, and Alte Pinakothek present the new construction as new, clearly differentiated from the historical remains, although they do so in different ways. And Falser considered these reconstruction strategies as a positive way of confronting the past:[34]

> *Progressive Architekten und Denkmalpfleger hingegen begriffen die zeitgenössische Aneignung von Ruinen als kreative und lebensbejahende Begegnung, die das Fragmentarische und die materiellen Verluste am teilzerstörten Denkmal als Faktum akzeptieren musste. ... Heute sind diese angeeigneten Kriegsruinen als historische "Trauerräume" der Nachkriegszeit zu verstehen, in denen Verlust, Trauer und ambivalente Gefühle der Mitschuld und Scham nicht tabuisiert wurden.[35]*

(Progressive architects and conservationists, on the other hand, saw the contemporary appropriation of ruins as a creative and life-affirming encounter that had to accept the fragmentary and material losses of the partially destroyed monument as a fact. ... Today these appropriated war ruins are to be understood as historical post-war "mourning rooms" in which loss, grief and ambivalent feelings of complicity and shame were not taboo.)

Kaiser Wilhelm Memorial Church, Berlin

Kaiser Wilhelm Memorial Church in Berlin is among the limited instances of keeping the ruin as a ruin while the postwar additions are separated, both physically and stylistically (Figure 1.14).[36] It was built by Kaiser Wilhelm II to commemorate his grandfather, Kaiser Wilhelm I. The original Memorial Church was designed in neo-Romanesque style with Gothic elements by Franz Schwechten, who also designed Anhalter Bahnhof, just southwest of the current Topography of Terror documentation center site. The church was heavily damaged during the

FIGURE 1.14 Kaiser Wilhelm Memorial Church, Berlin. The new additions are completely separated both physically and stylistically from the original building in ruin. Source: Gillermo Yanguez Bergantino.

30 Postwar Rebuilding and Coping with the Past

November 23, 1943, air raid, but not to the extent that it was not recoverable, and in 1947 the Kaiser Wilhelm Gedächtniskirche Stiftung [Foundation] decided in favor of rebuilding it. In 1956, a two-stage competition was announced, leaving the question open to the competitors whether to take down or preserve the remains of the spire. Egon Eiermann (1904–70) won the competition with a proposal to completely demolish the ruin for a new construction.[37] In the public outcry that followed, which many consider "the first moving public debate within the Berlin reconstruction,"[38] the original tower, in ruin, was identified as the "heart of Berlin." The architect wrote to the Pastor, Günter Pohl, who was the managing director of the Board of Trustees of the Foundation, on March 22, 1957:

> *Sehr geehrter Herr Pfarrer!*
> *Ich glaube, dass allen Beteiligten an dem Neubau der Kaiser-Wilhelm-Gedächtnis-Kirche klar war, dass mit einer Entscheidung des Preisgerichtes, wie auch immer sie ausgefallen wäre, die angestaute Flut der Meinungen in der Öffentlichkeit sich ergiessen würde.*
>
> *Mit der Gedächtnis-Kirche verbinden sich für die meisten von uns freundliche Jugenderinnerungen aus einer unbeschwerteren Zeit und symbolhaft die bitteren Zeiten des Krieges. Sich davon loszusagen, ist sehr schwer. Noch liegen mir die Stimmen der Berliner Zeitungen nicht vor; aber ich weiß schon jetzt, dass ich alle diesen Menschen, die den alten Turm behalten wollen, aus der gleichen inneren Einstellung recht geben möchte. Nach einer kurzen Notiz, die ich gelesen habe, soll Herr Bartning gesagt haben, dass auch er es für richtiger hielte, den Turm stehen zu lassen und die Kirche woanders zu bauen. Dieses Wort beweist, wie schwer auch ihm die persönliche Entscheidung fällt. Wir tragen alle sehr schwer an dieser Aufgabe. Insofern sind wir alle gleich am Beginn. So dürfte denn niemand, dem Tradition, Anhänglichkeit und menschliche Gefühle noch etwas bedeuten, imstande sein, die Verantwortung für das, was zu geschehen hat, allein zu übernehmen.*[39]

(Dear Pastor!
I believe that it was clear to all involved in the construction of the Kaiser Wilhelm Memorial Church that with a decision of the jury, however it had turned out, the pent-up flood of opinions in the public would pour.

With the memory church for most of us friendly youth memories from a carefree time and symbolically connect the bitter times of the war. Getting rid of it is very difficult. I do not yet have the votes of the Berlin newspapers; but I already know that I would like to justify all those people who want to keep the old tower, from the same inner attitude. After a brief note that I read, Mr. Bartning is said to have said that he, too, thought it best to leave the tower and build the church elsewhere. This word proves how hard his personal decision is. We all have a hard time on this task. In this respect we are all at the beginning. So no one who is anything more than tradition, attachment, and human sentiment should be able to take responsibility for what has to be done on his own.)

Accordingly, the architect revised the design.[40] Eiermann kept the ruined tower. With rich mosaics and sandstone and marble reliefs that originally were intended to commemorate Wilhelm I and other German emperors, but which now were showing the scars of the air raid of November 1943, the ruined building became a memorial against the war. Surrounding this tower, Eiermann placed four new buildings – the church with the octagonal plan to the west, the rectangular foyer further to the west, the hexagonal bell tower to the east, and the rectangular chapel to the northeast. In this ensemble of the five – one old and four new – buildings, each is separated physically, standing on its own from the shared platform. The four new buildings share the design vocabulary despite the differences in their overall shape, clearly resembling each other and contrasting against the ruined tower. The four are all enveloped by steel grids made of almost-square rectangles, each of which holds a concrete "honeycomb" panel of horizontal and vertical grids filled with colored glass of predominantly blue but also ruby red, emerald green, and yellow. Upon closer examination, the structures of the four buildings are different: The church has a double wall system, with the inner wall matching the outer steel frame, and the two separated by 2.45 meters for the sound insulating effect.[41] The chapel also has a double wall system, but its inner wall consists of sheets of glass, allowing the view to the outer gridded wall. By letting the five buildings stand on its own on the platform, the resultant physical separation of the buildings implies the separation of the religious life of the present from the war devastation of the past.

Alte Pinakothek, Munich

Alte Pinakothek, considered an exemplar of "Kritischen Rekonstruktion," or critical reconstruction, incorporates the war-damaged historical building with the new construction in a single building.[42] The original building was constructed by the order of King Ludwig I of Bavaria and by the design of Leo von Klenze as a gallery for the painting collection of the House of Wittelsbach and opened in 1836. The Alte Pinakothek was then the largest and one of the most important museums in the world.

During the war, the museum was burned down to a large extent because of bombing in 1943–44. And the south side, which is our current subject, was partially destroyed in the middle of its 150-meter-long façade. The postwar Munich community saw a fierce debate on what to do with the building, with one side arguing for a complete restoration, to which the Frankfurt Goethe House was referred as the model, and the other advocating for a total demolition. The former, "traditionalists," saw in the reconstruction a way to regain beloved old Munich and to invite order and stability into the chaos of the postwar society, while the latter, "modernists," saw the old Munich as irretrievable and longed for a new Munich by way of modern construction.[43]

In 1951 Hans Döllgast, a professor at the Technical University of Munich, together with his colleagues, put forward a proposal for a reconstruction. The

32 Postwar Rebuilding and Coping with the Past

FIGURE 1.15 Alte Pinakothek, Munich. South façade. Photo by author.

proposal was accepted in the following year, the south façade was closed in 1955, and the museum reopened in 1957. In order to fill the gaping south façade, Döllgast's design used rubble bricks from the area. These bricks imitated the geometry of the original classicist motif of arched openings, but without ornamented cornices. In order to support the new roof, seven steel tubes were used as vertical supports, which stood detached from the surface of the bricks (Figure 1.15). These slender columns were contrasted with the much thicker and semicircular pilasters of the original façade (Figure 1.16). These design elements can be understood as the modern interpretation of the classicist construction, and when seen in one gaze, make a clear statement about the scars of the war and the postwar coming to terms.

Winfried Nerdinger considers Alte Pinakothek as an example of "creative restoration," which is an "an architectural coming-to-terms with the National Socialist past and its legacy. In those spots, the traces of World War II are still readily apparent."[44]

Kolumba, Cologne

Kolumba in Cologne represents the design strategy in which the new construction surrounds the ruins of the historical building, turning the latter into part of an exhibition.

Kolumba in Cologne, opened in 2007 and located halfway between Cologne Cathedral and the documentation, is the work of the Swiss architect Peter Zumthor, who won the commission through the design competition in 1997. It is a case of

FIGURE 1.16 Alte Pinakothek, Munich. South façade detail. Showing the slender columns of steel pipes detached from the surface of the building. Photo by author.

an architectural design applied to a historical place, and it succeeds in presenting both the past and the passage of time. The past being presented is multi-layered. The church of St. Kolumba, a fifteenth-to-sixteenth-century Gothic structure, and the largest and most important parish church in medieval Cologne, was heavily damaged by the air raids, but a statue of the Virgin Mary survived the destruction, which gave the community hope. Gottfried Böhm (1920–) designed a chapel, much smaller than the original church, placing the chapel on the central nave of the now destroyed church.[45] The chapel was inaugurated on January 6, 1950, and the statue was nicknamed "Madonna of the Ruins."[46] The rest of the site surrounded by the remaining exterior walls of the original church was turned into a memorial garden. Two decades later, starting in 1974, archaeological excavations were conducted by Sven Seiler (1940–2015) and his colleagues, uncovering generations of constructions at the site. The dating went all the way back to the first to the third centuries, when Cologne was a Roman colony and the site was part of a residential development. A part of an apse from the seventh century also was unearthed, marking the beginning of the church dedicated to Saint Kolumba, as well as the remnants from the subsequent expansions that took place during the ninth, mid-eleventh, twelfth to fourteenth, and finally fifteenth to sixteenth centuries.[47]

In December 1996, the Cologne Archdiocese announced an open competition for a design of the new museum. They also invited a number of architects, including Peter Zumthor, Annette Gigon and Mike Guyer, and David Chipperfield. The task

34 Postwar Rebuilding and Coping with the Past

was to design a new building of the Diocesan Museum on the site of St. Kolumba Church, preserving all fragments of it. In June 1997, Zumthor was announced the winner; his proposal was to erect new walls on top of the remaining walls of the original church, to wrap around Böhm's chapel as well as the ruins. It also was to add a building wing to the side and above the archaeological site to provide for the exhibit spaces.[48] The building construction began in 2003 and was completed in 2007.

At Kolumba, Zumthor's intention to showcase the past is clear in his statement to that effect: "The new has to motivate us to better see the existing, the new building serves the old as its historical reference, and operates its own function of exhibition – displaying the continuous history and culture." Three distinct pasts are showcased: the times prior to the Second World War, that of the Second World War, and that of the Böhm chapel, after the war. The generations of construction prior to the Second World War, starting from the Roman time to Romanesque and then to the Gothic, are presented as an aggregated time period in the form of the ruined building. The second, that of the Second World War, is presented as the scars left in the ruined building. And the postwar time period is presented by Böhm's chapel. The passage of time from each of these three pasts is also clearly presented. The time's passage is visible in the stark differences in the forms and materials between the ruined church, Böhm's chapel, and Zumthor's building. Furthermore, Zumthor's walls on the one hand stands on the outer walls of the ruined church, extending the latter's lost height upward, and on the other wraps around Böhm's chapel without physically touching the latter's wall or roof. As well, Zumthor has set up a zig-zag path of circulation within this space, which hovers over the excavated ruins without conforming to its geometry (Figure 1.17). This pathway does not take the visitor into Böhm's chapel, and this also isolates Zumthor's and Böhm's times completely. Zumthor reflected on the visitor's experience he created:

> In a nutshell, the most interesting thing is perhaps, that you can read the history at the location and in the building. Normally people think history is written down in books. But history, time, has been stored in the landscape, at the location and in the building, and we can also read it here. This is what Kolumba is really all about, 2000 years of history, Roman excavations, Romanesque and Gothic churches, the heaps of rubble after World War II and the chapel from the 1950s as the symbol of the new beginning, unbelievable. And for an architect, to be able to write history here once again, recapitulating everything, assembling everything to form a new unity and to respectfully be able to say, we stand here and create a home for the dialogue between old and new art, this was, of course, not exactly easy, but it was a fantastic task.[49]

Seen from the point of view of *Vergangenheitsbewältigung*, Germany's rebuilding projects demonstrate varied motivations and methods. Postwar dealings with *Täterorte* varied, from merely stripping away the National Socialist symbols from

FIGURE 1.17 Kolumba, Cologne. The pathway, alike a bridge, hovers over the excavated ruins of the original church's foundations. Seen in the left is the chapel designed by Gottfried Böhm. Seen in the background is how Zumthor built up bricks on top of the remaining church wall. Photo by author.

the prominent location on the building to destroying the building altogether, and from repurposing the building for a totally unrelated function to turning it into a commemorative place. What looked straightforward actions of denazification had motives, from demonstrating the victorious army's power to marking the end of the dark era. When *Täterorte* were normalized, they may have started with the occupying forces who needed square footage for their own operation or demonstrated their victory against the oppressive military regime. When it comes to the reconstruction of buildings that are unrelated to the National Socialist operation, the design strategies varied, from full restoration that erases the memory of the war to different ways of overtly presenting the damaged buildings as commemoration of the war.

Notes

1 Alf Lüdtke, "'Coming to Terms with the Past': Illusions of Remembering, Ways of Forgetting Nazism in West Germany," *The Journal of Modern History* 65, no. 3 (1993): 542–72. Lüdtke complained that "public attention to ways of coping with the Nazi past in Germany tends to focus on gestures or speeches by representatives of the state and society," and that "the sentiments, opinions and practices of 'the masses' play no active

36 Postwar Rebuilding and Coping with the Past

role in these accounts." Jenny Wüstenberg focused on an important role the civil engagement played in the actions taken in Berlin and elsewhere. See: Jenny Wüstenberg, *Civil Society and Memory in Postwar Germany* (Cambridge: Cambridge University Press, 2017).

2 Michael S. Falser, "Trauerarbeit an Ruinen: Kategorien des Wiederaufbaus nach 1945," Michael Braum and Ursula Baus, eds., *Rekonstruktion in Deutschland: Positionen zu einem umstrittenen Thema*, Baukultur vor Ort – Potsdam (Basel: Birkhäuser, 2009), 60–97, 60.

3 Iris Lauterbach, "Austreibung der Dämonen: Das Parteizentrum der NSDAP nach 1945," Zentralinstitut für Kunstgeschichte, *Das Parteizentrum Der NSDAP in München* (Berlin: Dt. Kunstverl, 2009), 80.

4 Lauterbach, *Das Parteizentrum Der NSDAP in München*, 82. See also NS-Dokumentationszentrum München et al., *Munich and National Socialism: Catalogue of the Munich Documentation Centre for the History of National Socialism* (München: Beck, 2015), 308.

5 Hannah Arendt, "Eichmann in Jerusalem," *The New Yorker*, February 16, 1963, http://www.newyorker.com/magazine/1963/02/16/eichmann-in-jerusalem-i. This series ran weekly till no. 5, which was published in March 16 issue. See also Hannah Arendt and Amos Elon, *Eichmann in Jerusalem: A Report on the Banality of Evil* (New York: Penguin Classics, 2006).

6 In March 1939, German troops moved into the rest of Czechoslovakia and occupied Prague. On September 1, 1939, Germany invaded Poland, and on September 3, 1939, France and Great Britain declared war against Germany. The Munich Agreement turned out to be a failed appeasement. See: NS-Dokumentationszentrum München et al., *Munich and National Socialism*, 201.

7 Ulrike Grammbitter, "The NSDAP Centre," in *The NSDAP Centre in Munich*, ed. Ulrike Grammbitter, Klaus Bäumler, and Iris Lauterbach (Berlin [u.a.: Dt. Kunstverl., 2015), 30.

8 *The NSDAP Centre in Munich*, 69–70.

9 Grammbitter, "The NSDAP Centre," in *The NSDAP Centre in Munich*, 30.

10 *The NSDAP Centre in Munich*, 68–9.

11 *The NSDAP Centre in Munich*, 72–4.

12 NS-Dokumentationszentrum München et al., *Munich and National Socialism* (München: Beck, 2015), 203.

13 Iris Lauterbach, "Austreibung der Dämonen: Das Parteizentrum der NSDAP nach 1945," Zentralinstitut für Kunstgeschichte, *The NSDAP Centre in Munich*, 80.

14 Interestingly enough, these measures were undertaken by the construction firm Leonhard Moll, a company which, under the Nazis, had been considerably involved in the remodeling of Königsplatz. Iris Lauterbach, "Austreibung der Dämonen: Das Parteizentrum der NSDAP nach 1945," Zentralinstitut für Kunstgeschichte, *The NSDAP Centre in Munich,* 84–5.

15 NS-Dokumentationszentrum München et al., *Munich and National Socialism*, 379. See also: Lauterbach, "Austreibung der Dämonen: Das Parteizentrum der NSDAP nach 1945," *The NSDAP Centre in Munich*, 83.

16 Alexamder Schmidt, "Editorial: 'Das Gelände' – zum Umgang mit dem Reichsparteitagsgelände seit 1945," Alexander Schmidt, Martina Christmeier, and Museen der Stadt Nürnberg, *Das Gelände: Dokumentation, Perspektiven, Diskussion, 1945–2015: Ausstellungskatalog des Dokumentationszentrums Reichsparteitagsgelände* (Petersberg: Michael Imhof Verlag, 2015), 8–17; 9. For the history of Nuremberg's dealing with the perpetrator buildings, see also Sharon Macdonald's important scholarship: Sharon Macdonald, *Difficult Heritage: Negotiating the Nazi Past in Nuremberg and Beyond* (New York: Routledge, 2009).

Postwar Rebuilding and Coping with the Past **37**

17 Alexander Schmidt, Martina Christmeier, and Museen der Stadt Nürnberg, *Das Gelände*, 28–9.

18 Ibid. 95.

19 Ibid. 36–41.

20 Ibid. 119.

21 Bernd Ogan and Wolfgang W Weiss, *Faszination Und Gewalt: Nürnberg Und Der Nationalsozialismus: Eine Ausstellung* (Nürnberg: Pädagogisches Institut der Stadt Nürnberg, 1990).

22 Matthias Donath, *Architecture in Berlin 1933–1945: A Guide through Nazi Berlin* (Berlin: Lukas Verlag, 2006), 18–19.

23 Gavriel David Rosenfeld, *Munich and Memory: Architecture, Monuments, and the Legacy of the Third Reich*, Weimar and Now 22 (Berkeley: University of California Press, 2000).

24 Rosenfeld, *Munich and Memory*, 2. His references include: Leland Roth, *Understanding Architecture: Its Elements, History and Meaning* (New York: Icon Editions, 1992), for the concept of "built memory"; and Siegfried Kracauer's statement "steady transformation expunges memory" quoted in Wolfgang Sonne, "The City and the Act of Remembering," *Daidalos* 58 (1995): 90–101.

25 Theodor W. Adorno, "The Meaning of Working through the Past," *Critical Models: Interventions and Catchwords*, European Perspectives (New York: Columbia University Press, 1998), 89–103, 89. The lecture was originally titled "Was bedeutet: Aufarbeitung der Vergangenheit," and was given at a conference on education hosted by the Duetsche Koordinierungsrat der Gesellschaften für Christlich-Jüdische Zusammenarbeit (German Coordinating Council of Organizations for Christian-Jewish Cooperation) in Wiesbaden.

26 A related topic is the distinction we need to draw between forgetting and forgiving. On this topic, some references are: Adrian Forty and Susanne Küchler, eds. *The Art of Forgetting*. Materializing Culture (Oxford; New York: Berg, 1999). "Preface" by David Lowenthal, xi–xiii. See also: Simon Wiesenthal, Harry J. Cargas, and Bonny V. Fetterman, *The Sunflower: On the Possibilities and Limits of Forgiveness*, 2nd ed. (New York: Schocken Books, 1997). "… forgetting turns out to be more benefit than bereavement, a mercy rather than a malady" (xi).

27 Macdonald, *Difficult Heritage*.

28 Otto Peter Görl, "Der Wiederaufbau," *3 x Nürnberg: Eine Bilderfolge aus unserem Jahrhundert* (Nürnberg: Verlag A. Hofmann, 1988), 89–105; 97.

29 Clemens Wachter and Willy Prölß, "*Wiederaufbau*," in Stadtlexikon Nürnberg, ed. Michael Diefenbacher and Rudolf Endres (Nürnberg: W. Tümmels Verlag, 1999), 1178ff.

30 Nuremberg and Albrecht Dürer Haus Stiftung, *The Dürer House in Nuremberg* (Nuremberg: Albrecht Dürer Haus Stiftung, 1961).

31 Ernst Eichhorn, Georg Wolfgang Scramm, and Otto Peter Görl, *3x Nürnberg*, 120–1.

32 Michael S. Falser, "Trauerarbeit an Ruinen: Kategorien des Wiederaufbaus nach 1945," Michael Braum and Ursula Baus, eds., *Rekonstruktion in Deutschland: Positionen zu einem umstrittenen Thema*, Baukultur vor Ort – Potsdam (Basel: Birkhäuser, 2009), 60–97; 88–89.

33 Norbert Mühlen, "Das Land der Großen Mitte, Notizen aus dem Neon-Biedermeier" *Der Monat* 6 (1953), quoted in Michael S. Falser, "Trauerarbeit an Ruinen: Kategorien des Wiederaufbaus nach 1945," 89.

34 Alexander Mitscherlich and Margarete Mitscherlich, *The Inability to Mourn: Principles of Collective Behavior* (New York: Grove Press: distributed by Random House, 1975).

35 Michael S. Falser, "Trauerarbeit an Ruinen: Kategorien des Wiederaufbaus nach 1945," 90.

38 Postwar Rebuilding and Coping with the Past

36 Falser, 71–2.

37 Eberhard Schultz, "Kontrapunkt des Kurfürstendamms: Kaiser-Wilhelm-Gedächtniskirche, Berlin," *Deutsche Architektur Nach 1945: Vierzig Jahre Moderne in Der Bundesrepublik*, ed. Mathias Schreiber and Peter M. Bode (Stuttgart: Deutsche Verlags-Anstalt, 1986), 53–5.

38 Martin Wörner, *Architekturfuhrer Berlin* (Berlin: Reimer Verlag, 2013).

39 Günter Pohl, who was the managing director of the Board of Trustees of the Foundation.

40 Michael Braum and Ursula Baus, *Rekonstruktion in Deutschland: Positionen zu einem umstrittenen Thema* (Basel: Walter de Gruyter, 2012), 71.

41 Stiftung Kaiser-Wilhelm-Gedächtniskirche, *Kaiser-Wilhelm-Gedächtnis-Kirche: Zukunftsperspektiven Für Ein Nationales Denkmal* (Berlin: Stiftung Kaiser-Wilhelm-Gedächtniskirche, 2017). See also: Protestant Kaiser Wilhelm Memorial Parish Berlin, "Building Ensemble," gedaechtniskirche-berlin.de; and Eberhard Schulz, "Kontrapunkt des Kurfürstendamms," Mathias Schreiber and Peter M. Bode, *Deutsche Architektur Nach 1945: Vierzig Jahre Moderne in Der Bundesrepublik*.

42 Falser, 75.

43 Rosenfeld, *Munich and Memory*, 41–4.

44 NS-Dokumentationszentrum München et al., *Munich and National Socialism*, 350.

45 Dominik Duka, *Kolumba* (Prague: Krystal Publishers, 2011).

46 Wolfgang Pehnt and G. Böhm, *Gottfried Böhm*, Studio Paperback (Basel: Birkhäuser, 1999), 44–9. Svetlozar Raev, *Gottfried Böhm: Lectures, Buildings, Projects: Vorträge, Bauten, Projekte* (Stuttgart: K. Krämer, 1988), 76–7.

47 Kolumba (Körperschaft) and Römisch-Germanisches Museum, *Pas de deux*, 2018.

48 Kolumba (Körperschaft) and Römisch-Germanisches Museum, *Pas de deux*.

49 "If Everything I Planned Had Been Realized, I Would Not Be So Happy Now," interview with Peter Zumthor, in Dominik Duka, *Kolumba*, 123–33; 131–2.

2

FOUR DOCUMENTATION CENTERS – HISTORIES

This chapter describes the histories of the four documentation centers that are at the center of this book's investigation. They are: NS Documentation Center of the City of Cologne (opened in 1997) at the former Gestapo regional headquarters; Documentation Center Nazi Party Rally Grounds, Nuremberg (2001), housed in a portion of the building intended as a congress hall but which was still under construction at the end of the war; Topography of Terror, Berlin (2010), on the site of the buildings that had housed Gestapo and SS headquarters; and NS Documentation Center Munich (2015), on the site where the so-called Brown House had contained the National Socialist Party's regional headquarters. The goal of this chapter is to understand the opportunities as well as challenges the communities have faced along the way to the decision to set up a documentation center in each specific site, particularly with regard to the history of each one after the war.

Some opportunities as well as challenges are shared among the four locations: Each location was a *Täterort*, a perpetrator place of National Socialism, but prior to that had been a place of peaceful activities and after the war became part of people's everyday life. On the one hand, the authentic place provided an opportunity to make present material evidence of the community's involvement in National Socialism as its agents, corroborators, or bystanders where evil deeds were conceived. On the other, there was a desire for normalization, as seen in the perpetrator examples in Chapter 1, returning it to a peaceful place that was part of people's everyday life. The solutions varied, based on the differing roles the cities had played in the National Socialist regime, shifts in Germany's postwar memory culture and politics, and through the accumulated experience of designing such sites.

The following will illustrate each place's history, including the historical building's original construction, its use by the Third Reich, and its postwar treatment. The regime adopted preexisting buildings to their purposes in Berlin and Munich, took over a building still under construction in Cologne, and designed a new building in Nuremberg. The buildings in Berlin and Munich were damaged during the war and, although they were not irrecoverable, were torn down after it. A citizen's movement demanded excavation, and some remaining underground structures were unearthed in Berlin. In Cologne and Nuremberg, the buildings survived the war fairly unscathed, and subsequently were adopted to new uses before the documentation center projects.

History of the NS Documentation Center of the City of Cologne

The NS Documentation Center of the City of Cologne (NS-Dokumentationszentrum der Stadt Köln) (Figure 2.1) is located at 23–25 Appellhofplatz, about 500 meters west of the western portal of Cologne Cathedral. At the time of the building's original construction, its location must have been desirable to the owner, as it is today, because it is only a few hundred meters away from the core of the old city, Cologne Cathedral and the central railroad station. The centrality of the location goes back to the time when Cologne was the capital of the Roman colony Germania Inferior, called Colonia Claudia Ara Agrippinensium, when the site was within the walled city, with the northern portion of the city wall running just north of the site. One

FIGURE 2.1 Documentation Center, Cologne. Present. Appelhofplatz (left) and Elisenstraße (right) façades. The building was expanded after the war, from 6 to 12 bays on the Appelhofplatz side, and from 12 to 16 bays on the Elisenstraße site. Photo by author.

of the Roman towers, which marked the northwest corner of the walled city, is still standing 300 meters west of the site.

Appellhofplatz is the street that circles the nineteenth-century building originally designed and constructed as the Court of Appeals, which stands across from the documentation center building. Starting in the early nineteenth century, on this site stood a generation of large institutional buildings that accommodated various courts of the city and the district. The first such building was constructed during the 1820s according to the design by Johann Peter Weyer, a Cologne architect and master builder who had been educated at the Ecole des Beaux-Arts in Paris. It housed the Court of Appeals – Appellationsgerichthof, later shortened to Appellhof – which gave the street its name.[1] This building became too small fairly quickly because of the increasing population, and a new building was built on the same site, designed by Paul Thoemer and Rudolf Mönnich, and opened in 1887. The building once again turned out to be too small for its purpose, so the appeals court moved out, and the district court took it over at the end of the nineteenth century. After this building was heavily damaged during the Second World War, it

FIGURE 2.2 EL-DE House, Cologne. In the National Socialist newspaper *Westdeutscher Beobachter*, December 5, 1934. The interior was still under construction. After this article, the Gestapo took over and turned it into their regional headquarters.
Source: NS Documentation Center of the City of Cologne.

42 Four Documentation Centers – Histories

was reconstructed in a somewhat simplified manner and now houses the financial and administrative courts of the Nordrhein-Westfalen region.

The building that houses the documentation center goes back to 1934–35. Leopold Dahmen, a Catholic wholesaler of gold articles and clocks, who had lived with his family at Appellhofplatz 21 and ran a wholesale shop for gold goods and watchmaking supplies close by to the south,[2] had two residential buildings next door torn down to replace them with a new building intended for residential and commercial purposes. The new building was designed by Hans Erberich, *Regierungsbaumeister* (government builder) and architect, who was listed in the member directory of the Deutscher Werkbund in their 1913 publication.[3] It stretched the entire consolidated site at the corner of Appellhofplatz and Elisenstraße, and often was, and still is, referred to as EL-DE House for the original owner's initials.[4]

The building had four full stories above ground plus an attic on top and two additional floors in the basement. It was in somber neoclassical style, finished with tufa, a type of limestone. The building's elevation is composed of three horizontal layers, separated by horizontal cornices, which run at the tops of the ground (first), third, and fourth stories. Arranged perpendicularly to those horizontal lines of cornices were vertically proportioned windows running repeatedly on each floor, making 6 bays facing Appellhofplatz and 12 facing Elisenstraße. Where these two streets meet and the building's corner is rounded, a crest was prominently present, with the city arms engraved on the left and an emblem on the right with the letters EL DE for the owner's initials, with two pendula of a longcase clock, referring to the building owner's business. At the center of the crest was a winged helmet, symbolizing Hermes, the god of trade and commerce.[5] The letters "EL DE" were repeated on the glass pane above the entrance doors.

The building's general sternness that comes from its style and material and the window design details – with the frames protruding from the exterior wall surface – are common to typical National Socialist architecture, although it was not designed for the party but for a private citizen. Similar design elements are seen in buildings designed for the regime, for example, the pair of Führerbau and Administration Building in Munich, originally designed by Paul Ludwig Troost (d. 1934) in 1931 but whose construction was completed in 1937 after his death, or the Aviation Ministry building in Berlin, designed by Ernst Sagebiel and constructed in 1934–35. Likely because of the stylistic similarities, *Westdeutscher Beobachter* (*West German Observer*), the National Socialist daily in the Rhineland, praised the building as "modern" in its evening edition of December 5, 1934 (Figure 2.2): "*Kennen Sie schon das El-de-haus?*" ("Do you already know the EL-DE-Haus?") asked the newspaper. It explained that the new building was to provide 14 offices on the ground floor and "modern small apartments" on the three upper floors, in addition to an underground garage in the basement.[6]

After the newspaper article, and in the summer of 1935, the building was taken over by the Gestapo. It happened while the building was still under construction but after the topping-out ceremony and the completion of the exterior. In addition to the building's appearance, and more pragmatically, its proximity must have been advantageous. The

Gestapo at that time was stationed at Zeughausstraße 8, only about a hundred meters northwest of the building site. Just east of that and only one block away to the north of the site, also on Zeughausstraße, were the seventeenth-century Zeughaus, or armory, and the nineteenth-century Alte Wache, or guardhouse, both of which were used for National Socialist operations.[7] To the east of the site across Appellhofplatz street was the Court of Appeals, which also was involved in Gestapo operations as the Special Court of Cologne.[8] The Gestapo forced Dahmen to cancel the building's other lease agreements and had the interior remodeled for its own purposes. The ground floor originally had been intended for commercial use, and the upper floors and the attic for 12 rental residential units. Instead, it was refitted to accommodate offices above ground and ten prison cells in the upper basement. The Gestapo began operating from the building on December 1, 1935, using it as the headquarters for the administrative district of Cologne.[9] During the period of their occupation, which lasted just short of nine years and three months, EL-DE House became "in Cologne, and far beyond, the epitome of the National Socialist reign of terror."[10]

Of course, there were other National Socialist perpetrator buildings in Cologne. The introduction of *Die Wandinschriften des Kölner Gestapo-Gefängnisses im EL-DE-Haus, 1943–1945* provides a list of other places, while also acknowledging that comprehensive coverage is impossible. What makes it difficult is the incomplete nature of the records: "the dreaded Secret State Police, or Gestapo for short" "had every reason to destroy to the best of their ability all traces of their terrible activity,"[11] and records also were destroyed in the fire during the air raids as well as intentionally toward the end of and after the war.[12] However, a list of known National Socialist sites includes: Braunes Haus at Mozartstraße 28; the old university building on Claudiusstraße; the detonator factory at the corner of Frankfurter and Maarhäuser street; the old police headquarters at Krebsgasse 1–3, at the corner of Schildergasse; the building of the criminal police on Weidenbach 10; and the state police station at Burgmauer 118, which is close by EL-DE House.[13] Almost none of these buildings still exist, either having been damaged by bombs and/or demolished after the war.[14] Some places carry commemoration, typically for the victims.[15] There were *Opferorte*, or victims' places, too, including the expansive buildings of the Deutz trade fair center on the east side of the Rhine River.[16] There also were transit camps and labor education camps.[17] In this context, EL-DE House occupies an important place: The building survived with only insignificant damage while 90% of the buildings in the city's old town were destroyed in the war.[18]

The postwar development prior to the conversion of the EL-DE House into the NS Documentation Centre of the City of Cologne is a typical example of the memory politics and culture in Germany: It has gone through the process of forgetfulness and normalization, memorialization first as a victims', and then finally as a perpetrators', place, and it would not exist without citizen involvement.

After the war, as part of normalization, the building was returned to the original owner. In 1947–49 the EL-DE House was expanded. The next-door house on Elisenstraße and the owner's residential and commercial building at Appellhofplatz 21 were damaged during the war, which offered an opportunity.[19] The original

44 Four Documentation Centers – Histories

façade design of the EL-DE House was repeated, from 6 bays to 12 on the Appellhofplatz side and from 12 bays to 16 on the Elisenstraße side.[20] With the EL-DE House's roof having been damaged during the war, its attic was turned into a full story.[21] The building was rented to the City of Cologne, which used it for offices, including the Occupation Office, the Pricing Authority, the Office for Defense Expenses, the Registry, the Pension Office and the Legal and Insurance Authority, the last of which still rents a space in the building.[22]

For the postwar memory culture and politics in general, the commemoration victims' places came before that of the perpetrators', and the EL-DE House was not an exception. As a part of the Gestapo operation, which was held in the offices above ground, prison cells existed in the basement. Twenty years before the opening of the documentation center in 1997, attention was given to the building as a victims' place. The first step, therefore, was to restore the prison cells in the basement to create an information site on the victims of National Socialism and to install a commemorative plaque on the outside wall of the building, which was accomplished by the city council's resolution of December 13, 1979, and in agreement with Georg Dahmen, the building's owner. Civic activism brought this resolution: Since the 1960s, Sammy Maedge had drawn attention to the historical significance of the building; in 1969 VVN Köln or Vereinigung der Verfolgten des Naziregimes (Association of the Persecuted of the Nazi Regime), the SDS or Sozialistische Deutsche Studentenbund (Socialist German Student Union) in Cologne, devoted their interest to the Gestapo prison; in 1975 a group of students from the Hansa-Gymnasium reported on the house in their student newspaper; in 1977 the *Kölner Volksblatt* newspaper published an article about EL-DE House; and the television series titled *Holocaust* starring Meryl Streep raised public awareness in the spring of 1979.[23] In May 1979, the Council of Art and Culture demanded that the city administration "ensure, through negotiations with the owner of the EL-DE House, that … the basement rooms … be prepared as an information center about the victims of National Socialism and made accessible to the public." On December 4, 1981, the former prison in the basement was opened to the public by the mayor of the city as a memorial place with a small exhibition, and since the early 1980s the building has been a historically protected monument.[24] A commemorative plaque was attached to the house on November 6, 1980.

The resolution on December 13, 1979, also included a decision "to establish a documentation centre on the era of National Socialism in Cologne," whose functions at that time were limited to research and academic purposes and without any exhibits. Initially, the "documentation center" was understood as a collection point of historical records gathered for the purpose of reparation to the victims of National Socialist deeds in Cologne. In January of the following year, a citizens' initiative was formed, called "Initiative for a Documentation Center in the EL-DE House," requesting to set up the entire EL-DE House as a documentation and information center. Although this could not be realized at that time, a director's position was created within the Historical Archive of the City of Cologne. The position was filled on October 1, 1980, by Horst Matzerath, a historian who later became the first director of the NS Documentation Centre.[25] In 1985 a group of committed citizens founded the initiative for the establishment of an NS documentation center and organized demonstrations and other activities. In 1986 and 1987, the staff of the "center" was expanded: There were now five individuals dedicated to the research on Jewish victims and forced labor. And on June 11, 1987, another city council resolution passed, adding two more researchers, a librarian and a secretary. In early 1988 the work of the committed citizens' group resulted in the Friends of the NS Documentation Centre association, the EL-DE House Association. On September 19 of the same year, the documentation center staff finally moved into the EL-DE House, allocating their offices on the ground floor and a small library and a room for group work on the first floor. At this time the conversion of the building into an exhibition space was not possible, as the building was still, as it is now, owned by the original family, who at that time refused the implementation.

The opening of the Documentation Center at the EL-DE-House had to wait until 1997. In 1991, ten years after the opening of the Gestapo prison in the basement as a victims' memorial, the Cologne City Council resolved to convert a part of the House into a Documentation Center on National Socialism. Professor Peter Kulka, an architect based in Cologne, was commissioned and was to be assisted by Konstantin Pichler and Professor Gerd Fleischmann, a typographer and exhibition designer.[26]

Documentation Center Nazi Party Rally Grounds, Nuremberg

The Documentation Center Nazi Party Rally Grounds (Dokumentationszentrum Reichsparteitagsgelände) is located a couple of miles outside Nuremberg's old, albeit reconstructed, city wall, on the former Party Rally Grounds.[27] Hitler commissioned Albert Speer in 1934 to design the stretch of 25 square kilometers as well as several buildings on the Grounds draw an overall plan for the Rally Grounds.[28] Speer, after the unexpected death of Troost in January of that year, had just become Hitler's number-one architect for carrying out the leader's propagandistic schemes. However, the design of the Congress Hall, which the current documentation center occupies a portion of, was commissioned by the city of Nuremberg, even before Speer came on board for the site design, to Ludwig Ruff, who was local to Nuremberg but among Hitler's top architects. Ludwig Ruff also was a professor of the city's art craft school and a National Socialist member since February 1, 1933. After Ludwig's death in 1934, his son Franz Ruff took over the project.[29] Hitler was heavily involved in design consultation. Modeled after the Roman Colosseum, but even larger, and in a U-shape instead of an oval, the Hall was to consist of an auditorium with 50,000 seats and two orthogonal blocks terminating each end of the U.

The construction began in 1935. The building's exterior, which was completed except for the uppermost story, demonstrates some of the typical characteristics of National Socialist business and administration buildings. This style is sometimes called "stripped-off classicism" and features window design with pronounced frames

46 Four Documentation Centers – Histories

and the darker grayish polychrome granite finish, which came from more than 80 domestic quarries. The Congress Hall certainly had the stylistic characteristics that Matthias Donath has observed of the typical National Socialist architecture:

> The business and administration buildings were largely built in the monumental building style that reduced design to its essentials, functionalizing it and doing without any superfluous ornamentation. The unadorned, smooth surface, the accentuated two dimensionality and the objective severity is suggestive of modern architecture. Direct references to the historical feudal architecture of the ruling class can, however, be discerned. Entranceways are given emphasis through rows of columns and lateral extensions. The facades are often symmetrical. The window frames have sharp edges. ... The structure's facades are clad with large slabs of natural stone. The identical rows of windows contain sharp-edged rectangular frames. The ornamentation is limited to powerful eagle reliefs on the building corners.[30]

Despite the exterior showcasing these characteristics, and the planned completion date of 1943, the construction of the Congress Hall was never completed. The roof structure above the main hall, surrounded by the U-shaped building, still was being designed in 1938–40, with 12 companies coming together to establish an association for the purpose of constructing it in a steel cantilever system. The construction work was interrupted in 1939 at Hitler's invasion of Poland, which pulled his attention away from the project. It then restarted and proceeded between 1940 and 1941. Some masonry work and planning activities continued but were halted in 1943.[31] At the end of the war, the area for the auditorium, surrounded by the U-shaped building, was left without a roof (Figure 2.3).[32] The two end blocks were missing their topmost story, and the space between these blocks, intended for the main entrance hall, remained void. While the outer surface of the building and the U-shaped colonnade were finished with polychrome granite cladding, the rest was for the most part unfinished, with exposed bricks for the walls and raw concrete for the floor and ceiling. The Congress Hall building therefore was never actually used for its intended National Socialist purpose, although, with the U-shaped outer portion of the building finished, its propagandistic presence certainly was already in effect. At 275 meters wide, 265 meters deep, and 40 meters tall, it is the "largest preserved monumental building from the Nazi era in Germany."[33]

The City of Nuremberg's ties to the National Socialist past are at least threefold. First, it held the annual Reichsparteitage (Nazi Party Rallies). Second, the Race Laws, later known as the Nuremberg Laws, were announced there in 1935 during the Party Rally. Third, the propaganda newspaper *Der Stürmer* (*Stormtrooper*) was published there by Julius Streicher (1885–1946), a former schoolteacher and one of the Party's earliest members as well as the leader of its Franconian division. And fourth, during 1945–46 the major National Socialists responsible for the Holocaust were tried there at the Nuremberg Trials. But above all, the city's dark past is rooted in it having been the place of the Nazi Party Rallies, which involved the entire

FIGURE 2.3 Documentation Center, Nuremberg. The space intended for the main auditorium of the Congress Hall. With the structure of the roof over the space never resolved, it was left roofless at the end of the war. Photo by author.

city, physically and socially. And it also would be extremely difficult for the citizens to acknowledge this past because of their direct involvement in crimes against humanity. Hermann Glaser, an influential historian and Nuremberg's culture minister since 1964, retrospectively noted:

> "Eternal jubilation met the Führer of the Franconians when he appeared on Adolf Hitler Square. There was a storm of enthusiasm which subsided only after quite a while." The overwhelming majority of the women and men of Nuremberg could have avoided this event without any danger of retaliation. Instead, they applauded these national criminals.[34]

Nuremberg was chosen for the Party Rallies for a number of reasons. First, the city was fairly centrally located. Second, a large park called Luitpoldhain was available for congregation. It makes up the northern portion of a large city park called Volkspark Dutzendteich (people's park dozen pond), surrounding the lake with the same name. Beginning in the seventeenth century, the park was developed as a destination for the Nurembergers to enjoy gondolas and barges on the lake, and when it was frozen, sleighs or ice skates. The train station (Nuremberg Dutzendteich) was built in 1870. In 1906 the city hosted a jubilee on the 100th anniversary of

48 Four Documentation Centers – Histories

its membership in Bavaria. Luitpoldhain in particular had a municipal stadium and a field named after Ferdinand Graf von Zeppelin, who landed an airship there in 1909. Third, the Party could rely on its well-organized Franconian branch led by Streicher, and the police were highly sympathetic to the Party.

The selection also subsequently was justified by the Party in relation to the notion of the Third Reich. The National Socialists adopted the term to legitimize themselves in the historical lineage of the Holy Roman Empire (962–1806) and the German Empire (1871–1918). Nuremberg fit into this scheme, with its castle having been one of the places of the medieval Imperial Diet. Playing on the linguistic similarity, the National Socialists highlighted Nuremberg's transformation from the city of the Reichstage to that of the Reichsparteitage des deutschen Volkes.[35] The Rally was held for the first time in 1923 in Munich but moved to Nuremberg in 1924 and 1925, was held in Weimar in 1926, and returned to Nuremberg in 1927 and 1929. When Hitler became the Chancellor in 1933, the rally became an annual event in Nuremberg until its cancellation in 1939. The primary purposes were to stir National Socialism and anti-Semitism among the German people and to demonstrate power both nationally and internationally. Up to one hundred thousand soldiers marched through the city, and a growing number of onlookers, eventually reaching nearly a million, cheered and gave the Nazi salute.

The Rally involved the entire city, physically and socially. The procession started from the castle at the hilltop at the northern edge of the walled city where the Reichstag had met. It then descended on the sloped Burgstraße toward the river Pegnitz, passing St. Sebald church, and the Rathaus. It arrived at the Hauptmarkt, then called Adolf Hitler Square, where Frauen Kirche, the place of worship for the Holy Roman Emperors, stands. After crossing the river on Königstraße and climbing upward, it passed Lorenzkirche and reached the Frauentorturm at the southern end of the walled city in front of the Hauptbahnhof. From there, it continued southward on Allersberger Straße, which now is traced by tourists on a tram. The crowd's enthusiastic reactions were captured in numerous photographs and films.

It had taken half a century to designate the former Congress Hall as a place that recalls the city's involvement in National Socialism. Nuremberg's citizens and their leaders went through a number of ideological, political, and moral stances regarding the colossal material evidence of the genocide. Denial of the past and willful forgetfulness were prevalent during the 1950s and 1960s, and people in Nuremberg portrayed themselves as innocent victims, expounding that National Socialism had come from outside and that the city was a casualty of Allied bombing. These sentiments manifested in a number of different forms. They shifted the focus to different pasts: The city's medieval and Renaissance pasts were promoted. The castle and Albrecht Dürer House, damaged during the war and reconstructed, were elevated as examples of exemplary built heritage. The Party Rally Grounds, too, have returned to a place of leisure, taking back the original name Luitpoldhain. Since 1997 the area has hosted an annual music event called "Rock im Park" for several days in early June, and people set up tents throughout the park for overnight stays. A car race called Norisring also is held annually at the Zeppelin Field.

Four Documentation Centers – Histories **49**

On both occasions, Zeppelin Grandstand, famously used for the National Socialist Rally and also for the National Socialist symbol that is now absent because it was blasted by the city, is used either as the stage or as seating for spectators. In the former Congress Hall, the building block opposite the Documentation Center is occupied by the Nürnberger Symphoniker, and includes the Serenadenhof, an open-air venue for classical music that opened in 1986.

But the fate of the former Congress Hall had much to do with its large size and heavy structure, which made it difficult to do anything with the building other than keeping it. Once the former Congress Hall building became the property of the city, it was renamed the Round Exhibition Building to sever its ties with the National Socialist past, a type of denazification.[36] There were a number of attempts at normalizing the perpetrators' building: When the city held the German Building Exhibition in 1949, the expressed intention was to promote "the rehabilitation of the reputation of the City of Nuremberg," which "has suffered considerably … because of the political events of the past years." A restaurant was set up to offer a panoramic view of the courtyard. Other shows included the 900 years of Nuremberg exhibit in 1950 and a restaurant exhibition in 1951. There also were proposals to demolish the building: In 1963, the Association of German Architects proposed doing so because it "remains a contravention of the spirit of the new city. … We have the responsibility to erase this sign and to sacrifice it."

More attempts were made at adapting the building to other mundane purposes, in addition to the above use as an exhibition hall. Already in the 1950s the city administration attempted to apply some substantial work to the building for economic exploitation. Ideas included a football stadium (1955) and an event hall with a covered courtyard (1958), neither of which were pursued due to the prohibitive cost or the unsuitability of the structure. The U-shaped building was used as a storage facility with annual rental income going to the city. The Nürnberger Symphoniker gained the use of the southern end block. A practice room and a recording studio were set up, and a private recording company also rented space. Since 1986, the courtyard within the southern block was turned into the Serenadenhof, an open-air music venue. Other proposals, which were not realized, included a drive-in cinema or a home for the elderly.

Meanwhile a new perspective was emerging. The mid-1970s saw a development of interest in the central role architecture played in National Socialism. With the increasing willingness to confront National Socialist crimes, the Reichsparteipagsgelände were listed under the Bavarian State Historic Preservation Law in 1973. In 1985 an exhibition entitled "*Faszination und Gewalt*" ("Fascination and Violence") was installed in the Zeppelin Grandstand building designed by Albert Speer.[37] This is the beginning of the effort to use perpetrators' buildings for the explicit use of presenting that very past. There were some constraints: The exhibit was open only during summer months because the building was not heated, and it was not easily accessible because it was located at the farthest end of the former Rally Grounds. Still, the number of visitors to the exhibit climbed to 35,000, including many youths who did not have a personal memory of National

50 Four Documentation Centers – Histories

Socialism and the Holocaust. And yet, the idea of preserving the building was still highly controversial, in part because of the fear that doing so would promote and support the neo-Nazis.

A turning point came in 1987 when Nuremberg's businessmen proposed converting the former Congress Hall into a leisure center. Strong opposition was raised, among which was that of Michael Petzet, Conservator General of the Bavarian Conservation Department in Munich, a branch of the National Office for the Preservation of Monuments.[38] Petzet wrote to the city administration that the building was the "most important testimony of the gigantomania of the National Socialism" and should be left unused. He also acknowledged that there were different types of memorials, differentiating the *Mahnmal*, a critical statement about or a warning from the past, from the *Denkmal*, a mere reminder, or *Ehrenmal*, which honors someone or something from the past.[39] The Vereinigung der Verfolgten des Naziregimes (Association of Persecuted of the Nazi Regime) also protested the proposal, drawing attention to the exploitation of concentration camp prisoners as forced laborers at the site. Some Nuremberg citizens, welcoming the state office's position, offered a counterproposal of leaving the courtyard to a planned decay, which they said would "take care of its criminal world of thought."[40] According to their idea, a small pavilion in the space between the two end blocks would inform visitors of the National Socialist period and the history of the Nazi Party Rally Grounds, and a path in the center of the courtyard fenced with barbed-wire would symbolically exclude National Socialism from their lives.

An additional ten years had to pass before a resolution to face the artifact of the National Socialist past head-on. With a solid consensus formed among those involved by the mid-1990s, a board of trustees was established for a new documentation center in 1997, and on August 3, 1998, the city announced an invitational architectural competition for the Dokumentationszentrum Reichspartitagsgelände, to be housed in the uppermost floor of the northern end block.[41] Its explicit purposes were to serve as "a permanent establishment to the numerous visitors, who come to the site all year round and expect a comprehensive education about its history" and of presenting the "emergence, manifestations, and consequences of National Socialism."[42] The Center was to become the first step toward an overall concept for the future use of the former Nazi Party Rally Grounds. Based on having run the exhibit in the Zeppelin Grandstand building, the city expected 100,000 annual visitors.[43] Middle Bavarian and federal governments joined the city to fund the project, as did private sponsors and cultural foundations. Eight teams of architects were invited to the competition; three from Nuremberg and its environs and four from other German cities, including Peter Kulka from Cologne.[44] Günther Domenig (1934–2012), from Graz, Austria, was the only one from outside Germany. The deadline was October 23, and the jury met on November 11.

The first prize went to Domenig, the second to Johannes Hölzinger, and honorable mentions to Volker Staab and Frese and Kleindienst.[45] Domenig's design featured a "*Pfahl*," a stake, or a spear of steel and glass diagonally through the block (Figure 2.4).[46] The stake holds a space sized about 6' wide and 9' tall, which serves

FIGURE 2.4 Documentation Center, Nuremberg. The "*Pfahl*," or stake is the main design feature of the center design, which sticks out of the former Congress Hall, and the steel stairs lead the visitors to the center's entrance on the second floor. Photo by author.

as the museum entrance on one end and a platform overlooking the vast area on the other. Visitors enter the building at one end of the "*Pfahl*," meander through the orthogonal building through the permanent "Fascination and Terror" exhibit, reconnect with the spear, which jets out over the vast exterior court, and return to

52 Four Documentation Centers – Histories

the entrance foyer through the "*Pfahl*." The center also has 1,300 square meters of exhibition space and 450 square meters of the "International Learning Center" for films, lectures, and seminars.

Even after the competition, the city's leaders engaged in the debate on how best to create a memory place. On November 13 and 14, 1999, the Nuremberg City Museums held an international symposium titled "Future of the Past: How Should the History of the Third Reich be Transmitted in the 21st Century?" at the Deutsch-Amerikanischen Institut.[47] Invited speakers represented various Holocaust-related museums including the U.S. Holocaust Memorial Museum, which had opened in 1993. On this occasion, Franz Sonnenberger, Director of Nuremberg's City Museums since 1994, offered a retrospective of the city's attempts to deal with the built relics of the National Socialist past. The resolve and determination of those involved in the project to confront the past through the construction of a documentation center is clear in his statement:

> the historical burden of the former Reich Party Congress site is perhaps a unique opportunity. Where else would there be a comparable possibility of throwing critical light on the façade of the Third Reich, so giving the lie to new myths and legends? Where else would it be possible to analyse the "motivation machinery" of National Socialism?[48]

At the time of the competition, the city expected to have the construction completed by the fall of 2000, in time for the city's 950th anniversary. However, construction was delayed. The topping ceremony instead was held on November 15, 2000, and the building was opened a year later, on November 4, 2001. The permanent exhibit titled "Fascination and Terror" presents chronologically organized themes, including the rise of the National Socialist Party; mass myths and the Führer cult; Nuremberg as the city of the annual National Socialist Party Rally; the propaganda and reality of the Party; the Second World War and the Holocaust; and the Nuremberg Trials and after 1945.

History of the Topography of Terror Documentation Center, Berlin

The Topography of Terror Documentation Center (Figure 2.5), in Berlin, which opened in 2010, occupies the eastern half of a large city block bounded by Wilhelm Straße to the east, Prinz-Albrecht Straße (now Niederkirchnerstraße) to the north, Stresemanstraße (Königgrätzer Straße before 1930) to the west, and Anhalter Straße to the south. It is just one large city block southward from Potsdamerplaz, whose history goes back to the mid-eighteenth century. Then, the road to the city of Potsdam intersected with Berlin's city wall at Potsdam Gate, but now it is a large patch of land cut through by wide streets with heavy traffic and surrounded by skyscrapers. During the Third Reich, the site bound by these four streets contained the headquarters of the Secret State Police (Gestapo), the SA (Sturmabteilung, or

FIGURE 2.5 Documentation Center, Berlin. Photo by author.

"Brownshirts"), the SS, and the Reich Security Main Office (RSHA), the principal instruments of perpetration.[49] The site of this documentation center has been known as the Topography of Terror since 1987, after the title of an exhibit that opened that year as part of Berlin's 750th anniversary celebrations in a building designed by Jürg Steiner, who capped the underground kitchen cellars of a former SS mess hut.

Prior to 1933, the block had been occupied by a number of buildings and entities. At the northwest corner of the site was the Royal Museum of Ethnology (Königliches Museum für Völkerkunde, opened in 1886).[50] And moving eastward along Prinz-Albrecht Straße were found: the Museum of Applied Arts (Kunstgewerbemuseum), designed by Martin Gropius, great uncle of Walter Gropius and opened in 1881, at Prinz-Albrecht Straße 7;[51] the School of Industrial Arts and Crafts, built between 1901 and 1905, at Prinz-Albrecht Straße 8; and Hotel Prinz Albrecht, originally built as Hotel Römerbad in 1887–88, at Prinz-Albrecht-Straße 9 (Figure 2.6). Turning the northeast corner of the site onto Wilhelmstraße and moving southward, at 98–101 were several commercial and residential buildings; Prinz Albrecht Palais, built in 1737–39 originally as Palais Vernezobre, and remodeled by Karl Friedrich Schinkel for Prince Albrecht of Prussia in 1830–32, at 102; and the Palais's annex at 103 and 104; a commercial building at 106, built in 1903; and, at the southeast corner of the block, Hotel Wartburg. While the garden of Prinz Albrecht Palais originally occupied a large portion of the block, extending

54 Four Documentation Centers – Histories

FIGURE 2.6 Prinz-Albrecht-Straße, Berlin. 1933. Looking west. The building in the center is the former School of Industrial Arts and Crafts, which was turned into RSHA (Reich Security Main Office (Reichssicherheitshauptamt)). Beyond it, Museum of Applied Arts (now Martin-Gropius-Bau, exhibition venue) and, further on, the Royal Museum of Ethnology (demolished, now open space) are seen. Source: Bundesarchiv, Bild 183-R97512 / Fotograf: o.Ang.

to Königgräter Straße, a portion facing the street was sold, and the Europahaus, a commercial and office complex, was built during 1926–31.

During the National Socialist regime, an increasing number of these buildings that had existed on the site had been taken over by various functions of the National Socialist government. By the end of the 1930s, all buildings in the block except two, at Wilhelmstraße 105 and 107, were occupied by National Socialist organizations, including the Gestapo (Geheime Staatspolizei), the SS (Schutzstaffel or the Protection Squadron), the SD, and by the Reich Security Main Office. A commercial building was used by the National Socialist newspaper *Der Angriff* (*The Attack*). The block's location was advantageous because of its proximity to various government departments. The Ministry of Aviation was immediately to the north, and beyond that, one block further north on Wilhelm Straße, was the Reich's Chancellery complex.[52] The Old Chancellery originally had been Palais Radziwiłł, a city residence of the Polish prince Radziwiłł, but since 1875 was the Reich Chancellery to which Hitler entered in 1933 after being named Chancellor.[53] In 1930 the Chancellery Annex was completed next door to the south, designed by Eduard Jobst Siedler, to which Speer added a balcony for Hitler for public appearance in 1935. The large

FIGURE 2.7 Documentation Center, Berlin. In its context, looking west. Also seen are: at the far right of the image, the southwest corner of the former Aviation Ministry; the remains of the Berlin Wall running along Niederkirchnerstraße, former Prinz-Albrecht-Straße; and Martin-Gropius-Bau in the center. Photo by author.

New Reich Chancellery, designed by Speer and dedicated in 1939, stretched the entire city block from Wilhelm Straße to Hermann-Göring-Straße (now Ebert Straße) along Voßstraße. Anhalter rail station also was only a block away to the west.

Gestapo Headquarters were located at the former School of Industrial Arts and Crafts. The hotel building on Prinz-Albrecht-Straße was turned into the SS House by 1934, Heinrich Himmler, the SS Leader, having moved the most important offices there. The Prinz Albrecht Palais was use by the SD (Sicherheitsdienst), or the Security Service of the Reichsführer, since 1934 and by the RSHA (Reichssicherheitshauptamt), or the Reich Security Main Office, since 1939. The commercial building at Wilhelm Straße 106 was used, from 1932, by the National Socialist newspaper *Der Angriff*, founded by Joseph Goebbels.

At the end of the war, many buildings in the block carried various degrees of damage from the Allied Force's air raids, some heavily and others not to the extent that they were unrecoverable. Those that were less damaged – Europa House and Martin-Gropius-Bau – were then restored. Some of the buildings, including the former School of Industrial Arts and Crafts, were recoverable but destroyed in the mid-1950s. When the Berlin Wall was constructed in 1961, it ran along Niederkirchnerstraße, the former Prinz-Albrecht-Straße at the northern boundary of the block (Figure 2.7), and as a result, this area, which had been in the center of

56 Four Documentation Centers – Histories

the city, became the edge of West Berlin and lost its geographical importance. The block then became a dumping ground for demolition debris from throughout the city. One portion of the block was flattened and a driving circuit was laid, called Autodrom, where driving was permitted without license.

In 1982, Berlin's parliament held a debate over the future use of the site, and the Berlin Senate had held a national competition with international invitations, which now is considered the first of the series of three competitions for the site. The Berlin landscape architects Jürgen Wenzel and Nikolaus Lang won the first prize, and the Italian architect Giorgio Grassi the second. In 1984, however, the Berlin Senate decided not to execute the winning design. The cancellation was at least partially because of the question of whether artistic treatment of the site was the right way to go.[54] The piece written by Benedict Erenz and published in *Die Zeit* demonstrated the fact that the people perhaps were not ready to meaningfully confront the physical place with the difficult past:

> A competition for a memorial, organized as early as 1983–84, brought to light a lot of embarrassing facts: mythical landscapes, eternal flame and giant pillars – many of them reminded in a macabre manner of the monuments of the perpetrators, of Totenburg and Heldenhain. Even the impressive proposal of the first award winners, the sculptor Nikolaus Lang and the landscape architect Jürgen Wenzel, the entire area with terror documents (file sheets, deportation lists, command telegrams), poured into metal plates, to "seal" was placed for the time being in the drawer. The discomfort remains too great: if what was invented and commanded here can be remembered and remembered for the industrial murder of millions of people in stone and bronze, aestheticise? Does not all monument architecture of this kind – and examples abroad, whether the Warsaw ghetto memorial or the Parisian memorial for the deportees on the Ile de la Cité, prove this – does not this all have to be upscale grave-care art?

On May 5, 1985, citizens' groups, Active Museum Association (Verein Aktives Museum) and Berlin History Workshop, gathered together at the site and held a symbolic event focused on "digging" into the past called "Let's Dig." With the public interest in the historical significance of the site raised, in 1987, a temporary exhibition titled "Topography of Terror: Gestapo, SS and RSHA Reichssicherheitshauptamt (Reich Security Main Office) on the 'Prinz-Albrecht-Terrain'" opened as a part of Berlin's 750th anniversary celebrations. The exhibition, organized by the historian Reinhard Rürup, was a part of "Berlin, Berlin," the history exhibit held at the Martin-Gropius-Bau next door. The "Topography of Terror" was held in a temporary structure, designed by the architect Jürg Steiner of Berlin and built over the underground cellars of a former SS mess hut, which had been unearthed during construction work. The "Topography of Terror" exhibit was successful, resulting in the Berlin Senate's decision to extend it indefinitely. A book was published both in German and English based on the exhibition's contents.[55]

Four Documentation Centers – Histories **57**

In 1992, two years after German reunification, a foundation bearing the name of the exhibit "Topography of Terror" was established. The following year the State of Berlin held an international invitational competition for a permanent museum, and a year after that announced the Swiss architect Peter Zumthor as the winner. Construction began in 1997; however, it was halted in 1999. Technical and financial difficulties were immediate reasons. The concrete cores of the building stood on the site. In 2004, the State of Berlin and the Federal Government, the joint sponsors of the project, terminated it altogether, and the construction thus far accomplished was demolished during 2004–5. Andreas Nachama later reflected on the failure of this competition:

> When the history of this eradicated Berlin block between Niederkirchnerstraße and Wilhelmstraße was documented during the festivities in (West) Berlin commemorating the city's 750th anniversary in 1987, it was clear to everyone that this exhibition devoted to the history of the command centers of Nazi terror would not be displaced. The question soon (after 1987) arose as to how this (former command centers of Nazi terror) site should be designed so as to fit into the context of such memorials as Daniel Libeskind's prize-winning proposal for the Jewish Museum in Berlin, the U.S. Holocaust Memorial Museum in Washington and Yad Vashem in Jerusalem, which had been progressively expanded through the addition of new buildings and sculptures since the 1950s. Yet this frame of reference was wrong for a number of reasons. None of the places cited, not even Eisenman's Memorial to the Murdered Jews of Europe, was an original scene of Nazi terror. And they all shared the common objective of honoring the victims of the National Socialist system. What is unique about the "Topography of Terror" is that it was here that the desks of the perpetrators stood, perpetrators who left their desks from time to time to take command of infamous units composed of murderers and killers operating in occupied regions of Europe. All that remained of the original complex were isolated exterior walls and other fragments of foundations, which were exposed to view and later declared historical monuments in response to popular initiative.
>
> The design of this site cannot be accomplished by a sculptural structure that seeks to unite form and content. It requires an architecture that neither ducks its head nor hides in the ground nor imposes its form on the historical setting. One should not visit the "Gestapo grounds" in hopes of admiring sculptural inventions but instead to learn how a murderous, anti-democratic system emerged within only a few short months.
>
> When the decision was made to terminate the preceding project in late May of 2004, many people including employees of the Foundation, had little hope that a new plan could be found.[56]

Despite the pessimism Nachama described, another competition was held, organized by the BBR of Bundesamt für Bauwesen und Raumordnung (Federal

58 Four Documentation Centers – Histories

Office for Building and Regional Planning). The announcement of the competition was in April 2005, and the submission deadline was set in early December, with the announcement of the results in January. The management of the competition was performed by the same office, and in particular, Beate Hückelheim-Kaune, Architect, Head of the Unit; Philipp Dittrich, Architect; and Angela L. Kauls, Landscape Architect, the latter two of whom, with the Topography of Terror Foundation, were the authors of the competition brief, which gave a history of the site and referred to the two preceding competitions. The brief also explained why a building was needed: namely, the increasing number of visitors to the site, 350,000 per year, which is comparable, it stated, to those to the Jewish Museum and the Memorial to the Murdered Jews of Europe. Additionally, it stressed the site's significance: "a place not only of German but also of European history, and with national and international significance." It also resolved to find a design that confined the building within the specified budget, likely a reference to what happened with Zumthor's design. Out of 309 submissions to the first stage, 23 were selected for the second stage. At the end of the second stage, the first prize went to the team of the architect Ursula Wilms, of Heinle, Wischer und Partner, Berlin, and the landscape architect Heinz W. Hallmann, Aachen.

The construction of the new documentation center according to a prize-winning design was finished in 2010. The new documentation center was officially opened on May 6, 2010, by Federal President Horst Köhler on the occasion of the 65th anniversary of the end of the Second World War and was opened to the public the next day. The Documentation Center Topography of Terror had over one million visitors in 2016 and is one of the most visited memorial sites in Berlin.

History of the NS Documentation Center Munich

The NS Documentation Center Munich (Figure 2.8), which opened on May 1, 2015 is the newest addition to what is now identified as the city's Kunstareal, or Art District.[57] The center is only one kilometer away both from the Central Rail Station to the south, and from the Residenz to the east, the seat of government and the residence of the dukes, electors, and kings of the House of Wittelsbach of Bavaria from 1508 till 1918.[58] The designation of the area as a cultural zone goes back to early nineteenth century. Brienner Straße, on which the documentation center stands, is one of the road systems planned by Karl von Fischer (1782–1820), an academy professor and architect, and Friedrich Ludwig von Sckell (1750–1823), a court garden designer, for King Maximilian I Joseph of Bavaria and his successor Ludwig I, its construction beginning in 1812. The street originates in Odeonsplatz, immediately west of the Residenz's Hofgarten, and runs westward in the direction Nymphenburg Palace, the House of Wittelbach's main summer residence. It passes through Wittelsbacherplatz, Karolinenplatz, and Königsplatz, all designed by von Klenze. Especially Königsplatz (King's Square), called Königslicher Platz (Royal Square) till Hitler renamed it, was planned as a cultural zone, designed in reference to the Acropolis in Athens. At the west end of the square is Propyläen, in Doric style, designed as a city gate. It recalls the Propyläen of Acropolis. At the north of the square is Glyptothek, with Ionic columns, for the collection of sculptures from antiquity. And at the south, facing Glyptothek, is the Staatliche Antikensammlungen (State Antiquity Collection), in the manner of a Corinthian temple, to hold small Greek, Etruscan, and Roman art objects. The first two were designed by von Fischer and the third by Georg Friedrich Ziebland.

The documentation center is on the site on which Palais Barlow had stood, east of Königsplatz. This building had been designed by von Klenze's colleague Johann Baptist Métivier in neoclassical style and completed in 1828 for the aristocrat Karl Freiherr von Lotzbeck. But in 1930, it was owned by Elizabeth Stefanie Barlow, the widow of William Barlow (1869–1928), an English wholesale merchant, when it was purchased by the National Socialist Party. Paul Ludwig Troost, a favorite of Hitler till his unexpected death in 1934, was tasked with converting the Palais Barlow to a Parteiheim, or home of the party. Hitler is said to have been heavily involved in the renovation and to have enjoyed it, according to the journalist Konrad Heiden, a contemporary of Hitler.[59] On January 1, 1931, the party leadership moved into the building, often referred to as the Brown House (Figure 2.9). The stately building gave the party status even while the Weimar government was still in operation. Hitler, Heinrich Himmler, Hermann Göring, and Joseph Goebbels all had their offices in the building.

When Adolf Hitler became the Chancellor in January 1933 and Führer in August 1934, Munich was identified as the city of the National Socialist Movement. Königlicher Platz became Königsplatz and was changed according to the design by Troost. The square was enlarged by extending its bilateral symmetry eastward, toward the Brown House. The new eastern edge of the square was defined by the buildings designed by Troost: Führerbau and Verwaltungsbau der NSDAP (Administration Building of the National Socialist Party), constructed 1933–37, making a pair, and, between these two buildings, two Ehrentempelen (Honor Temples), constructed in 1935. The square, which had been full of green vegetations, was stripped bare, and became the NSDAP's demonstration grounds (Figure 1.1). The Brown House was damaged heavily during an Allied bombing raid in October 1943. Although its damage was not completely unrecoverable, it was decided to demolish it.

Immediately after the war, various ideas were put forward as to commemorating the National Socialist past. The American army, with the Allied Control Council Directive No. 30, which came into effect in July 1945, demanded that all monuments, names, and signs recalling the National Socialist regime be removed by January 1, 1947. General Eisenhower ordered that the Honor Temples be blown up. There also was a proposal by Munich's mayor, Karl Scharnagl, in July 1945, to melt down the 16 sarcophagi to make bells and to hang them in the "Temples of Honour," for "the idea of world peace."[60] In 1946, Cardinal Faulhaber proposed converting the Temples into a Catholic and a Protestant chapel. In the following month after the Temples were blown up, on January 9 and 16, 1947, the Bavarian

FIGURE 2.8 Documentation Center, Munich. View from northern Honor Temple eastward. Photo by author.

government invited a number of architects to submit proposals on what to do with the bases of the Temples, which remained fairly intact, and with the adjoining sites of the Brown House and the former Palais Degenfeld across the street. Some proposed to build and others to grow vegetations. After enduring heavy criticism of the winning design for its stylistic resemblance to National Socialist architecture, and

FIGURE 2.9 Brown House, Munich. 1930. View from Brienner Straße eastward. Note the swastika and the propaganda "Dem Wachenden Deutschland" ("Awakening Germany") atop the cornice. Photograph: Heinrich Hoffmann. Source: Bayerische Staatsbibliothek München/Bildarchiv, hoff-6982.

62 Four Documentation Centers – Histories

after yet another unsuccessful competition, the government decided in 1948 not to build, but to fence the bases in wood, and to plant vegetation to hide the Temples, Führerbau, and the Administration Building.[61] The exhibit in the center explains this as "the advent of a long-standing defensive approach to the Nazi past which sought to avoid a direct and productive confrontation with it."[62] In the same year a proposal was put forward to turn the Führerbau and the Administration Building into a hotel complex to attract foreign visitors, but it was rejected. There also was an idea in late 1945 to rename Königsplatz "Platz der Opfer des Nationalsozialismus" ("Square of the Victims of National Socialism") and Brienner Straße "Straße der Opfer des Nationalsozialismus" ("Streets of the Victims of National Socialism"), which met the rejection that the name Königsplatz should be retained as a "positive" reference to the past.[63]

As to the idea of establishing a place of commemoration of the National Socialist past in the city of the Party movement, a number of sites were considered: Wittelbachers Palais and the northern end of Maximiliansplatz, both of which are on Brienner Straße. Wittelbacher Palais was built as a royal prince's palace in the 1840s but beginning in 1933 was used as the headquarters of the Gestapo, and as its prison the following year. It was damaged heavily during the 1944 air raids and was demolished in 1951. The 1955 application to build a "House of Culture," submitted by former concentration camp prisoners, now members of the city council, was rejected by the Bavarian Prime Minister.[64] In 1961, the City of Munich purchased the site, but the area previously occupied by the palace remained in the hands of the Bavarian State. With both governments intending to turn it into a green space with a memorial to the victims of National Socialist persecution, in 1964, the Gestapo prison, which remained on the site as commercial property, was demolished.[65] The idea of building a "House of Culture" in this site dwindling, the city sold its share of the site to the Bavarian State Bank in 1974. With the 1982 completion of the Bank building occupying the entire site, the notion of a memorial was completely discarded.[66]

Maximiliansplatz was discussed because of its location – the site of Wittelbacher Palais was visible from there across Brienner Straße – and because of the monument there of Friedrich Schiller, a friend of Goethe and a thinker on questions concerning human freedom.[67] The first move was in 1946, when on the "Day for the Victims of Fascism," Mayor Karl Scharnagl announced that the site would be dedicated to the victims of National Socialism. In the mid-1960s, a memorial stone was placed to commemorate "the victims of National Socialism." It must be noted that Winfried Nerdinger recognizes, as Mayor Hans-Jochen Vogel realized then, too, that this was not an effective memorial as it helped support the population's self-victimization.[68] In 1983, a competition was held for the design of a monument to be placed in the Platz der Opfer des Nationalsozialismus. A granite column with a gas flame, designed by Andreas Sobeck, was put up in 1985, carrying an inscription, "To the victims of the National Socialist regime of tyranny."

Debate over what to do with the Königsplatz area resurfaced at the end of the 1970s. In 1986 the governments of the city of Munich and the state of Bavaria made

Four Documentation Centers – Histories **63**

a joint decision and in the following year removed the granite slabs on Königsplatz from the National Socialist era to restore the square back to its nineteenth-century appearance, with the exception of a new traffic pattern. The square had been used as a parking lot since after the war. The Bavarian government planned a competition to build new cultural institutions over the bases of the Honor Temples, intending to "expunge the former 'Forum of the Movement' from the collective memory." The city council rejected this plan, however, and instead a "Haus der Zeitgeschichte" (House of Contemporary History) was proposed on the site of the former Brown House. This idea was not included in the competition and demonstrated the general lack of awareness of how to deal with the historical site.[69] This prompted a civic outcry, and as the idea for a documentation center started to gain public support, the Bavarian government abandoned the project.

In the 1990s a number of exhibitions, symposia, and publications were organized. Two of the more notable were "Bauen im Nationalsozialismus. Bayern 1933–1945 (Buildings in National Socialism. Bavaria 1933–1945)," a City Museum exhibit and resulting publication; and "München: Hauptstadt der Bewegung (Munich: Capital of the Movement)," in 1993–94.[70] In the early 2000s, the city received requests to approach the Bavarian government to establish a documentation center either in the area around Königsplatz or specifically at the site of the former Brown House; these requests were in vain because the Bavarian government was not forthcoming. But finally after an event in November 2001 titled "A Documentation Centre for Munich," and a lecture on how Munich had treated its National Socialist past was printed in *Süddeutsche Zeitung* and commented on in a Swiss newspaper as well as in *Frankfurter Allgemeine Zeitung*, the Bavarian parliament decided to establish a documentation center.

In 2002, Initiativkreis für ein NS-Dokumentationszentrum was formed, although the concept for a documentation center still was not on firm ground: At one point, the Bavarian government and the city government intended to treat the involvement of Munich in National Socialist history lightly, and felt that a comprehensive documentation center was unnecessary given those at Nuremberg and Obersalzberg. There also were two different directions for a center: one that advocated a House of the History of National Socialism with original exhibits, and another, put forward by Winfried Nerdinger, that promoted a center focused on Munich without any original exhibits. In 2004, the city council unanimously approved the latter. A scientific advisory board of 15 members was established in 2005. The board, although made up of members with diverse opinions, persuaded the Bavarian government to make the site of the Brown House available. The funding was to be shared equally between the city, state, and federal governments.[71]

In December 2005 the Bavarian government announced its plans to establish a Documentation Centre for the History of National Socialism at the site. A two-stage competition was held, and the office of Georg Scheel Wetzel Architekten was announced the winner in 2009. The foundation stone was laid in March 2012. The documentation center opened to the public in 2015, coinciding with the 70th anniversary of the occupation of Munich and of liberation from National Socialism.

64 Four Documentation Centers – Histories

In 2009 Irmtrud Wojak was appointed founding director; however, the contract was suspended in 2011, and Nerdinger was then appointed founding director in 2012.

When it was decided to construct a documentation center, the site was excavated, and some remaining foundations were found. The competition program specified the footprint of the Brown House on the site.[72] While others followed the rectangular floor plan for the Brown House, the winning design proposed a square floor plan instead.

While the four documentation centers examined in this book have had varied histories, they all were characterized by their prestigious and advantageous locations to the benefit of the National Socialist regime, either for their adjacency to the city center or because the large area already well established as a city park or an urban cultural square was suitable for the party activities. And the sites remain advantageous at the present as documentation centers. On the road to establishing a documentation center, citizens' or citizens groups' involvement cannot be overlooked, who drew attention to the sites' National Socialist past. Additionally, there had been forerunners in the form of either documentation depository or a smaller or more temporary exhibitions. The communities engaged the professions of designers in an increasing degree in soliciting design proposals. The sequence began with a commission to a specific design group, but moved to an invited competition involving German and Austrian designers, then to invitational international competition finally to international open competitions. The widening of the net that were cast as well as openness of solicitation may mean an increasing interest in the communities and also increasing trust in the profession.

Notes

1 Petra Leser, "Die Baugeschichte des Rheinischen Appellations-gerichtshofes in Köln," in Udo Mainzer and Petra Leser, *Architektur Geschichten Festschrift für Günther Binding zum 60. Geburtstag* (Köln: J.P. Bachem, 1996), 183–96.

2 Manfred Huiskes and Alexandra Gal, eds., *Die Wandinschriften des Kölner Gestapo-Gefängnisses im EL-DE-Haus, 1943–1945* (Köln: Böhlau, 1983), 14.

3 Deutscher Werkbund was closed in 1938 by the National Socialist regime.

4 "Mitgliederverzeichnis Bundesämter Satzung des Deutschen Werkbundes," ("Member lists of the federal offices statute of German Werkbund") dated May 1, 1913, lists Hans Erberich as "Regierungsbaumeister, Architekt, Köln Mozartstraße 1." http://www. werkbund-initiativ.de/PDF/1913%20DWB%20Gesamt-Verzeichnis.pdf

5 "The History of the EL-DE House," NS Dokumentationszentrum der Stadt Köln, https://museenkoeln.de/ns-dokumentationszentrum/default.aspx?s=715. See also: NS-Dokumentationszentrum, ed., *Cologne during National Socialism: A Short Guide through the EL-DE House* (Köln: NS Documentation Centre of the City of Cologne: Emons, 2011).

6 Huiskes and Gal, *Die Wandinschriften des Kölner Gestapo-Gefängnisses im EL-DE-Haus*, 14.

7 These two buildings now house the City Museum.

8 Huiskes and Gal, *Die Wandinschriften des Kölner Gestapo-Gefängnisses im EL-DE-Haus*, 11.

9 Ibid., 15.

10 Ibid., 14.

11 Ibid., 9.

Four Documentation Centers – Histories **65**

12 Ibid., 10.
13 Ibid.
14 Huiskes and Gal, *Die Wandinschriften des Kölner Gestapo-Gefängnisses im EL-DE-Haus*, 11.
15 Ibid.
16 Ibid., 12.
17 Ibid.
18 Ibid., 14 and 46.
19 Ibid., 14.
20 Ibid.
21 Ibid.
22 Ibid., 48.
23 Ibid., 50.
24 Ibid., 52.
25 Ibid., 49, 51. Matzerath retired from this position in 2002. He is the author of: *Köln in der Zeit des Nationalsozialismus 1933–1945* (Köln: Greven, 2009).
26 "Architecture of the Exhibit" NS-Dokumentationszentrum der Stadt Köln, https:// museenkoeln.de/ns-dokumentationszentrum/default.aspx?s=770 (Accessed August 7, 2017).
27 After the allied bombing destroyed much of the city, the old fabric was reconstructed, taking four decades. See: "Nuremberg Rebuilt – City at the Crossroads." *New York Times* (April 8, 1984) NYTimes.com, accessed July 27, 2017, http://www.nytimes.com/1984/ 04/08/travel/nuremberg-rebuilt-city-at-the-crossroads.html?pagewanted=all.
28 Hans-Christian Täubrich ed., *Fascination and Terror: Documentation Centre Party Rally Grounds: The Exhibition* (Nürnberg: Museen der Stadt Nürnberg, 2006), 41–3.
29 Alexander Schmidt, *Geländebegehung: das Reichsparteitagsgelände in Nürnberg* (Nürnberg: Sandberg Verlag, 2002), 177.
30 Matthias Donath, *Architecture in Berlin 1933–1945: A Guide through Nazi Berlin* (Berlin: Lukas Verlag, 2006), 13.
31 Täubrich, *Fascination and Terror*, 9–10.
32 Schmidt, *Geländebegehung*, 48. See also: Nuremberg City Museums, "*Dokumentationszentrum Reichsparteitagsgelände*," pamphlet (November 4, 2001); and H.-W. Lübbeke, Chief Conservator of Bayern state office for the preservation of monuments, Munich, an attachment (WU14) to "*Eingeladener Realisierungswettbewerb Dokumentationszentrum Reichsparteitagsgelände Nürnberg, Anslober: Stadt Nürnberg, Tag der Anslobung*: 03.08.1998," ("Invitational realization competition Documentation Center Nazi Party Rally Grounds Nuremberg, Issuer: The City of Nuremberg, Day of Issue: August 3, 1998") (competition program hereafter), Architekturzentrum Wien (Az-W hereafter).
33 Museen der Stadt Nürnberg, "*Neues Zeichen – Die Architektur des Dokumentationszentrums Reichsparteitagsgelände*," news release (November 15, 2000), Az-W.
34 Hermann Glaser, "The Majority Could Have Stayed Away without the Risk of Repression," *The German Public and the Persecution of the Jews, 1933–1945*, ed. Jörg Wollenberg and Rado Pribić (Atlantic Highlands, NJ: Humanities Press, 1996), 15– 21, 15–16. Glaser is quoting a reporter from the Fränkische Tageszeitung, November 11, 1938.
35 An exhibition titled "Stadt der Reichsparteitage" ("The City of the Nazi Party Rally") was held on September 8–30, 1937, at the Germanic National Museum of Nuremberg, organized by the *Amt Schrifttumspflege bei dem Beauftragten des Führers für die Überwachung der gesamten geistigen und weltanschaulichen Erziehung der NSDAP*, or the Office of the Führer's representative for the supervision of the entire spiritual and ideological

66 Four Documentation Centers – Histories

education of the or National Socialist German Workers' Party. The poster announcing this exhibit highlighted the city's transformation from that of the Imperial Diet to that of the Nazi Party Rally.

36 For the postwar history of the former Congress Hall, see: Alexander Schmidt, "'Ein Felsklotz, der in der Gegend Steht': Die Kongresshalle nach 1945," Hans-Christian Täubrich, ed., *Die Kongresshalle Nürnberg: Architektur Und Geschichte* (Petersberg: Michael ImhofVerlag, 2014), 90–111.

37 Franz Sonnenberger, Eckart Dietzfelbinger, and Nuremberg Municipal Museums, *Faszination und Gewalt, das Reichsparteitagesgelände in Nürnberg (Fascination and Terror, The Nazi Party Rally Grounds in Nuremberg)* (Nürnberg: Museen der Stadt Nürnberg, 1996). See also: Bernd Ogan and Wolfgang W Weiss. *Faszination und Gewalt: Zur politischen Ästhetik des Nationalsozialismus* (Nürnberg: Tümmels, 1992).

38 Michael Petzet later became the President of the German National Committee of ICOMOS (1989-) and the President of ICOMOS International (1999 and 2008). See: "Michael Petzet, Advisor, Conservationist,"'"dOCUMENTA (13) – dOCUMENTA (13)," accessed May 25, 2017, http://d13.documenta.de/#participants/participants/michael-petzet/.

39 Sharon Macdonald, *Difficult Heritage: Negotiating the Nazi Past in Nuremberg and Beyond* (New York: Routledge, 2009).

40 According to their idea, a small pavilion in the space between the two end blocks would inform visitors of the Nazi period and the history of the Nazi Party Rally Grounds, and a path in the center of the courtyard fenced with barbed-wire would symbolically exclude National Socialism from their lives.

41 Competition program, section 2. Az-W.

42 Competition program. Az-W.

43 Franz Sonnenberger, "A City Confronts Its Past: Nuremberg's Documentation Centre on the Reich Party Congress Site; 1999." *Museum International* 51, no. 3 (July 1999): 53–7, 54, accessed May 25, 2017, www.unesco.org/ulis/cgi-bin/ulis.pl?catno=116849&set=0059274FF7_2_321&gp=1&lin=1&ll=1. For information on Franz Sonnenberger, see: "Nürnberger Museen-Chef Geht in Ruhestand," *Nürnberger Nachrichten [Nuremberg News]* (August 23, 2008), accessed July 19, 2017, www.nordbayern.de/cm/2.244/kultur/nurnberger-museen-chef-geht-in-ruhestand-1.853649. See also: *Nuremberg: The Imaginary Capital*, 272; Mcdonald, *Difficult Heritage*, 207.

44 Dürschinger & Biefang; Frese & Kleindienst; and Arbeitsgemeinschaft Hennig & Mihm with Dietrich Lohmann from Nuremberg and its environ; Johannes Hölzinger from Bad Nauheim (north of Frankfurt); Architekten am Pündterplatz with Jörg Homeier and Gerold Richter from Munich; Johann Peter Kulka from Cologne; and Volker Staab from Berlin. Az-W.

45 *Wettbewerbe Aktuell*, March 1999, 44–5.

46 The pun of Speer and spear, which works in English, is from: Steven Erlanger, "Nuremberg Journal; The Architect Who Speared His Own Nazi Demon." *The New York Times*, November 8, 2001, http://www.nytimes.com/2001/11/08/world/nuremberg-journal-the-architect-who-speared-his-own-nazi-demon.html.

47 Franz Sonnenberger et al., eds., *Die Zukunft der Vergangenheit: wie soll die Geschichte des Nationalsozialismus in Museen und Gedenkstätten im 21. Jahrhundert vermittelt werden? (The Future of the Past: How Should the History of the Third Reich Be Transmitted in the 21st Century?)* (Nürnberg: Museen der Stadt Nürnberg, 2000).

48 Franz Sonnenberger, "A City Confronts Its Past," 54–5.

49 "Topography of Terror," accessed May 21, 2017, www.topographie.de/.

Four Documentation Centers – Histories **67**

50 The building was demolished after the war and now the site is left open space.
51 Martin-Gropius-Bau is a new now an exhibition venue.
52 For the significance of Wilhelmstraße, see also Laurenz Demps, "Wilhelmstraße" in *Die Wilhelmstrasse 1933–1945: Aufstieg und Untergang des NS-Regierungsviertels* (*The rise and fall of the Nazi Government Quarter*) by Claudia Steur (Berlin: Topographie des Terrors, 2012), 161–4.
53 Steven Lehrer, *The Reich Chancellery and Führerbunker Complex: An Illustrated History of the Seat of the Nazi Regime* (Jefferson, NC: McFarland & Co, 2006), 24ff.
54 Erika Bucholtz et al., *Site Tour "Topography of Terror" History of the Site* (Berlin: Stiftung Topographie des Terrors, 2016), 94.
55 Reinhard Rürup ed., *Topography of Terror: Gestapo, SS and Reichssicherheitshauptamt on the "Prinz-Albrecht-Terrain": A Documentation*, trans. Werner T. Angress (Berlin: Willmuth Arenhövel, 1989).
56 Andreas Nachama, "Topographie Des Terrors: Wittbewerb Für Ein Dokumentationsgebäude," *Bau Und Raum: Jahrbuch, Bundesamt Für Bauwesen Und Raumordnung*, 2006, 118–29; 121.
57 The Art District includes: museums such as Alte Pinakothek, built in the first half of the nineteenth century by the order of King Ludwig I of Bavaria and designed by Leo von Klenze and inaugurated in 1836; and Staatliches Museum Ägyptischer Kunst (State Museum of Egyptian Art), which had been housed since 1970 in the Hofgarten wing of Munich Residence but now has been moved to the new building designed by Peter and Gottfried Böhm; cultural institutions such as Amerikahaus Münich; and universities such as Akademie der Bildenden Künste München (Academy of Fine Arts Munich).
58 In 1918 King Ludwig III released his officials from their oath of loyalty on the day following the Armistice.
59 Konrad Heiden, *The Führer*, trans. Ralph Manheim and Richard Overy (New York: Skyhorse Publishing, 2012). Konrad Heiden was a journalist and contemporary of Hitler.
60 Winfried Nerdinger, *Erinnerung gegründet auf Wissen / Remembrance Based on Knowledge. Das NS-Dokumentationszentrum München / The Munich Documentation Centre for the History of National Socialism* (Berlin: Metropol-Verlag, 2018), 11.
61 Winfried Nerdinger, *Remembrance Based on Knowledge*, 13–15. See also NS-Dokumentationszentrum München et al., *Munich and National Socialism: Catalogue of the Munich Documentation Centre for the History of National Socialism* (München: Beck, 2015), 85.
62 NS-Dokumentationszentrum München et al., *Munich and National Socialism*, 86.
63 Nerdinger, *Remembrance Based on Knowledge*, 13.
64 Ibid., 17.
65 Ibid., 21.
66 Ibid., 23.
67 Ibid., 15.
68 Ibid., 21.
69 Ibid., 29.
70 Ibid., 31.
71 Ibid., 37–9.
72 Klaus Bäumler, "The Munich Documentation Centre for the History of National Socialism: 'Munich's Belated Path,'" NS-Dokumentationszentrum München et al., *Munich and National Socialism*, 91.

3

IN THE SHADOW OF PROPAGANDA ARCHITECTURE

Complex issues surround the question of how, if at all, the architectural design converting historical *Täterorte* into documentation centers on National Socialism can contribute toward the meaningful presentation of the past. The issues have to do with what we expect from today's architectural design in general as well as what roles architecture played in the National Socialist era in particular, which resonate in historical buildings. On the one hand, we expect architecture to be artistic: Especially when a well-known architect is involved, we often consider the work as an object of art and as the designer's self-expression. On the other, we also have utilitarian expectations: We often assume architectural design is a provider of a well-functioning container. Additionally, when we confront the historical perpetrator buildings that still exist on the project site either physically or in memory, we cannot but be reminded of the propagandistic power they exuded or of the evil actions that were committed in them during the National Socialist era. Especially under this particular circumstance, endowing architectural design with the ability to evoke the past can be met with ambivalence, suspicion, or contention. This chapter will review the expectations toward historical buildings as well as toward architectural design in the context of the documentation centers that stand on perpetrators' places. In particular, it will examine Adolf Hitler's view of architecture, which inevitably accompanies historical perpetrator buildings, and the resistance against architectural design that seems to be laden with the architect-artist's self-expression as it was exemplified in the criticism against the winning scheme by Peter Zumthor for the 1993 competition for Topography of Terror documentation center in Berlin.

Hitler's View of Architecture

In Germany, the symbolic value of architecture is a laden topic, particularly because of how Hitler used architecture for propaganda and domination. It is

In the Shadow of Propaganda Architecture **69**

understandable that, when faced with the perpetrators' buildings, especially in the early postwar period, people often desired to demolish them, as if demolishing the buildings would destroy the political ideology they represented as well as the memories associated with them. Given this context, converting historical perpetrator buildings into documentation centers is controversial. To begin with, just as in the early postwar period, there is, understandably, a question of whether to encourage using historical buildings to reflect on the past and its ideology and deeds. Second, there is another question of whether to bestow the new architecture with expressive power. We only have to refer to Günther Domenig's statement to know the architect's recognition of this challenge. In this statement, Domenig recalled his first visit to the former Congress Hall in preparation for the competition for the Nuremberg center.[1] The building tour took place on September 16, 1998, as part of a colloquium offered by the City of Nuremberg to the invited competitors.[2] Domenig stated: "During the visit, icy coldness came over me. The dust of the dead in the interior spaces and the architectural translation of the power – there were only right angles and axes."[3] How Domenig tried to destroy this "power" will be discussed later (Chapters 5 and 6), but in this chapter, we will examine how Hitler and his architects saw the symbolic power of architecture and its lasting legacy even after the makers' death and the buildings' ruination.

Hitler and his strong interest in architecture and involvement in designing are well known. In *Mein Kampf*, the two-volume book published in 1925 and 1926, he recounted his path to anti-Semitism and laid out his political ideology and future plans for Germany. The account included how the young Hitler had tried to gain admission to an art school in Vienna, thinking that he would become a painter, how he did not succeed, and how instead he was told his aptitude would be more suited to the study of architecture. At about the same time of the book's publication, Hitler also was making plans for buildings. In 1936, after taking power, he handed some drawings to Speer, adding a note: "I made these drawings ten years ago. I have always held onto them, because I never doubted that one day I would build them. And now we want to make them happen."[4] Hitler had favorite architects, first Troost, and, after his unexpected death in 1934, Albert Speer, who was made General Inspector for the Redesign of the Capital on January 30, 1937, and was accountable to the Führer directly.[5] But Hitler himself was involved heavily in the design of buildings that various functions of his regime were to occupy. For example, according to Jochen Thies, in 1936 Hitler "sat for many hours" surveying the models of buildings being designed for the five "Führer cities," Berlin, Munich, Nuremberg, Hamburg, and Linz.[6] Hitler also produced some sketches of the balcony to be added to the Chancellery Annex and for the New Reich Chancellery building.[7]

Hitler believed in the effectiveness of architecture as political propaganda, and what we characterize as stripped-off classicism was the style he favored. Accordingly, as Daniel Grinceri noted, "the building constructed by the National Socialists," and the buildings adopted for their important headquarters, were "not intended to be 'ordinary' buildings. Their colossal scale and unified aesthetic make the buildings of

70 In the Shadow of Propaganda Architecture

the Third Reich some of the most recognizable and studied objects in the world."[8] Grinceri stated further:

> Many of the public and government buildings constructed by the Third Reich are easily identifiable as a result of their adherence to a particular brand of "stripped back" neo-classical architecture. There buildings are typically out of scale with other surrounding buildings and distinguished by their stone masonry structures. This brand of neo-classicism was intended to link the National Socialist movement with the imperial power of Athens and Rome, and present the Reich as indomitable and all-powerful. However, the Nazis were not the only governing authority to embrace this architectural style.[9]

Hitler's conviction and preference for Roman architecture were rooted in his obsession with its power's geographical reach, as he desired his own domination. According to Alexander Scobie, "Hitler was more fascinated by the scale of Rome's political power [than that of the Ancient Greek's], and by the size of the state buildings that symbolized and represented it."[10] Hitler's enthusiasm toward Rome commented in a conversation how wide the empire's political reach was: "The Roman Empire never had its like. To have succeeded in completely ruling of the world! And no empire has spread its civilization as Rome did."[11]

Rome, with its wide reach of power, was Hitler's political model. He also had Mussolini to compete with and refer to because the other man had a way of taking advantage of Roman architecture as the background of his political propaganda. The Colosseum in particular was a backdrop against which Mussolini showcased his power and lineage, and planned his parades' routes strategically to have the ruin of Roman architecture in the background. When Hitler visited Mussolini on May 3, 1938, the latter took the former to a military parade through the city from Ostia station to Quirinale Palace, and no doubt Hitler experienced the propagandistic effects.[12] Hitler, in parallel, used Nuremberg Castle as the starting point of his annual party parade. When photographed, the parade would show the castle in the backdrop. Situated atop the ridge and on the northern edge of the city's medieval fortifications, Nuremberg Castle had been one of the Imperial seats of the Holy Roman Empire. As the empire did not have a fixed location, the emperor traveled the realm, from one Imperial city to another. When the emperor was in residence, Nuremberg Castle was a place for both the Imperial Diet (Reichstag) and the Imperial Courts of Law (Reichsgerichte). Dominating the view of the city, the castle symbolized the power of the emperor and of the important role the city of Nuremberg played, as can be seen in many medieval drawings of the city. Hitler took advantage of this historical significance of the city and the Roman Empire's power and reach. In 1933, when he decided to make Nuremberg the fixed location for the annual party rallies, which previously had been held in Munich (1923), Weimar (1926), and Nuremberg (1927 and 1929), he called them "Reichsparteitage (Reich's party rallies)," in a direct reference to the Imperial Diet, "Reichstag." Not only did Hitler begin his parade at

Nuremberg Castle but the wide street (named Große Straße), constructed as part of the Reichsparteitagsgelände (Reich's Party Rally Grounds), was aligned in the direction of the castle. Here again, just like Mussolini, Hitler was using the historically significant building to showcase his power.

He stated: "Roman history in broad outline, and correctly understood, is and remains the best instructress, not only for today, but indeed for all periods."[13] And he even argued that Germans were the descendants of the Ancient Romans.[14] And now, to Hitler, it was his Germany that would, with its architecture, even surpass the glory of Rome. Hitler stated:

> With an arch of triumph, the military Pantheon and the square of the people – things that will take your breath away, we will now be able to outdo our only rival in the world, Rome. It shall be built according to such dimensions that St. Peter's and the square in front of it will seem like toys by comparison.[15]

And, according to Hitler, the persuasion that architecture exudes was not to be limited to the contemporaneous audience. It was to last centuries, even after the regime's power declined and the buildings became ruins, just as it had done in Rome. The future generations were to look back at the greatness of his monuments as a reminder of the greatness of the regime that had created them. On April 29, 1929, in a speech, he compared his architecture to that of Napoleon I and Napoleon III, who, according to Hitler, did not just make their buildings central points of France: "but rather to make it the shining central point of the whole world."[16] In 1936 Hitler stated that "eternal works" built in Berlin would be "comparable only to Ancient Egypt, Babylon and Rome."[17] In the following year he stated:

> … the major cultural documents of humanity made of granite and marble have stood for millennia. And these are the only true stationary poles in the flood of all other manifestations. In times of decay, humanity has continued to return to them in search of eternal magical power and it has always found it there as a means to gain control of its confusion and establish a new order / from the chaos. This is why our buildings should not be built for the year 1940 and not for the year 2000, but like the cathedrals of our past they shall reach into the millennia of the future.[18]

How did architecture's persuasion compare to that of written text, speeches, or military parades? According to Albrecht Koschorke, *Mein Kampf* is long and not meant for a mass audience but for select readers. It is in two volumes; it refers to the masses in the third person plural; and it treats them in a derogatory mode. Although Hitler of course did express his will and desire in it, according to Koschorke, he did not see *Mein Kampf* as a means of mass persuasion. In comparison, the parades, and the speeches he gave at these occasions, were intended to convince the population at large. Architecture was similar to these because it was public, and was always there as the backdrop when he used the parades and speeches

72 In the Shadow of Propaganda Architecture

for mass demonstrations.[19] He would locate himself in front of a certain building for maximum effect to observe the parade or to give a speech. Similarly, just as Mussolini had a balcony on the eastern façade of Palazzo Venezia for appearances and speeches, Hitler had his own – first the one in the old President's Palace facing Wilhelmstraße, and later, the one he was heavily involved in designing, on the Chancellery building.

Because, as scholar Jordan Thies notes, under oppressive governments, "[A]rchitecture, especially, is in a position to be misused, as it gives the propaganda of a totalitarian regime the chance to develop a very permanent form of demonstration,"[20] it is natural in the postwar era for the German community leaders to be cautious about the symbolic nature of architecture and to try to remove its power. This was manifested in the demolitions of the National Socialist buildings but also extended to structures that were not perpetrator buildings but that merely had references to classicism. The 1977 international invitational competition for the design of Neue Staatsgalerie in Stuttgart is one indication of this, and especially its use of Postmodernist form, as pointed out by Gavriel Rosenfeld.[21] When in 1979 the jury's unanimous selection of James Stirling was announced, his reference to historic forms, including the floor plan of the Altes Museum in Berlin designed by Schinkel, was abundantly clear. To many of those who operated within Modernist design, this blatant historical reference in architectural forms was greatly problematic, not the least in relation to the postwar era architecture that had tried to get away from National Socialist architecture.

Léon Krier's project to publish Albert Speer's works could be understood as another manifestation of this impulse. When Krier published a book on Albert Speer's architecture in 1985, his purpose was to strip the National Socialist associations and implications out of the National Socialist architecture. Krier advocated looking at the buildings' form as devoid of meaning, and called them beautiful. This invited many objections, most very forceful. Joan Oakman has put forward a well-argued opposition that even if the form on its own may be devoid of any specific meaning, the National Socialist buildings can never be disassociated in people's minds from the atrocities of the regime. In 1989, in his article in *Werk: Bauen + Wohnen*, Dieter Hoffmann-Axthelm referred both to Aldo Rossi, whose work had strong historical references if only through typology, and to Rob Krier, brother of Léon.[22] Here, Hoffmann-Axthelm characterized postmodernism take on history as "… ist eine Architektur, die sich damit begnügt, Vergangenheit in Objektform zu produzieren, nicht genug (an architecture that is content to produce past in object form is not enough)," and that this is where the difficulty of the "Architektur als Gedächtnis (architecture as a memory)" lies.

And the concerns about the expressive architecture, rooted in the apprehension and trepidation toward architecture as a vehicle of National Socialist propaganda, seem to have cast some shadows on documentation center projects to varied degrees, but especially in Berlin and Munich. These concerns were, if not the only, at least one, reason behind the cancellation of the execution of Peter Zumthor's winning design for the 1993 Topography of Terror competition in Berlin. They also seem to have loomed over the subsequent Berlin and Munich competitions, whose program included a statement in its program to argue against the symbolic use of architecture.

Peter Zumthor's Topography of Terror Design and "Speaking Architecture"

"Nur kein zweiter Zumthor! (Just no second Zumthor!)" With this interjection, in the February 24, 2006, issue of the architectural journal *Bauwelt*, the sentiment that had governed the 2005 Topography of Terror competition was summed up by Dieter Hoffmann-Axthelm, a Berlin architecture critic who was one of the first to draw people's attention to this former site of the Gestapo, SS, SD, and RSHA headquarters, and who was to become an influential critic on the treatment of the site through the opening of the current documentation center.[23] In this article, Hoffmann-Axthelm was analyzing both the program of the competition issued in April 2005 and the jury selection of eight winning designs announced in January 2006. The sentiment represented in this article demonstrates the difficulties, especially in the context of Germany's postwar *Vergangenheitsbewältigung*, of exploiting architecture's symbolic power, and in turn, of allowing architecture to play a role as something other than a container. But, in order to understand the sentiment, we need to go back to what Hoffmann-Axthelm referred to when he said "Zumthor," the competition held a decade earlier and its aftermath, which Eckhardt Barthel, a member of the Deutsches Bundestag (Federal House of Representatives), characterized as the "ordeal."[24]

The Swiss architect Peter Zumthor had won the international invitational competition held in 1993 for the Topography of Terror documentation center. Work was begun in 1997, but was halted in 1999. In May 2004, the federal government publicly announced the termination of the project. Accordingly, what already had been built of Zumthor's design up to that point, including vertical shafts of poured-on-site concrete, was demolished. Escalating cost was cited as the reason for terminating the project. Hoffmann-Axthelm, in his 2004 article in the journal *Ästhetik und Kommunikation*, listed three contributing faults. The first on his list was the cost. According to Hoffmann-Axthelm, the client, the State of Berlin, commissioned the project to the construction company with the lowest bid, which turned out to lack the necessary technical competency, which in turn led to "endless problems of feasibility, delays, opinions on appraisals." However, there were a number of additional issues that are more complex. Hoffmann-Axthelm's second and third reasons are intricately related to each other and bear significance to the present discussion: In them, Hoffmann-Axthelm saw two "contradictions": one was between the desire of the architect who "realizes an aesthetic dream" and the expectation of the user who "wants a comfortable cover," and the other was between "speaking terrain and state commemorative culture."[25] It is important to

74 In the Shadow of Propaganda Architecture

note that in the article, Hoffmann-Axthelm acknowledged Zumthor's intention of letting the terrain speak on its own. And yet, he concluded that the architect "believed more in his own project than in the language ability of the terrain." Further, he stated:

> Zumindest hätte Zumthor, angesichts gleich zweier Gegner, Bauverwaltung und Ausstellungsinstitution, radikal vcreinfachen müssen, um durchzukommen. Statt dessen hat er durch Veredelung seines Projekts – eine Holzkonstruktion,die experimentell in Beton ausgefohrt werden soll, bei der aus dem Rohbeton des Wettbewerbsentwurfs im Ausführungsprojekt weißer Beton wird – selbst seine Unterstützer enttäuscht.[26]

> (At least Zumthor would have had to radically simplify in the face of two opponents, the building administration and the exhibition institution, in order to get away with it. Instead, by refining his project – a wooden structure to be experimentally drilled into concrete, which turns the raw concrete of the competition design into white concrete in the execution project – he even disappointed his supporters.)

How the point about allowing the place speak on its own somehow gets equated to the architect exercising his artistic self-expression is curious. But to Hoffmann-Axthelm, Zumthor's project for Topography of Terror, as revised in the course, was not of the same type as his earlier project in Chur:

> in Holz zu bauen, wie das Museum in Chur, des sentwegen man einst Zumthor zugeladen hat … wäre, unter den gegebenen Umständen, mit Abstand die beste Lösung.[27]

> (to build in wood, such as the Museum in Chur, which is why Zumthor was invited, … would have been, under the given circumstances, by far the best solution.)

In order to appreciate the complexity surrounding a project to turn an authentic perpetrator site into a documentation center, it would be beneficial to examine Hoffmann-Axthelm's observation and summation, and to do so, we must study Zumthor's scheme, which is available in the exhibition catalog published on the occasion of the exhibition "Peter Zumthor: Topografie des Terrors – Internationales Besucher- und Dokumentations-zentrum Berlin (International Visitor and Documentation Center)" held at the gallery Aedes Architekturforum in Berlin, from December 1995 to February 1996, that is, just before construction began at the site. The catalog is titled *Stabwerk* (*Framework*), in reference to the architect's concept of the structure as a framework to encase the terrain laden with history and demonstrated the Topography of Terror Foundation's affirmative support at

In the Shadow of Propaganda Architecture **75**

that time as well as the architect's intentions.[28] A brief introduction by Andreas Nachama, Director of the Foundation, characterized the winning design:

> The area should be covered by a "plain shed." The structure housing these relics of the Third Reich, leaving an ugly void in the midst of a city now rapidly resuming the functions of a national capital, must be without ornament of any kind. What will be exhibited under its roof is a wound on the face of the earth – a gash (to paraphrase what Dan Diener has said of Auschwitz) in the fabric of civilization.[29]

The "plain shed" was explained in an essay by Zumthor in the same catalog, which comes with studies of the model, materials, and drawings of the proposed design. Zumthor's statement is clear as to containing the excavated historical buildings and accommodating the institutional functions:

> After a competition held in spring, 1993, a design was adopted based on the concept of enclosing the remains of the buildings used by the National Socialist terror and for accommodating the Centre's staff and visitors. The design was to be pure structure, speaking no language but that of its own materials, composition, and function.[30]

The proposed structure's deference to the excavated remains of the historical building is clear: its orientation was skewed from both that of Niederkirchnerstraße and nearby Martin-Gropius-Bau or that of Wilhelm Straße and instead aligned with that of the excavated kitchen cellars, the site of the gallery designed by Jürg Steiner for the "Topography of Terror" exhibition. Zumthor's structure treated the excavation site as an important part of the exhibition, adding a stair tower to its west and extending the vast elongated gallery to its east. The structure was a "Stabwerk" or framework, an assembly of "prefabricated vertical and horizontal concrete members" made of concrete with white aggregate mixed in.[31] The structure was to consist of three floors, with an open "great hall" for permanent and temporary exhibitions on the ground floor. Between the vertical concrete members are narrow panes of glass, which allow the light to come into the interior. The ground floor was to be left "bare but for the simplest covering of natural materials" so that "one can sense the smell of earth."[32] Despite Hoffmann-Axthelm's differentiation, the design does remind us of Zumthor's earlier design for the shelter for Roman archaeological site (1987) in Chur, Switzerland; it also reflects his later work at Kolumba in Cologne (opened 2007). In both buildings, the ground is an excavated historical site, and Zumthor's structure sits over it, barely touching the ground. The light comes into the interior through narrow openings between the narrow building elements, wooden slats in Chur and bricks in Cologne. The ground floor is barely finished with small cracked stones covering the ground in Chur and with a bridge for visitors crossing over the excavation in Cologne.

76 In the Shadow of Propaganda Architecture

Overall, it seems that the architect, the Foundation (Nachama), and the involved architectural critic (Hoffmann-Axthelm) all agreed that the pure and simple form and the materials of the proposed design were to create a place of quiet contemplation of the past. What happened between the initial assessment and the above statement by Hoffmann-Axthelm indicates the difficulty of the project to turn the place laden with the difficult past into a documentation center on that past.

Why was Zumthor's statement of intention construed as the architect's self-realization? Why did it not receive sympathy from those, like Hoffmann-Axthelm, who felt strongly about the significance of the historical site? As if to consider these questions and set up a new direction, two colloquia were held after the announcement of the cancellation of Zumthor design, to regroup and reconsider the whole project, one in the summer (July 9) of 2004, titled *"Historischer Ort Und Historische Dokumentation: Bauen Für Die Topographie Des Terrors,"*[33] and the other in the autumn of the same year, both open to the public and involving a number of politicians, specialists, and the general public as speakers, for the purpose of disseminating their opinions and to help formulate the new direction of the project. Subsequently, in April 2005, the federal government announced another competition, which this time consisted of two stages and was open to international teams of architects and landscape architects.

The answer to my questions above can be found in the transcripts from the above colloquia, the subsequent competition's programs, the competition winners' statement of intention, and the competition jury's report. They all point to the people's understanding of what role architecture should play when providing for the documentation center at a historical perpetrator site, which was characterized by two seemingly incompatible yet dominant goals. And, in the conflict between creating a functional container for the institutional program and furnishing an artistic and symbolic expression of the institutional goals in the form of a building, the former seemed to take over. Zumthor's design itself, when one takes time to closely examine both his textual and visual presentations, proves to have been neither a formal expression that symbolizes the past nor a functional container that satisfies the pragmatic needs. In fact, Zumthor's design existed elsewhere outside the dichotomy, though neither in the sense that the design ignored the program nor in the sense that its form was uninteresting. But it did so in the sense that the design was to contribute to the memory process by incorporating the presentation of what physically remained from the past and the exhibition of textual and visual documentations of the past. But in the political context of the time, the sum of the historical, economic, and technical backgrounds was such that few must have seen beyond the dichotomous schematization above.

Subsequently, the competition program and the jury's selection stayed away from the notion of "speaking architecture." Hoffmann-Axthelm observed, in the program, "Eine (bau)künstlerische Überhöhung in der Gestaltung der zukünftigen Bebauung sol les zu Gunsten einer hohen Aufmerksamkeit für das Gelände ... nicht geben" (A (constructional) artistic exaggeration in the design of the future development should not give in favor of a high attention for the area ...).[34] And further,

In the Shadow of Propaganda Architecture 77

"Bei dem zu planenden Gebäude … handelt es sich vorrangig um ein Gebäude der wissenschaftlichen und pädagogischen Arbeit, nicht um eine Gedenkstätte" (The building to be planned … is primarily a building of scientific and educational work, not a memorial).[35] Note that the program even rejected the notion of "Gedenkstätte." Hoffmann-Axthelm further observed that the result of the first stage makes it clear that the jury chose designs that were modest: "no large-scale excavation, no strong symbolism of the terrain, strict functionality of the building and long-term care perspective for landscape." The designs that were selected to proceed to the second stage of the competition shared a consensus: "no relapse into those attempts of speaking architecture, which characterized the competition of 1983 and still played a role in 1993." Instead, the jury selections are made of "… younger people who have no relationship to the discussions of the eighties …" "more relaxed, … more impersonal.…"[36]

As seen in this chapter, the symbolic or expressive value of architecture is met with suspicion or at best ambivalence, and this could get in the way of considering architectural design's contribution toward meaningful presentation of National Socialist past. Behind the contention may be the reaction against Hitler's view and use of architecture as a tool of political persuasion. While the level of expectations toward architectural designs in the presentation of the past in meaningful ways are commonly low, they need to be reconsidered. As Winfried Nerdinger suggested, the presentation of the past by a historical place is important.[37] And, as Edward Casey suggested, the engagement in such historical imagination is an important human experience that cannot be overlooked.[38] Needless to say, a historical place's presentation of the past is ontological, that is, it does not happen to everyone and every time. Then, not despite but because of the above, I believe architectural design can and should play a role in assisting in making the past present in meaningful ways when applied to a preexisting building that carries a notable and troubling past. In order to promote such architectural design, this study will take existing designs and explore the potential of architectural design in assisting historical places bring the past to the present needs serious consideration.

Notes

1 Presentation script, by Günther Domenig (November 15, 2000), Az-W.
2 Competition program, page 14. Az-W.
3 On September 16, 1998, as a part of a colloquium the City of Nuremberg organized for the invited competitors Presentation script, by Günther Domenig (November 15, 2000), Az-W. Competition program, 14.
4 Jochen Thies, *Hitler's Plans for Global Domination: Nazi Architecture and Ultimate War Aims* (New York and Oxford: Berghahn Books, 2014), 32.
5 Matthias Donath, *Architecture in Berlin 1933–1945: A Guide through Nazi Berlin* (Berlin: Lukas Verlag, 2006), 9.
6 Thies, *Hitler's Plans for Global Domination*, 80.
7 Steven Lehrer, *The Reich Chancellery and Führerbunker Complex: An Illustrated History of the Seat of the Nazi Regime* (Jefferson, NC: McFarland & Co, 2006), 40, 64.

78 In the Shadow of Propaganda Architecture

8 Daniel Grinceri, *Architecture as Cultural and Political Discourse: Case Studies of Conceptual Norms and Aesthetic Practices* (New York: Routledge, 2016), 92.

9 Grinceri, *Architecture as Cultural and Political Discourse*, 93.

10 Alexander Scobic, *Hitler's State Architecture: The Impact of Classical Antiquity*, Monographs on the Fine Arts 45 (University Park: Published for College Art Association by the Pennsylvania State University Press, 1990), 20–1.

11 Adolf Hitler et al., *Hitler's Table Talk, 1941–1944: His Private Conversations* (New York: Enigma Books, 2008). The quotation is from Alexander Scobie, 21.

12 Scobie, *Hitler's State Architecture*, 25.

13 Ibid. no page number.

14 Ibid. 20.

15 Thies, *Hitler's Plans for Global Domination*, 80.

16 Ibid. 34.

17 Quoted in Donath, *Architecture in Berlin 1933–1945*, 7–8.

18 Ibid. *1933–1945*, 7–8.

19 Albrecht Koschorke, *On Hitler's Mein Kampf: The Poetics of National Socialism*, trans. Erik Butler (Cambridge, MA: The MIT Press, 2017).

20 Thies, *Hitler's Plans for Global Domination*, 62.

21 Gavriel D. Rosenfeld, "The Architects' Debate: Architectural Discourse and the Memory of Nazism in the Federal Republic of Germany, 1977–1997," *History and Memory* 9, no. 1/2 (1997): 189–225.

22 Dieter Hoffmann-Axthelm, "Architektur Als Gedächtnis: Über Die Möglichkeiten, Abwesendes Abzubilden," *Werk, Bauen & Wohnen* 76, no. 1/2 (1989): 28–31. For Léon Krier's book on Albert Speer architecture, refer to Léon Krier, *Albert Speer Architecture, 1932–1942* (A Bruxelles: Aux Archives d'architecture moderne, 1985).

23 Dieter Hoffmann-Axthelm, "Die Topographen Sind Am Ziel, Der Ort Geht Unter: Zur Entscheidung Eines Weiteren Wettbewerbs Zur 'Topographie Des Terrors' in Berlin," *Bauwelt* 97, no. 9 (February 24, 2006): 14–31.

24 Eckhardt Barthel, "Statement Zur Podiumsdiskussion Beim Öffentlichen Symposium Der Stiftung Topographie Des Terrors Am 9. Juli 2004," in *Historischer Ort Und Historische Dokumentation: Bauen Für Die "Topographie Des Terrors"*, 2004, https://www.topographie. de/veranstaltungen/veranstaltung/nc/1/nid/historischer-ort-und-historische-dokumentation-bauen-fuer-die-topographie-des-terrors/y/2004/m/07/d/09/z/1/?type=98.

25 Dieter Hoffmann-Axthelm, "Zur Zeit: Notizen: Topographie Des Terrors," *Ästhetik Und Kommunikation*, no. 126 (2004): 4–5.

26 *Hoffmann-Axthelm, "Zur Zeit," 4.*

27 Ibid., 5.

28 Peter Zumthor, *Stabwerk: Internationales Besucher- und Dokumentationszentrum "Topographie des Terrors," Berlin: Ausstellung 6. Dezember 1995–4. Februar 1996* (Berlin: Aedes Galerie und Architekturforum, 1995).

29 Andreas Nachama, "Gestapo Headquarters: The Site and the Evidence," *Stabwerk*: 6–7, 7. For further discussion on Hoffmann-Axthelm's influence, see Franz D. Hofer, "Memorial Sites and the Affective Dynamics of Historical Experience in Berlin and Tokyo," A Dissertation Presented to the Faculty of the Graduate School of Cornell University In Partial Fulfillment of the Requirements for the Degree of Doctor of Philosophy (2012).

30 Zumthor, *Stabwerk*, 15.

31 Ibid. 15.

32 Ibid. 16–17.

33 Eckhardt Barthel, "Statement Zur Podiumsdiskussion Beim Öffentlichen Symposium Der Stiftung Topographie Des Terrors Am 9. Juli 2004," in *Historischer Ort Und Historische Dokumentation: Bauen Für Die "Topographie Des Terrors"*, 2004, www.topographie. de/veranstaltungen/veranstaltung/nc/1/nid/historischer-ort-und-historische-dokumentation-bauen-fuer-die-topographie-des-terrors/y/2004/m/07/d/09/z/1/?type=98.

34 Competition Program, Anlass und Ziel, S.7 (Reason and goal, p.7). See also: Dieter Hoffmann-Axthelm, "Die Topographen Sind Am Ziel, Der Ort Geht Unter: Zur Entscheidung Eines Weiteren Wettbewerbs Zur 'Topographie Des Terrors' in Berlin," *Bauwelt* 97, no. 9 (February 24, 2006): 14–31.

35 Competition Program, Wettbewerbsaufgabe, S.50 (Competition Task, p. 50). See also: Dieter Hoffmann-Axthelm, "Die Topographen Sind Am Ziel, Der Ort Geht Unter: Zur Entscheidung Eines Weiteren Wettbewerbs Zur 'Topographie Des Terrors' in Berlin," *Bauwelt* 97, no. 9 (February 24, 2006): 14–31.

36 Dieter Hoffmann-Axthelm, *Bauwelt*, 14–31.

37 Winfried Nerdinger, "Umgang Mit Den Spuren Der NS-Vergangenheit – Indizien Zu Einer Geschichte Der Verdrängung Und Zum Ende Der Trauerarbeit," *Wolfgang Ruppert, "Deutschland, Bleiche Mutter" Order Eine Neue Lust an Der Nationalen Identität*, 1992, 51–60.

38 Edward S. Casey, *Remembering: A Phenomenological Study*, 2nd ed., Studies in Continental Thought (Bloomington: Indiana University Press, 2000).

4

PRESENTING PASTS THROUGH ARCHITECTURE – INTELLECTUAL FRAMEWORK

There is no denying that historical buildings and places have the potential for presenting the past; many thinkers have discussed this in the affirmative. However, Edward Casey recognizes this area to require further consideration:

> Yet it is just this importance of place for memory that has been lost sight of in philosophical and common sense concerns with the temporal dimensions of memory. … it is a fact that memory of place, of having been in a place, is one of the most conspicuously neglected areas of philosophical or psychological inquiry into remembering.[1]

Casey continues by saying that, while the "[p]lace is selective for memories; that is to say, a given place will invite certain memories while discouraging others,"[2]

> … it is still not clear just how such an intimate relationship between memory and place is realized. … if it is the body that places us in place to start with, it will be instrumental in re-placing us in remembered places as well.[3]

To address the question of "[w]hy is place so potent as a guardian of memories?"[4] Casey suggests

> we need to notice the way in which the functions of memory and place are strikingly parallel. They accomplish a similar task at a quite basic level. This task is that of congealing the disparate into a provisional unity.[5]

If there is a parallel between the functions of memory and place, as Casey observes, and if memory of a place is synonymous with that of being in a place, we need to acknowledge the fact that there are fewer and fewer people who experienced the place during the Third Reich. The implication for the architectural designs that convert historical perpetrator places into documentation centers on National Socialism is the question of how to assist in making those historical buildings' past intelligible to audiences that include people who do not have direct experience. In fact, the significance of a memory place, at least partly, is to allow the imagining of a particular past by those who may not have experienced it. That way, the past is shared, empathy is exercised, and the lesson is learned.

And yet, people do not always agree as to how effective places could be in presenting the past in a meaningful way. In addition, when it comes to the architectural designs that are applied to the historical buildings or places, the primary expectation is to have them as the architect's self-expression or as the provider of a container for the exhibition. It is not always the case that architectural design is expected to assist the historical buildings and places in presenting their past in meaningful ways. In order to observe how the architectural designs of the four documentation centers are doing just that, it is necessary for us to have a systematic understanding of various mechanisms that are at work. For this reason, this chapter offers an intellectual framework of how historical buildings and places present a certain past, in preparation for analytical studies of the four documentation centers at hand.

The following framework has been developed by looking at architectural design from the points of view of representation (a piece of architecture as an artifact that represents ideas) and interpretation (the viewers take certain meanings out of their experiences), and in reference to philosophical works in semiotics and hermeneutics. In particular, I have borrowed some concepts from the works of Charles Sanders Peirce and Hans Georg Gadamer, specifically Pierce's classification of signs – icon, index, and symbol – and Hans Georg Gadamer's concept of memento.[6] My framework identifies four distinct mechanisms: First, a building may refer to the time of its origin by way of its *formal characteristics*. Second, a building may recall an otherwise neglected past by bearing *physical traces*. Third, a building may commemorate a particular event or individual by being *designated* to do so. Fourth, as a *memento*, a building is a reminder of a past simply because an event took place there, even when there is no deliberate designation, formal characteristics, or material trace.

The resulting intellectual framework can be applied not only to the four documentation centers at hand but also to a wide range of projects that involved historical places' presentation of the past. And the ensuing Chapters 5–8 will be organized by this framework.

Semiotics and Hermeneutics: Icon, Index, Symbol, and Memento

Charles Sanders Peirce was an American philosopher who left an enormous volume of texts on the relationships between a sign and its object, which he called semiotics. In the 1970s scholars from different disciplines became acutely interested in his

82 Presenting Pasts through Architecture

body of work as well as the semiology of the Swiss linguist Ferdinand de Saussure, and architects and architectural theoreticians were among them. It turned out that the interests were a passing trend, and the contributions, some possibly not so productive, seem for the most part forgotten. However, I see Peirce's basic categorization of signs as useful for understanding architecture's presentation of the past, although it requires some adjustments. In the semiotics of Peirce, a sign stands for an object in some conditions.

> A sign, or *representamen*, is something which stands to somebody for something in some respect or capacity. It addresses somebody, that is, creates in the mind of that person an equivalent sign, or perhaps a more developed sign. That sign which it creates I call the *interpretant* of the first sign. The sign stands for something, its *object*. It stands for that object, not in all respects, but in reference to a sort of idea, which I have sometimes called the *ground* of the representamen.[7]

For Peirce, signs can be classified into three kinds: icon, index, and symbol, which is useful for the current study. His definitions of these three concepts are:

> A sign is either an icon, an index, or a symbol. An icon is a sign which would possess the character which renders it significant, even though its object had no existence; such as a lead-pencil streak as representing a geometrical line. An index is a sign which would at once, lose the character which makes it a sign if its object were removed but would not lose that character if there were no interpretant. Such, for instance, is a piece of mould with a bullethole in it as sign of a shot; for without the shot there would have been no hole; but there is a hole there, whether anybody has the sense to attribute it to a shot or not. A symbol is a sign which would lose the character which renders it a sign if there were no interpretant. Such is any utterance of speech which signifies what it does only by virtue of its being understood to have that signification.[8]

In order to adopt these concepts to the current study, it is more useful to refer to the examples he offered. Marco Frascari once explained them thus: The icon is a sign of an object based on the formal similarities; the index based on the cause–effect relationship; and the symbol based on a societal agreement.[9] An example of an icon is a traffic sign for a pedestrian crossing. Even a person who has not studied the drivers' manual likely would recognize the meaning of the graphic composition of a black figure on a yellow background. The index corresponds with its object on the basis of the cause–effect relationship. An example is that of a traffic sign bent in the middle, telling us there was a traffic accident there. The significant nature of an index is that it does not require any prior knowledge for the viewer to know something has happened which caused the damage, although they may not be able to identify the exact cause. An example is the stop sign. It does not mean anything

Presenting Pasts through Architecture **83**

to the viewer who does not know the language – the societal agreement – that connects the white pattern on the red background to the meaning of "stop."

For the current study, we need to add one more concept, drawn from the hermeneutics of Hans Georg Gadamer (1900–2002), a German philosopher of phenomenology and hermeneutics. In his magnum opus *Truth and Method*, in the section titled "Aesthetic and Hermeneutic Consequences," Gadamer defined "memento" thus:

> Of all signs, the memento most seems to have a reality of its own. It refers to the past and so is effectively a sign, but it is also precious in itself since, as a bit of the past that has not disappeared, it keeps the past present for us. But it is clear that this characteristic is not grounded in the being of the object itself. A memento has value as a memento only for someone who already – i.e., still – recalls the past. Memento lose their value when the past of which they remind one no longer has any meaning. Furthermore, someone who not only uses mementos to remind him but makes a cult of them and lives in the past as if it were the present has a disturbed relation to the reality.[10]

While ordinarily a memento may be a fairly small object that recalls something positive from a certain past, making that recalling a pleasant experience, Gadamer's characterization can be applied to a much larger physical object, a building, which reminds us of a different type of past, the recalling of which is painful or derisive. In this sense, a building can be a "bit of the past that has not disappeared," which "keeps the past present for us." Now, what assets of a memento endow such a potential for its holder (or beholder) recalling the past? The above passage from Gadamer has an answer: "But it is clear that this characteristic is not grounded in the being of the object itself. A memento has value as a memento only for someone who already – that is, still – recalls the past."

First, a building may refer to the time of its origin by way of its *formal characteristics*, carrying a certain style or other special features the viewer can observe in the form. On the National Mall, people are shown the near and far pasts through the contrasting styles of the National Gallery's East and West Buildings. Here, the observer may not be able to name the particular style correctly but can recognize its historical nature. Second, a building may recall an otherwise neglected past by bearing *physical traces*. At the southwest corner of the East Building, astute observers would have noticed an erosion of the Tennessee Marble and determined it to be a result of past visitors' repeated brushing against the stone's sharp edge. Third, a building may commemorate a particular event or individual by being *designated* to do so. An example would be the Washington Monument in Washington, D.C.; without the knowledge of the specific designation, what it commemorates is obscure, as is true of any other obelisk or singular column that stands in open ground. Its form suggests to the viewer that it is a commemoration of something venerable, but that is the extent that the form can suggest. When it comes to what it is commemorating, we need to rely on the designation, and the disclosure of that

84 Presenting Pasts through Architecture

information. These three categories roughly correspond to Peirce's classification of signs into, respectively, symbol, icon, and index. The fourth category is Gadamer's concept of *memento*. That is, a building also may be a reminder of a past simply because an event took place there, even when there is no deliberate designation, formal characteristics, or material trace. For example, a family may remind each other of their previous visit to the nation's capital while standing at the same spot on the Mall as before to purchase ice-cream bars from a food truck. In a similar manner, a place may induce a past recollection in a person who experienced an event there, even if no one else did. Of course, in reality, a building might be more than just one thing, but instead a combination of any of the four. Additionally, a particular building can be taken differently to different people, or it may affect in multiple ways to a person while not affecting at all to another.

Formal Characteristics

A building may refer to the time of its origin by way of its *formal characteristics*, carrying a certain style. A historical building's form – either that of the whole or that of a part – would inform the viewer about its origin because particular styles are associated with particular time periods. The viewer may not identify the style accurately, but if not, then they do so in approximation.

There are many buildings in German cities which carry formal characteristics of National Socialist architecture and are easily noticeable by form today. And in the neighborhoods of the documentation centers there are quite a few: in Nuremberg, the Zeppelin Grandstand building in the former Party Rally Grounds; in Berlin, the former Aviation Ministry building, standing across the street from the Topography of Terror Documentation Center; and in Munich, the former Führerbau adjacent to the NS Documentation Center and Führerbau's counterpart of the bilateral symmetry, the Administration Building, as well as the building that houses the State tax office and others, just two blocks south. In addition to what often is referred to as stripped-off classicism, there are a number of more specific formal characteristics common among National Socialist architecture, which are visible from the exterior: The walls often are clad with stone slabs; and the windows are rectilinear, and their edges are sharp, often articulated by frames, made of the same stone material as the exterior finish, which protrude from the rest of the exterior surface. With the above buildings, our recognition of them being National Socialist architecture may possibly come from our prior knowledge, based on designation. However, when we recognize these formal characteristics in a building in an urban fabric, without our prior knowledge of the building's history, and if the building's current designation is silent about that history, then we certainly are using the formal characteristics in associating the building to the past. This happens, for example, in Munich on the way from Odeonsplatz to Haus der Kunst, with the building currently used as the office of Bavarian State Ministry of Food, Agriculture and Forests at the corner of Ludwigstraße and Von-der-Tann-Straße. Compared to other classicist buildings that stand on each side of Ludwigstraße, this building is strikingly stern. Additionally, especially on its first-story façade, the building uses darker toned stone, in this case limestone, and a strong articulation of windows, all typical of National Socialist architecture. The windowsills prominently protrude out of the building's surface and the large elements support those windowsills from underneath, all in limestone. The window frames are pronounced boldly, in this case not protruding as in the case of Führerbau but inset. underneath. It turns out that it had been constructed as the Central Ministerial Building for the Third Reich's operation, completed in 1938–39. It was designed by Fritz Gablonsky, a member of the German Werkbund, who in 1938 became the chair of architecture at the Technical University of Munich under the National Socialist government.

Some readers may automatically relate the historical building's presentation of the past by way of "formal characteristics" to those monuments that are based on "figurative" representation, sometimes called symbolic representation, or that which relies on the formal resemblance to what they commemorate. But a clear distinction is necessary to separate the two. To return to examples from the National Mall, the National Gallery's East and West Buildings, present near and far pasts through their styles. In comparison, the Vietnam Women's Memorial is a bronze lump molded to resemble human figure and is a figurative representation. Its sculptor Glenna Goodacre explained that she "arranged the four figures" around the "stacks of sandbags," which she observed in many photographs from that time. Although she "deliberately included no identifying insignia, to symbolically include all the women – military, medical and even civilian volunteers – who served in Vietnam," the four figures resemble humans in the war in kind: "a nurse" who "serves as the life support for a wounded soldier lying across her lap"; the standing woman who "looks up, in search of a mede-vac helicopter or, perhaps, in search of help from God"; and the kneeling figure, or "the heart and the soul" of the piece, in whom "so many vets see themselves," who "stares at any empty helmet, her posture reflecting her despair, frustrations, and all the horrors of war."[11] The use of the figurative representation in commemorating a certain past can be seen not only in sculpture such as the Vietnam Women's Memorial but also in architecture. In designing the Jewish Museum, Berlin, Daniel Libeskind arranged the lines of the floor plan in the shape of the star of David. If we say that the form of the building's floor plan reminds us of the past in which Jewish people were forced to wear the yellow star on their chests, then our association is by the figurative representation, and the figure in the building is the product of the present. Formal characteristics of the building by way of which we associate it to the past are the product of the past. At any rate, the contemporary building's reference to the past by way of its figurative representation must be clearly differentiated from the historical building's presentation of its own past.

Physical Traces

Second, a building may recall an otherwise neglected past by bearing *physical traces*. On the western façade of Victoria and Albert Museum in London, damages of

86 Presenting Pasts through Architecture

flying bombs during the Second World War are visible, which are physical traces of human actions that present the past.[12] If a building's fabric is scarred, the viewer would guess correctly that there was some force at work in the past, although, like the American tourist at the Victoria and Albert Museum, they may not be able to identify the exact cause of the damage. In this case, neither knowledge nor formal resemblance is a prerequisite for a representation for a historical place to represent its past. This can be very powerful in the sense that, first, only an authentic building can perform this task, and second, it is possible for the past to be shared among many people from different backgrounds and levels of education.

In the context of the reconstruction of German cities, examples of historical buildings presenting the past include Kaiser Wilhelm Memorial Church in Berlin, Kolumba in Cologne, and Alte Pinakothek in Munich. As discussed in Chapter 1, in all three cases, the postwar architectural design was applied to the historical building damaged by the Allied Forces' air raids. And the architectural design makes the scars clearly visible, though in three totally different ways.

Designation

A building may commemorate a particular event or individual by being *designated* to do so. In a manner similar to the societal agreement in the case of a symbol, the designation of a memory place would endow a connection between the physical entity and the specific past, which the former otherwise does not possess in its physical attributes. This designation may be done by the naming of an institution, which could appear in tourist brochures or on a plaque placed in front of the building. For many National Socialist perpetrator buildings and places, designation is the only way to allow the presentation of the past, especially where the building had survived the war but had been adopted to a new purpose or where the building had been destroyed or demolished. The agency of heritage protection typically functions as the agent of designation; however, in Germany, not every building or place with a National Socialist past, even if registered as historical, carries a visible designation. Possibly even worse, when buildings and places have significant pasts in addition to that of the Third Reich, their designation sometimes refers to the former but not the latter. Or, in some cases the building's designation refers to the victims' past but not the perpetrators'.

Many authentic perpetrator buildings from the Third Reich were damaged by the Allied bombing during the war and demolished or converted for mundane purposes afterward, and thus need to rely predominantly on designation in order to present the past. The Führerbunker in Berlin is an exemplary case of a building that was demolished and only recognizable because of the designation. Hitler had bunkers built as a protective measure against enemy forces. The first bunker, built in 1935–36, was located underground in the garden of the Old Chancellery, on Wilhelm Straße, north of the current Topography of Terror Documentation Center, which had been a palace before Hitler took over, and which Hitler expanded westward along Voßstraße. In January 1943, Hitler commanded Speer to build a new bunker directly to the west of the original one. It was 8.5 meters deep underground, and the inner dimensions were 20 × 15.6 meters. It accommodated Hitler's bedroom, living room, and office and Eva Braun's dressing room and bedroom. It also housed Hitler's doctor (later Joseph Goebbel's room), a hospital room, a conference room, and servant's room. After learning of the execution of Benito Mussolini, on April 30, 1945, Hitler committed suicide in the bunker.

After the war, there were numerous attempts at eradicating the bunker, but each time, the heavy concrete structure remained. In 1947 soldiers tried to destroy them with explosives. In 1949, the Red Army, decreeing that nothing of the National Socialist megalomania was to be kept, razed the Chancellery complex, but could not eradicate the Führerbunker remnants. In 1959, with the area now under the control of East Germany, they set dynamite. When the Berlin Wall was built, in 1961, the East German police entered the bunker to close subterranean escape hatches. In 1973 they explored the Führerbunker's underground passageways and found pages from Goebbel's diary. Between 1986 and 1989, the East Germans dynamited it and carried away some concrete remnants. In 1999 more structural remnants were found by construction workers near Wilhemstraße. The excavation was filled with dirt and closed. The site now is the parking lot of a housing complex.[13] A sign board stands at the site, explaining the extent of the structure and the activities that went on there. It is a stop for guided tours, but except for the board, there is no visible indication of the past.

The former Aviation Ministry building, also in Berlin, immediately north of the documentation center, was discussed in Chapter 1. It had generations of varied uses after the war, including those during the time the site was part of East Berlin, with the Berlin Wall running on the northern boundary of the documentation center site. The most prominently commemorated past here is the 1953 Uprising during the time of East Germany. On the northeast corner of the building is a sizable plaza, which is dedicated to commemorate the event. Here, in addition to the plaque that pronounces it, there also are a monument, a mural on the north face of the building, and exterior exhibition boards. In comparison, its past during the Third Reich is much less overt by way of designation. While the building's designation focuses on its roles in East Berlin, a new board was created across Wilhelmstraße that shows a timeline of the building's varied uses.

In contrast to the Führerbunker or the former Aviation Ministry above, at National Socialist perpetrator buildings and sites in Germany, a lack of designation sometimes is a frustrating but unfortunately familiar occurrence. For example, in Munich, at the east end of Brienner Straße on which the NS Documentation Center stands, Feldherrnhalle facing Odeonsplatz is an example of a building that, despite its significant role during the Third Reich, no longer carries the memorial plaque from that time or contemporary designation. Constructed in the 1840s to honor the Bavarian army, Feldherrnhalle was given a new identity by Hitler to commemorate the fallen soldiers during the 1923 Munich putsch and played a significant role in asserting the National Socialist propaganda. It was guarded by soldiers, and the citizens were required to give the Nazi salute when passing by

88 Presenting Pasts through Architecture

the building. While the National Socialist memorial long destroyed immediately after the war in June 1945, by ordinary Munich citizens, there is no designative plaque that refers to the building's National Socialist propaganda role.[14] Other National Socialist buildings whose past designation is obscured include the former Führerbau, the Administration Building, and the Honor Temples. In fact, the district now is given the nomenclature of "art district," which conceals its dark past. Also, within the art district, not far from the cluster of buildings mentioned above, is the former Haus der Deutschen Kunst, which now is called Haus der Kunst to distance it from its National Socialist past. The building does not carry a plaque on the building referring to its dark origin.

Memento

The physical environment working as a memento is a powerful way to recall the past. In Casey's statement about place and memory quoted above, "the place" is in fact working as a memento. The memento does not rely on the knowledge of history as the person had a direct experience of the past, and it does not rely on the knowledge of architectural style for the same reason, which the recall of the past by the building's form does. In this sense, the memento's ability to recall the past in the person is similar to the physical traces discussed in an earlier chapter. The difference is that, while the physical traces do not require direct experience of the past in order for the person to recognize some physical action that took place, which caused the physical traces the memento proper does require the person to have had a direct experience of the past.

The memento's requirement that the person who recalls the past event to have actually experienced it makes the memento in the purest sense of the term limiting. Strictly speaking, then, a person who does not have that direct experience does not have a way of connecting the memento to the past. A particular action that took place in a building only can be recalled by persons who actually were involved in the event. Memento, therefore, is a challenging mechanism in the context of documentation centers on National Socialism in Germany. On the one hand, the people with direct experiences with the National Socialist past are aging or already have passed away. On the other, institutions such as documentation centers need to address a wider, international audience and make it possible for those with no experiences, either direct or indirect, through relatives or acquaintances, to still imagine the past and exercise their empathy. Therefore, it may seem a great, if not impossible, challenge to take advantage of the memento.

In order to find ways to turn a memento into something to be shared, the concept of quasi-memento is worth exploring. We can consider ways in which, with some help from the characteristics of the environment itself or the supplying of knowledge of the past that took place there, the individual is led to have memento-like experiences at the place that definitely is a memento to some other people. This is where architectural design, applied to convert the former perpetrator building into a documentation center, could contribute.

An example of a quasi-memento in the context of the memory of the Third Reich is the station of Wannsee, just outside of Berlin. At Wannsee, the sense of the National Socialist past is actually felt when one gets off the train and stands on the platform. The signage board carrying the station name is in Blackletter font, similar to the one used in *Der Stümer*, a propaganda newspaper, or on political posters. Using a particular font that refers back to a particular past the area is known for is part of a larger project throughout Berlin, seen at 81 listed subway stations.[15] In this case, the sign board creates a quasi-memento to those who have had experiences of seeing these newspapers or posters.

It is important here to distinguish the quasi-memento discussed above from another experience, which may be mistaken as being of the same kind. In particular, Peter Eisenman's Memorial to the Murdered Jews of Europe, Berlin, has been reported to induce a sense of unease, characterized by some as "a space within which the viewer feels physically disoriented, and is thus put in the position of victimhood,"[16] or a "peripatetic journey" in which "the visitor may feel lost, or at least removed and isolated from the rest of the world."[17] The reported sense of unease does relate to the architect's intention for the design. Eisenman once explained thus:

> The project manifests the instability inherent in what seems to be a system, here a rational grid, and its potential for dissolution in time. It suggests that when a supposedly rational and ordered system grows too large and out of proportion to its intended purpose, it loses touch with human reason.[18]

At the memorial, the rational system is represented by the "rigid grid structure composed of ... stelae, each 95 centimeters wide and 2.375 meters long, ... spaced 95 centimeters apart." But within this "seemingly rigid order," the architect sought "the instability," by setting up two planes – the one of the ground, created by lowering the existing fairly flat land deeper by 8 feet toward the middle of the field, and the other of the top of the stelae, which vary in their height. The result is "a slippage in the grid structure," destroying "the illusion of the security of order." While the architect's intention is directed to the geometrical composition, that is, at the abstract level, the physical space created by the design reportedly has created a physical environment that induces a sense of unease in those who experience it. Further, while the architect's critique of the Third Reich is again at the abstract, geometrical level, the physically experienced sense of unease may be considered parallel to that of victims of National Socialism. Because of this parallel, some readers might consider the physical experience at Eisenman's work as a quasi-memento of those persecuted under the National Socialist regime.

However, it is important to note that the experience created by Eisenman's work is nowhere near the actual experience of those persecuted. The experiences in Eisenman's field of stelae – the loss of the sense of balance, the deception that one is alone in the space, which gets negated soon enough by the appearance of another who occupied a close quarter but was hidden by the stelae – are comparable, if at

90 Presenting Pasts through Architecture

all, to the real experience of the persecuted only at the most remote and abstract level. As Henry W. Pickford has clearly articulated, Eisenman's memorial does not stand on an authentic site or refer to one nearby, and as a result lacks the historical relation to the very past to which it is assumed to refer.

The architectural design can take advantage of these four mechanisms and assist the historical site in presenting the past. Two important considerations need to be made. First, in the real world and in real human experiences, any particular building referring back to a past more likely than not carries not one but two or more of the above four mechanisms. Considering just one aspect of a design, we can find multiple mechanisms at work. But classifying is useful as it allows an analysis of a design at hand, which would promote deeper understanding of its effects. Second, some of the design strategies that are identified and analyzed in the following chapters are not necessarily intentional on the part of the architects who designed the building. But instead the designers may have made those design choices intuitively or from experience. My aim for the anatomical study here is to cut open what is otherwise obscure and to make those strategies visible, so that they become available and employable to other designers for future projects. Third, that the physical attributes of the buildings are visible and the past events did in fact happen in place does not guarantee that the building turns into a place of memory for everybody. In other words, the mechanisms identified in this chapter may not affect every visitor. In fact, buildings have a tendency of receding into the background. By offering the intellectual framework, I am hoping to eventually elevate the visitors' level of engagement with architecture.

The following four chapters are close examinations of the four documentation centers. The discussions will be organized based on the four mechanisms that were established in this chapter.

Notes

1 Edward S. Casey, *Remembering: A Phenomenological Study*, Second edition, Studies in Continental Thought (Bloomington: Indiana University Press, 2000), 182–3.
2 Casey, *Remembering*, 189.
3 Ibid., 190.
4 Ibid., 201.
5 Ibid., 202.
6 The deliberate designation, formal characteristics, and physical traces identified here are parallel to Charles Sanders Peirce's categorization of signs – that which stands for something for somebody – into symbol, icon, and index. Charles S. Peirce, *Philosophical Writings of Peirce, Selected and with an Introduction by Justus Buchler* (New York: Dover Publications, 1955), 102. Hans-Georg Gadamer, *Truth and Method* (New York: Crossroad, 1989), 152–3.
7 Charles S. Peirce, *Philosophical Writings of Peirce*, selected and with an introduction by Justus Buchler (New York: Dover Publications, 1955), 99.
8 Peirce, *Philosophical Writings of Peirce*, 104.
9 Refer to His lectures in the course titled semiotics in architecture, University of Pennsylvania, 1980s.

10 Hans-Georg Gadamer, *Truth and Method*, 152–3.

11 Vietnam Women's Memorial Foundation, www.vietnamwomensmemorial.org

12 Rumiko Handa, *Allure of the Incomplete, Imperfect, and Impermanent: Designing and Appreciating Architecture as Nature* (New York: Routledge, 2015), 132–8.

13 Steven Lehrer, *The Reich Chancellery and Führerbunker Complex: An Illustrated History of the Seat of the Nazi Regime* (Jefferson, NC: McFarland & Co, 2006), 117–60.

14 NS-Dokumentationszentrum München et al., *Munich and National Socialism: Catalogue of the Munich Documentation Centre for the History of National Socialism* (München: Beck, 2015), 308.

15 Philip Oltermann, "From Grotesque to Quirky: A History of Berlin Told through U-Bahn Typography." *The Guardian*, March 11, 2015.

16 Christian Saehrendt, "Holocaust Memorial, Berlin." *Burlington Magazine* 147, no. 1233 (2005), 845.

17 Suzanne Stephens, "Peter Eisenman's Vision for Berlin's Memorial to the Murdered Jews of Europe." *Architectural Record* 193, no. 7 (2005), 120–7.

18 Peter Eisenman, *Blurred Zones: Investigations of the Interstitial* (New York: Monacelli, 2003), 14.

5

FORMAL CHARACTERISTICS

This chapter will focus on historical buildings' formal characteristics and will deal with the question of how architectural designs, when turning perpetrator places into documentation centers, might take advantage of those formal characteristics in order to present the places' pasts in a meaningful way. Every building has a form, but it is not always the case that visitors or passersby notice it as being a representation of a particular past. They may be oblivious when passing by because the building is a part of their everyday physical environment. Even when they are purposefully visiting the building, their attention may be focused on the exhibits, and the building's form may not receive their scrutiny. It therefore would be advantageous if the architectural design applied to the historical building could draw the viewer's attention to that form in a clear and inescapable manner. This chapter, through close on-site observations, will reveal a number of strategies that are working effectively at the four documentation centers, including:

1. physically isolating the National Socialist–era building from the postwar additions;
2. contrasting between the new and the old by way of form, including style, geometry, and materials; and
3. creating a place from which to view the historical.

By the time a decision was made to establish a documentation center on National Socialism in Cologne, Nuremberg, Berlin, and Munich, each perpetrator building had gone through changes of a varying degree that were caused by the destructive war and by the postwar economy and politics. In Cologne and Nuremberg, the buildings still stood, having survived the air raids during the war and having been used for various purposes after it. Both buildings carried significant characteristics of the historical style of National Socialist–era architecture: One, at Nuremberg, had been purposefully designed and built by the regime. And the other, at Cologne, had been built during that time. Although it had originated as a commercial and residential property before being taken over by the Gestapo while under construction, the building carried formal characteristics, if a somewhat softened version, of stern classicism. These buildings did not remain the same after the war, however. At Cologne, the building was expanded significantly, taking up next-door properties, altering the original vertical, imposing composition to a more horizontal, mundane one. And at Nuremberg, while much of the exterior was left unchanged from the end of the war, with the stone-cladding of the outer wall completed, the main space intended for the large auditorium left without a roof and raw bricks exposed, the southern end block was converted into a music venue, with a glass box for the main entrance and steel exterior stairs leading to it. Especially at night when music lovers approach the venue, the light coming from the glass box and the signage "NÜRNBERGER SYMPHONIKER," lit yellow, obscure the former Congress Hall's heavy historical form.

In comparison, the situations were quite different for the buildings in Berlin and Munich. To begin with, both Palais Barlow in Munich and the buildings along Albrechtstraße and Wilhelmstraße in Berlin had been built before the National Socialist era and carried the stylistic characteristics of the prior era. These buildings were damaged severely during the war, and, although the damages were not necessarily irreparable, the decision was made after the war to demolish the buildings. There were some underground remains excavated in Berlin, both along Wilhelmstraße and of the kitchen cellar. However, being the basement structures, they did not carry much of the formal characteristics to refer to the times of their origin, either of the National Socialist's utility construction or of the buildings from the prior era. Instead, the architectural forms representing the National Socialist era were available, both in Berlin and Munich, in a different way: Some perpetrator buildings built by the regime were still standing in the neighborhood, with their formal characteristics visible from the project sites. These neighboring buildings were: in Berlin, the former Aviation Ministry building, north of the project site across Albrechtstraße;[1] and, in Munich, the former Führerbau, immediately adjacent to the documentation center site to the north.[2] Interestingly, in fact, in all four cases the project site was part of a cluster of National Socialist perpetrator buildings, providing the architects of the documentation centers with possible opportunities to take advantage of these expanded lists of extant historical buildings. In Cologne, two buildings – the seventeenth-century Zeughaus, or armory, and the nineteenth-century Alte Wache, or guardhouse – both only one block north of EL-DE House as well as the Court of Appeals across the street to the east were preexisting buildings adopted by the Party. In Nuremberg, the project site belongs to the Party Rally Grounds. In Berlin, Wilhelmstraße ran at the project site's eastern edge, along which many government buildings stood. In addition to the Aviation Ministry mentioned above, further north, on Mauerstraße, one block east of Wilhelmstraße, the former Reichsministerium für Volksaufklärung und Propaganda (Reich Ministry of Popular Enlightenment and Propaganda) survived the war and now houses the

94 Formal Characteristics

Federal Ministry of Labor and Social Affairs.[3] In Munich, the Brown House was a part of the National Socialist party district. Nearby, in addition to the Führerbau mentioned above, are the former Administration Building as well as Königsplatz. There also are the remains of the Honor Temples, although these are mostly hidden by overgrown vegetation as a part of *Vergangenheitsbewältigung* strategy.

Physically Isolating the Past

The first notable strategy to make the historical form stand out for the viewer is that of physically isolating the past from the documentation center's design elements. This strategy in principle is not so dissimilar from the one seen at Wilhelm Memorial Church in Berlin, discussed in Chapter 1. But, unlike at the Memorial Church, constructing a new building totally detached from the remaining structures was not an option in Cologne and Nuremberg. Also, identifying the perpetrator building meant, in Cologne in particular, to separate it not only from the documentation center project but also from the postwar additions made previously.

Cologne

At Cologne, at the end of the war, the EL–DE House stood practically unscathed by the Allied Forces' air raids. That building's formal characteristics, which were those favored by the Gestapo even though the building was designed for a private citizen, were intact, and the National Socialist newspaper praised the design, as discussed in Chapter 2. At the time the building was taken over by the Gestapo for its regional headquarters, the exterior had been finished, and some its formal characteristics were common to National Socialist architecture: the classicist style, while slightly more ornate than was typical; the darker color of stones of the exterior finish; and the prominent articulation of rectilinear windows of vertical proportion, with the window frames protruding from the surface of the body of the building. The exterior, including an emblem on the corner referring prominently to the owner, was unaltered by the National Socialists while the interior was redesigned to accommodate the Gestapo's purposes.

After the war, the building was returned to its owner, who rented it to the city government whose various offices occupied the former Gestapo offices and served the citizens from there. In 1947, the building was enlarged by repeating the façade motif, from 6 bays to 12 along Appellhofplatz and from 12 to 16 bays Elisenstraße (Figure 2.1). Peter Kulka observed the lack of separation between the original structure and the postwar addition:

> Der 1947 angebaute Gebäudeteil wurde –wie auch der Büroteil in der Elisenstraße –ohne bauliche Differenzierung, mit gleicher Fassade, an das ursprüngliche EL-DE-Haus angefügt, sodaß ein Erkennen des eigentlichen EL-DE-Hauses als Mahnmal nicht mehr gegeben ist.[4]

(The 1947 attached part of the building was – as well as the office part in the Elisenstraße – without structural differentiation, with the same facade, attached to the original EL-DE-house, so that a recognition of the actual EL-DE house as a memorial is no longer given.)

It should be noted that, as a result of the postwar addition, the building lost its original proportion of verticality, especially in its main façade on Appellhofplatz, and became horizontal and rather mundane instead.

"Das Haus selbst als Exponat" (the house itself as an exhibit) was an explicit intention of the architect, Peter Kulka,[5] who applied this concept to both the exterior and interior of the building. For the exterior, this meant isolating the original façade of the EL-DE House from those postwar extensions, which otherwise are indistinguishable stylistically from each other. Kulka observed this problem:

> Der 1947 angebaute Gebäudeteil wurde –wie auch der Büroteil in der Elisenstraße –ohne bauliche Differenzierung, mit gleicher Fassade, an das ursprüngliche EL-DE-Haus angefügt, sodaß ein Erkennen des eigentlichen EL-DE-Hauses als Mahnmal nicht mehr gegeben ist.[6]

> (The 1947 additions of the building was -as well as the office part in the Elisenstraße – without structural differentiation, with the same facade, attached to the original EL-DE-house, so that a recognition of the actual EL-DE house as a memorial is no longer given.)

The architect's original design strategy can be seen in the diagrammatic drawings included in a bound document among the collection at the Deutsches Architekturmuseum in Frankfurt, which is a design report dated May 1993, submitted by Kulka.[7] It includes a proposed main façade, that is, on the Appellhofplatz street side. Here, Kulka has drawn a vertical line, described by him as a "visible dividing line in the façade," to be created to separate the original façade from that of the addition (Figure 5.1).

A second design element that isolates the original façade from the postwar extension was a diagonal translucent glass wall that was to be inserted in the addition, which would protrude through the façade and serve as the boundary of the special exhibition space on the second and third floors (Figure 5.2). The insertion of the different material in a different geometry, together with the separating vertical line, would have made the original façade independent, and would have provided, to the people on the street, a visual point that would draw their attention to the center building.

> Das Aufbrechen der Fassade umfaßt eine aus der Fassade herausgedrehte Wandscheibe, die einerseits die Gleichmäßigkeit der bestehenden Fassade durchbrechen soll, andererseits, einer Plakatwandähnlich, das Museum nach außen präsentiert. Die Wandscheibe besteht aus einer

96 Formal Characteristics

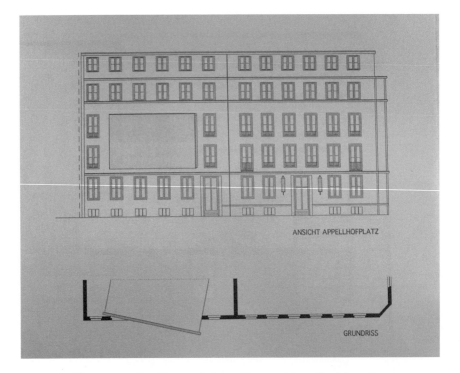

FIGURE 5.1 Documentation Center, Cologne. Proposed Appellhofplatz elevation, not executed. 1993. The vertical line on the building's façade shows the architect's intention to separate the original EL-DE House from the postwar extension. Source: © Peter Kulka-Archiv, Deutsches Architekturmuseum, Frankfurt am Main; und Peter Kulka Konzept für die Gedächtnisstätte El-DE Haus, Köln.

> Mattglas-Stahlkonstruktion, sodaß Licht zwar in den Innenraum hineinfallen, keineswegs aber der Eindruck einer großen Schaufensterscheibe entstehen kann.[8]

(The break-up of the façade comprises a wall panel turned out of the facade, which on the one hand is intended to break through the uniformity of the existing façade, on the other hand, similar to a billboard, presenting the museum to the outside. The wall panel consists of a frosted glass steel construction, so that light may fall into the interior, but by no means can give the impression of a large shop window.)

These, however, could not be executed for financial reasons:

> Ein anfanglicher Versuch, die für die Zeit typische und noch vorhandene Fassadengliederung mit einem sie durchdringenden Baukörper innen und außen zu stören, konnte aus Kostengrunden nicht zur Ausführung kommen.[9]

Formal Characteristics **97**

(An initial attempt to disrupt the facade structure, typical of the time and still existing, with a structure penetrating it inside and outside could not be carried out for cost reasons.)

At present, the façade on the Appellhofplatz street is smooth and continuous, without any indication of the separation. On the Elisenstraße side, however, the division is marked by the indent in the exterior wall and the insertion there of the drainpipe (Figure 5.3).

In the interior space, too, Kulka intended to differentiate the original building from the postwar addition. He accomplished this by allocating different programs. Especially along the Appellhofplatz street side, the postwar addition was assigned to serve as a library on the second floor and a learning center on the third:

> Mit der Idee des "Aufbrechens" des neueren Gebäudes, sowohl der Fassade als auch der beiden Geschosse, wird neben dieser Unterscheidung auch die funktionale Bedeutung ablesbar. Im originalen EL-DE-Haus befindet sich die NS-Ausstellung, im Anbau die Sonderausstellungen, Bibliothek, Kommunikationsbereich und Gruppenräume.[10]

> (With the idea of "breaking up" the newer building, both the façade and the two storeys, the functional meaning becomes readable in addition to this distinction [of the façade and the two stories]. In the original EL-DE-Haus there is the Nazi exhibition, in the annex the special exhibitions, library, communication area and group rooms.)

Additionally, Kulka had planned, although not executed, a "bridge" over the boundary between the original and the postwar addition on the second floor (Figure 5.2), which were to make the separation between the two even stronger.

> Den Übergang von der Ausstellung in den Anbau bildet ein Steg, über den man die Sonderausstellungsebene erreicht. Diese Stahlkonstuktion mit Holzbelag liegt als Galerie in einem Luftraum zwischen 1 und 2 Obergeschoß und dreht sich entsprechend der Wandscheibe aus der Fassade.

> (The transition from the exhibition to the annex forms a footbridge, through which one reaches the special exhibition level. This steel construction with wood covering is located as a gallery in an air space between 1 and 2 upper floor and turns according to the wall panel from the facade.)[11]

To isolate the original building meant not only to separate the postwar addition discussed above but also to detach the documentation center's new design elements from the historical building fabric. This is seen in the way the exhibition panels are kept away from the wall's surface. In this relationship, the building's wall is not merely a background that holds the exhibition panels. Instead, the building fabric is

98 Formal Characteristics

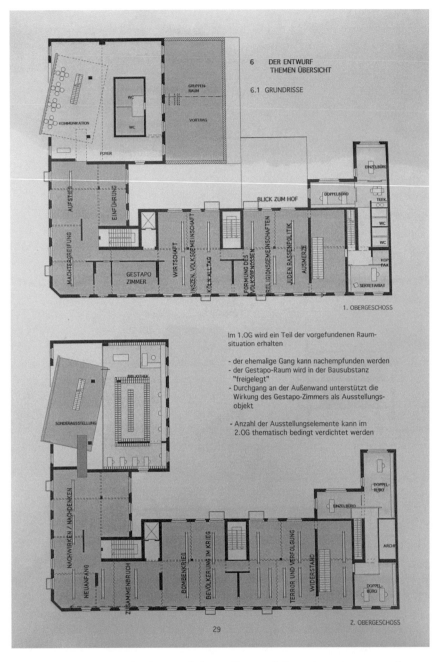

FIGURE 5.2 Documentation Center, Cologne. Proposed floor plans, not executed. 1993. The floor plans show the protruding frosted glass wall of the temporary exhibition space and a bridge over the boundary of the original building and the postwar addition. Source: © Peter Kulka-Archiv, Deutsches Architekturmuseum, Frankfurt am Main; und Peter Kulka Konzept für die Gedächtnisstätte El-DE Haus, Köln.

Formal Characteristics **99**

FIGURE 5.3 Documentation Center, Cologne. Drainpipe on Elisenstraße façade. They visually separate the original EL-DE House from the postwar extension. Photo by author.

100 Formal Characteristics

treated as if it were an independent material with its own identity. The detachment of the panels from the wall created a way for the two to coexist as important objects of exhibition, sometimes drawing attention to the panel and other times allowing the visitor's focus to dwell upon the stained wall, at which time the exhibit on the panel recedes from the attention, as occurs in cases of more straightforward historic preservation. The detached relationship between the historical building fabric and the exhibition panels is not a rare treatment when it comes to projects of historic preservation, in which the historical fabric is treated as precious object. However, in the context of National Socialist perpetrator buildings converted into a documentation center, the minimal contact between the new elements, in this case the exhibition panels, and the historical fabric, also suggests a sense of abhorrence felt by contemporary society toward the National Socialist past.

Nuremberg

In Nuremberg, different from Cologne's EL-DE House, the Congress Hall was designed purposefully for use by the National Socialist regime as a part of the larger Party Rally Grounds, and accordingly, intentionally carried the style of National Socialist architecture. Similar to the EL-DE House, although the building was still under construction, the Congress Hall's exterior appearance already revealed its stylistic characteristics and material finishes. Different from the EL-DE House, the Congress Hall building was never put to use by the Party, with its interior left unfinished, still in raw concrete and bricks. The Congress Hall, just like the EL-DE House, stood unscathed at the end of the war.

After the war, portions of the building were used by the city for exhibition and storage, and the southern orthogonal end block, the twin to the northern end block in which the documentation center exists, was turned into a music venue for Nürnberger Symphoniker. But otherwise, no major work, either toward demolition or completion, was applied, mostly because of the enormous cost such deeds would have required. As a result, when the architect Günther Domenig came on board having won the design competition for the documentation center, the former Congress Hall stood fairly unchanged since the Third Reich.

At Nuremberg, just as at Cologne, the exhibition panels are kept at a distance from the preexisting walls, in this case the raw bricks. But more importantly, Domenig's design insertions throughout the building are detached from the preexisting walls and floor slabs of the historical building fabric. They include the most prominent design element, the "*Pfahl*" or stake of steel and glass, which cuts diagonally through the orthogonal block of the National Socialist building, all the way from one end at the entrance to the other at the courtyard. The stairs and elevator shaft in the entrance hall and the bridge at the upper exhibition floor, all also in steel and glass, are also newly added design elements that are inserted by cutting into the existing brick walls and floor slabs. All these insertions create the visitors' processional route through the exhibits. And at every insertion point a space is maintained to detach the steel element of the new design from the cut bricks or concrete of the original building (Figure 5.4). This consistent design strategy throughout the center succeeds in presenting to the visitor the historical building as the product of the National Socialists' actions. While typically a building tends to recede into the background of any activities that take place within it, the detachment strategy keeps the large-scale building as an object of the center's exhibit.

The isolation of the Congress Hall from the documentation center extended further, beyond the newly inserted exhibition panels and the steel-and-glass "*Pfahl*." While the architect could keep the ceilings and walls in their unfinished state, the floors presented a design challenge, which Domenig successfully turned into an opportunity. The rough surface of the preexisting concrete slabs needed to be finished for the sake of visitors' safety. While Domenig's text states only, "To the

FIGURE 5.4 Documentation Center, Nuremberg. Insertion of new elements. Separating the glass-and-steel elements from the historical building fabric.

102 Formal Characteristics

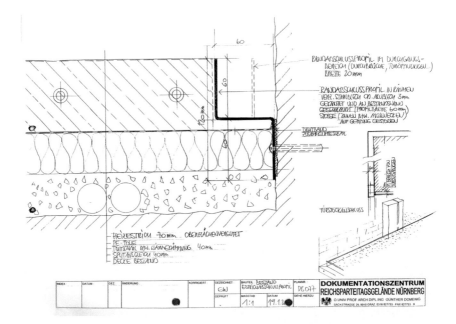

FIGURE 5.5 Office of Günther Domenig, detail drawing for the Documentation Center, Nuremberg. Source: Architekturzentrum Wien, Collection, Architekturzentrum Wien, Collection, N54 218 000 P 01.

existing bare floors we added industrial floor coverings (sealed concrete screeds),"[12] a drawing shows an explicitly intentional strategy to how the floor finish was applied (Figure 5.5). The drawing, dated January 19, 2000, drawn while construction was underway by Gerhard Wallner, Domenig's assistant, and titled "Screed Finishing Profile," is now part of the Domenig Archive of the Architecture Center in Vienna. According to this drawing, the rough raw surface of the existing floor was first leveled with mortar of 40 mm thickness, on which insulation of 40 mm, foil, and heated floor of 70 mm were applied, and the surface was treated. Notable for the present discussion is the treatment of where the floor meets any vertical surface, either wall or column. The drawing specifies a bent metal piece of either steel or aluminum of 120 mm tall and 60 mm wide along the preexisting vertical surface, which is fixed to the preexisting floor before the mortar was laid, which created a gap of 60 mm × 60 mm separating the finished floor from the preexisting wall (Figure 5.6). As a result, the new smooth floor never touches preexisting columns or walls, while at the same time clearly indicating the thickness of the newly added floor finish to the visitors. Clearly separating the raw surfaces of walls and columns from the newly finished, smooth surface of the floor emphasizes the contrast, which succeeds in showcasing the existing building fabric as the trace of the incomplete and unsuccessful operations of the perpetrators. At the same time,

FIGURE 5.6 Documentation Center, Nuremberg. Floor and wall joint detail. Photo by the author.

this detail – contemporary construction not touching the historical – can suggest the present abhorrence toward the National Socialist past.

Berlin

The design strategy to physically isolate the past building from the documentation center design, formally separating the past from the present, also is found at the Topography of Terror. However, here, the physical conditions at the site led the architect–landscape architect team to consider not only the past of the National Socialist era but also that of the postwar era.

At both the Cologne and Nuremberg sites, the original buildings that the National Socialist perpetrators occupied were still standing. In contrast, in Berlin the buildings were damaged during the war and were demolished after it. The former School of Industrial Arts and Crafts, at Prinz-Albrecht-Straße 8, which was built in 1901–5 and used as the Secret State Police Office headquarters in 1933–45 and as the Reich Security Main Office from 1939, was partially demolished in 1958–59, and the remaining walls were blown up in 1956. To the east, the former Hotel Prinz Albrecht, at Prinz-Albrecht-Straße 9, built in 1887–88 originally

104 Formal Characteristics

as Hotel Römerbad and used as the SS House, accommodating various offices including their main office, had been completely destroyed in 1943. The buildings on Wilhelmstraße, which form the eastern boundary of the site, also were damaged during the war. They included the former Prinz Albrecht Palais at Wilhelmstraße 102, built in 1737–39 originally as Palais Vernezobre and remodeled in 1830–32 by Karl Friedrich Schinkel as Prinz Albrecht Palais, and at Wilhelmstraße 106, a former commercial building, built in 1903, which housed the editorial offices of the National Socialist newspaper *Der Angriff* (*The Attack*) from 1932, and from 1937 to 1945 also the SD and the SS offices. And although some of these buildings along Wilhelmstraße were reported to have only "partial damage," they were demolished after the war, the Prinz Albrecht Palais in 1949 and the others in the 1950s. Only a limited number of small patches of building materials are visible on the ground level, making it impossible to consider the buildings' origins.

At the time of the competition, the remains of the basement walls along Niederkirchnerstraße, or the former Prinz-Albrecht-Straße, at the northern boundary of the site, had been used as the backdrop of the "Open-Air-Ausstellung" ("Open-air Exhibition"), with a roof overhead sheltering both the exhibits and the building remnants.[13] Although definitely presenting the age and suggesting human actions of the past, they could not specifically point to the National Socialist operation, as these buildings originated prior to the Third Reich, and they carried no formal characteristics from that era. Additionally, because the remnants were of the underground parts of the buildings, it was difficult to decipher their stylistic characteristics at all. Along Wilhelmstraße, some building remnants were to be found on the ground surface, also without any indication of the formal characteristics of the buildings.

In addition to the remains of historical buildings along Prinz Albrecht Straße and Wilhelmstraße, there also were some remains of the buildings in the interior of the site's field. Among them were the National Socialist air raid protection structures on which construction had begun in 1933. They consisted of both an above-ground bunker and underground ditches. The bunker was blown up in 1954, but in 1996 some remnants – the entrance staircase and an anteroom – were discovered.[14] Additionally, there was the former SS mess hut for the members of the Reich SS leader's personal staff, constructed during 1942 and 1943 by prisoners from the Sachsenhausen concentration camp. The cellar rooms were discovered in 1987, and the 1989 exhibition hall was built on top of this basement.[15]

The project's site carried additional postwar history, which was presented by the physical elements that remained. The site was used by the city as a dumping ground for demolition debris and also as a driving circuit. The Berlin Wall stood along the northern edge of the site. It also was the location of the temporary exhibit, "Topography of Terror," which opened in 1987 in the exhibition hall created by constructing a steel structure over the excavated kitchen basement.[16] There also was a memorial at the excavated Gestapo Prison cells. Lastly, some concrete segments still remained from the construction of Zumthor's winning design for the documentation center, which was halted and demolished in 2004.

Given the amount of physical remnants representing multiple layers of time – the pre–, during, and post–National Socialist eras – at so many locations throughout the project site, how does one accomplish the idea of physically isolating the past building from the documentation center design? It was accomplished by treating the site as a whole as the multiple pasts and separating the documentation center from it. In doing so, the "past" includes not only that of National Socialism but also of its treatment during the postwar era embodied physically at the site and of its aftermath, the divided Germany and Berlin. This is clear in the statement of the architect of the center, Ursula Wilms, who is treating the postwar wasteland of the site as something significant to be preserved and presented to the visitor:

> Das Gelände fiel bereits vor seiner Neugestaltung als städtebauliche Brache auf. Diese "irritierende" Leerstelle soll nicht nur erhalten werden, vielmehr soll der Eindruck der Leere und Kargheit verstärkt werden durch die neue, vegetationsfreie Bodenschicht aus gebrochenem, grauem Natursteinschotter.[17]

> (Even before it was redesigned, the site stood out as a wasteland. This "irritating" empty space should not only be preserved, rather the impression of emptiness and barrenness should be reinforced by the new, vegetation-free floor layer made of broken, gray natural stone gravel.)

She also considered the Berlin Wall as a part of the exhibit:

> Von hier sind die selbstsprechenden Zeugen der Geschichte unmittelbar sichtbar: die Berlier Mauer und der Gebäudekomplex des ehemaligen Reic hsluftfahrministeriums.[18]

> (From here, the self-speaking witnesses of history are immediately visible: the Berlin Wall and the building complex of the former Reich Aviation Ministry.)

The reviewer of the proposal, too, sees the presentation of the postwar Germany's treatment of the National Socialist past in the design of the documentation center. According to Hoffmann-Axthelm, the terrain, the rubble hills, meant the unconscious, and correspondingly fruitless, atonement attempt. The site was so much of a reminder of the mass murder by the National Socialist regime, the destruction of the city during the war, and the neglect of the past in the postwar era.[19] The site not only carries the difficult past that the documentation center deals with, but also it demonstrates how the postwar citizens dealt, or did not deal, with that difficult past.

This was accomplished by two strategies combined: First, they covered the terrain with "gebrochenem, grauem Natursteinschotter (broken, gray natural stone gravel)" (Figure 5.7), and then devised a detail that visually lifted the center building off the ground, not dissimilar to Mies van der Rohe's Farnsworth House (Figure 5.8).[20] However, this design strategy of the "handling of the terrain" does

106 Formal Characteristics

FIGURE 5.7 Documentation Center, Berlin. Ground cover. Photo by author.

FIGURE 5.8 Documentation Center, Berlin. View of the entrance. Isolating the building from the terrain. Photo by author.

reflect Peter Zumthor's winning design in the 1993 competition as well as his design for the shelter for the Roman archaeological site in Chur, Switzerland, not as a formal recreation but as an idea of separating the building from the ground.

What breaks this detachment of the documentation center building from the terrain of the pasts, not only that of the Third Reich but also that of the postwar neglect of the difficult past, is the design's treatment of the basement. Here the documentation center design tried to distance itself from Zumthor's design, which was vertically prominent, by keeping the above-ground structure to a single story. In order to accommodate the required programs, it was necessary to place substantial spaces in the underground, including the learning center, library, staff offices of the Foundation, and visitor's restrooms. To provide natural light to these areas, the central courtyard was created by making void the center square of the nine-square plan, and by creating a slope between the ground level to the basement level on the east side of the building, as well as by digging a sunken space west of the building. These three excavated areas bring natural light into the spaces of the basement; but as a consequence, the notion of the building block lifted up from the ground, which is accomplished successfully on the north and south sides of the building, is lost on the east and west sides and the central area of the building.

Munich

At Munich, the former Brown House was damaged during the war, and in 1947 was demolished to the level of the vaults of the cellar. At this time, the cellar's interior finishes were removed down to the raw structure, and the underground spaces were then filled. In 2006, the same year that the city's council decided to start the project of the competition for the documentation center, the remains of the cellar were uncovered, measured, and documented. At this time, the State Office for the Preservation of Monuments (Das Landesamt für Denkmalpflege), having examined the remaining traces of the cellar but not finding anything particularly significant for potential monument status, had the remains of the cellar demolished. When the competition was announced in 2008, its program directed the competitors to consider the formal characteristics of those structures that remained nearby: "The architecture of the building and the design of the exterior space must impressively mark the fundamental break with the history of the location and the traditional NSDAP administrative buildings in the neighborhood."[21] It went further by identifying those buildings: the Königsplatz, Führerbau, Administration Building, and two Honor Temples.

Munich's documentation center project site was immediately adjacent to Führerbau and the remains of the northern Honor Temple. While no effort is needed to physically isolate the documentation center building from these two historical structures, the ground is continuous. The documentation center design marked a clear separation on the ground by differentiating the ground surface finish. There is a patch of grass around the Honor Temple, which clearly is distinguished from the forecourt of the documentation center, which is paved in stone (Figure 5.9). There

108 Formal Characteristics

FIGURE 5.9 Documentation Center, Munich. Ground surface. Separation of the center building from the Honor Temple by way of ground surface materials. Photo by author.

also is a clear separation from the Führer Building by way of paving materials, as well as shrubs.

Contrast: Stylistic, Geometrical, Material

In laypeople's encounter with a documentation center building or any building for that matter, keen observation of the building's form is sometimes hard to come by, when they are either just passing by it or their attention already has been directed to the exhibition. Furthermore, while the formal characteristics of National Socialist architecture are recognizable to those with training, they may not be so apparent to every member of the population. If the architect is to make people aware of certain formal characteristics of a historical building, one way to do so is to create a contrast through the insertion of a new element. This may be done by way of the style, geometry, or material. As a general design strategy applicable to other projects, this was seen at Kaiser Wilhelm Memorial Church, examined in Chapter 1. There, the contrast is established in all three of the ways mentioned above. The original church was contrasted by the modernist vocabulary of the new construction, made of straight lines without any reference to classical order, and using the materials of steel, concrete, and glass blocks. To compare, the new insertion at the southern façade of Alte Pinakothek is much more subtle in contrast to

Formal Characteristics **109**

the historical form, the former being the modern interpretation of the historical motif. Still, there is a difference created by the use of steel pipes for columns and of the choice of the color tone of the bricks. At Kolumba, too, the most notable contrast exists in the wall that surrounds the excavated church. Zumthor's walls are constructed on top of the remains of the original church, and the straight horizontal lines of small regular intervals created by bricks of the upper part are in contrast with the organic lines of the much larger and irregular stone blocks in the lower.

Cologne

In Kulka's design proposal for the documentation center design dated May 1993, two geometrical contrasts created by the introduction of new forms, one much subtler than the other, can be observed.[22] The subtler one is a right-angled contrast between the existing linear, east–west axis of the building's form, which runs along Elisenstraße, and the sequence of exhibition panels arranged perpendicularly to that axis. And the other is a contrast between the orthogonal geometry of the historical building and the diagonal one of the new special exhibition space, created by the translucent wall, mentioned earlier, which was to be newly inserted and breaks the façade of the postwar addition on Appellhofplatz.

The idea of formal contrast ("genenüberstellen") is clear in Kulka's description of his design concept in the proposal. He commented on the perpendicular relationship ("Quer zur Gebäudeachse") between the linear axis of the historical building and the insertion of the proposed exhibition panels (Figure 5.10):

> Die Ausstellungsidee sieht vor, dem Gebäude eine neue Raumstruktur gegenüberzustellen. Quer zur Gebäudeachse stehende Wandelemente symbolisieren "Zeitschichten" bzw "Geschichte als geschichtete Zeit". Die Erschließung wird als "Zeitachse" entlang der Schichten an die Fassade Elisenstraße verlegt, sodaß die Fensterreihung an der gesamten Ausstellungsebene sichtbar bleibt. Die ursprünglich durch den Gang bestimmte Gebäudeachse wird von Wandelementen verstellt; ein Durchblick bzw eine Schlupfmöglichkeit von ca. 50 cm Breite bleibt jedoch erhalten.

> Die ca. 3.80 m breiten und 2.10 m hohen schichten- und raumbildenden Wandelemente, die gleichzeitig als Ausstellungsträger dienen, setzen sich aus halbtransparenten Rasterflächen zusammen. Diese Kleinelemente lassen sich für verschiedenste Formatgrößen und Ausstellungsobjekte auswechseln oder öffnen. Innerhalb der ca. 35 cm tiefen Elemente können Beleuchtungstechnik und Stromführung untergebracht werden.[23]

> (The idea behind the exhibition is to contrast the building with a new spatial structure. Wall elements standing crosswise to the building axis symbolize "time strata" or "history as stratified time." The development is laid as a "time

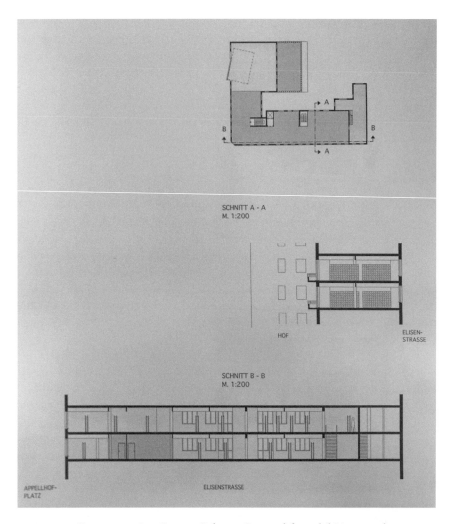

FIGURE 5.10 Documentation Center, Cologne. Proposal for exhibition panels, not executed. Source: © Peter Kulka-Archiv, Deutsches Architekturmuseum, Frankfurt am Main; und Peter Kulka Konzept für die Gedächtnisstätte El-DE Haus, Köln.

axis" along the layers of the facade Elisenstraße, so that the row of windows on the entire exhibition level remains visible. The building axis originally determined by the corridor is adjusted by wall elements; a view or a slip possibility of about 50 cm width is retained.

The approx. 3.80 m wide and 2.10 m high layer and space-forming wall elements, which also serve as exhibition bearers, are composed of semi-transparent

Formal Characteristics **111**

grid areas. These small elements can be exchanged or opened for a wide variety of format sizes and exhibits. Lighting elements and power supply can be accommodated within the approx. 35 cm deep elements.)

At the time of this proposal, the idea was to take down the existing lines of interior walls, which formed the central corridor, keeping only some of them, especially on the second ("the first" in German) floor, in order to treat "die Wirkung des Gestapo-Zimmers als Ausstellungsobjekt" (the effect of the Gestapo room as an exhibition object).[24] The proposed exhibition panels were made of "Auswechselbare Kleinelemente aus halbtransparentem Material" [interchangeable elements made of semitransparent material], each measuring 30×30 centimeters, with a total height of 2.10 meters. Any number of these units can be removed to place exhibit cases, photographs, or lighting.[25] The height of the panels would maintain the openness of the room whose height is 3.20 meters, and the semitransparent material of the panel would recall the translucent wall on the Appellhofplatz street side.

As to the second, diagonal contrast (see Figures 5.1 and 5.2), Kulka explained it thus:

> Das Aufbrechen der Fassade umfaßt eine aus der Fassade herausgedrehte Wandscheibe, die einerseits die Gleichmäßigkeit der bestehenden Fassade durchbrechen soll, andererseits, einer Plakatwand ähnlich, das Museum nach außen präsentiert. Die Wandscheibe besteht aus einer Mattglas-Stahlkonstruktion, sodaß Licht zwar in den Innenraum hineinfallen, keineswegs aber der Eindruck einer großen Schaufensterscheibe entstehen kann.[26]

> (The opening of the facade includes a wall pane [Wandscheibe] that has been twisted out of the facade, which on the one hand is intended to break through the uniformity of the existing facade, and on the other hand, like a billboard, presents the museum to the outside. The wall panel consists of a frosted glass steel construction, so that light may fall into the interior, but by no means can give the impression of a large shop window.)

Elsewhere in the proposal, Kulka called the diagonal element a "Scheibe" (slice).[27]

> Das NS-Dokumentationszentrum präsentiert sich nach außen
> - Neues Element durchbricht die Regelmäßigkeit der Fensterfront
> - "Scheibe" aus halbtransparentem Glas dreht sich aus dem Geäude heraus
> - Plakatwirkung – schon frühzeitig aus Richtung Breitestrasse zu Erkennen
> - Seitliches Fenster gibt den Blick auf das gegenüberliegende Gerichtsgebäude frei[28]

> (The NS Documentation Center presents itself to the outside world
> - New element breaks through the regularity of the window front
> - "Slice" made of semi-transparent glass turns out of the building

112 Formal Characteristics

- Poster effect – recognizable early on from the direction of Breitestrasse
- Side window gives a view of the courthouse opposite)

And Kulka devised a couple of design strategies to make the original historical building stand out separately from the postwar addition, in the following:

> Fassaden des originalen EL-DE-Hauses sind nicht von den Fassaden der Anbauten zu unterscheiden.
>
> Ziel: Kenntlichmachen des ursprünglichen Gebäudes
> Möglichkeiten:
>
> - Sichtbare Trennungslinie in der Fassade
> - Zurückhängen der 2 Eingangsleuchten an ihren ursprünglichen Platz in der Elisenstrasse
> - Bauliche Eingriffe in die nach 1947 errichtete Fassade[29]

> (Facades of the original EL-DE House cannot be distinguished from the facades of the annexes.
>
> Objective: To highlight the original building
> Possibilities:
>
> - Visible dividing line in the façade
> - Hanging back the 2 entrance lights to their original place in Elisenstraße
> - Structural interventions in the after 1947 built façade)

Although these proposed design elements were not executed, they demonstrate the architect's attempts at creating formal contrasts. In the executed design, the interior walls were kept, leaving the central hallway intact, and the diagonal wall was not inserted in the façade of the annex facing Appellhofplatz. What has remained from the proposal in the executed building is the idea of geometrical contrast, which appeared within the exhibit design. A diagonal line was drawn on the floor, in red, representing the chronological timeline (Figure 5.11). It travels through a sequence of rooms.

Nuremberg

As acknowledged both by the architect himself and the community leaders involved in the project, the most striking of feature of Domenig's design is the "*Pfahl*" or stake of glass and steel, which cuts diagonally through the orthogonal mass of the preexisting building of stone, bricks, and concrete. The stake presents a stark contrast in form – style, form, and materials – against the National Socialist building. Domenig explained the "*Pfahl*" in his speech at the building's opening ceremony:

FIGURE 5.11 Documentation Center, Cologne. Chronological timeline on the floor. Geometrical contrast between the diagonal line and the orthogonal building. Photo by author.

A "stake" cuts the right-angled geometry of the north wing. It begins across from Bayern Street, penetrates diagonally spatially the building, and floats in the void space of the inner courtyard of the congress hall. This "stake" is formed into the longitudinal and vertical main access of all intended functional areas.[30]

114 Formal Characteristics

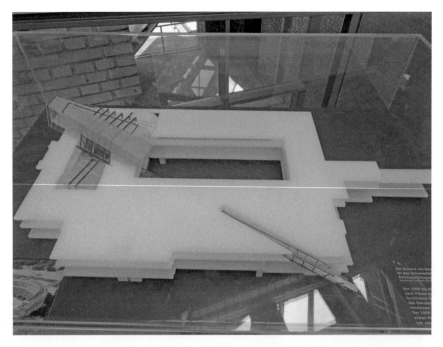

FIGURE 5.12 Documentation Center, Nuremberg. Model. Displayed in front of the learning center over the entrance foyer. Photo by author.

Domenig saw in the historical building's orthogonal geometry the National Socialism's "architectural translation of the power," observing that "there were only right angles and axes."[31] His idea was to destroy this "power" by cutting into it, and doing so using a contrasting geometry, the diagonal, both in plan and in elevation (Figure 5.12). Critiques also acknowledged how the new "surgical incision" of steel and glass in deconstructivist style contrasted against the monumentality of the National Socialist propaganda architecture of marble, bricks, and concrete based on right angles and bilateral symmetry.[32] The north end of the "*Pfahl*" thrusts out of the polychrome marble building, providing a clearly marked entrance to the documentation center that is visible from afar (see Figure 2.4).

The clash of the two styles are presented in a number of strategic locations in the visitors' sequential experiences with the center. From afar, the end of the "*Pfahl*" that thrusts out of the massive polychrome marble building works as an unequivocal marker for the entrance. Visitors climb up the steel steps, pass through the opening made into the heavy wall of marble and brick, and arrive at the entrance hall. In the entrance hall, the study center's auditorium hovers above the space, with its underside composed of diagonal planes. The visitor is led to the main stairs and the elevator, of steel and glass, which are aligned with the stake, and which lead visitors up to the exhibit floor. Once upstairs, and after the room for an introductory video and a couple of orthogonal exhibit rooms, the visitors come onto the top of the

FIGURE 5.13 Documentation Center, Nuremberg. The insertion of the "*Pfahl*". Overlooking the entrance foyer. The floor is of frosted glass. Photo by author.

stake, which forms a lookout to the front street on one side and the entrance hall on the other (Figure 5.13). The floor here is of frosted glass, making clear the notion of incision. After another set of exhibition rooms, visitors now cross a bridge over the space located on the central axis of the old orthogonal block, which was to become a secondary entrance to the Congress Hall and is the only space whose interior finish

116 Formal Characteristics

FIGURE 5.14 Documentation Center, Nuremberg. Balcony at the end of the "*Pfahl*". Overlooking the space intended for the main auditorium. Photo by author.

of polychrome marble was completed during the National Socialist era. Given the size of the space, Domenig could not have set up the bridge diagonally on the floor plan. His choice was to give an incline downward to the middle point of the bridge's span, creating the diagonal vertically. Visitors go through the exhibit sequence, set in the dark and orthogonal rooms of bricks and concrete. And before the end of the sequence where the floor slab is raised to accommodate a large space with a higher ceiling below, visitors traverse a new set of stairs upward and a ramp downward. After the last gallery space, visitors meet up with the stake at its other end, which provides a balcony over the courtyard (Figure 5.14). Visitors then return to the entrance hall, walking the full length of the stake and descending the full height of the floor.[33] Referring to the device set in a canal which controls the flow of water, the City Museums characterized this descent as a kind of "lock from the past to the present."[34]

Berlin

As discussed earlier, at Berlin and Munich, the historical perpetrator buildings had been torn down. In Berlin, however, there were numerous remnants of historical structures below ground as well as on the ground's surface. In both Berlin and Munich, there were authentic National Socialist pieces of architecture still standing that are visible from the documentation center project sites.

At the Berlin center, the glass and steel of the new construction make a clear material contrast to the historical buildings' remnants of stone, brick, and concrete. Stylistically, too, the documentation center building clearly is in the camp of modernism, making a stark difference from the historical buildings that accommodated the National Socialist operation, which, although not so apparent from the excavated remnants along Niederkirchnerstraße, are shown in the exhibit. In terms of geometry, contrast is not as evident. Rather, the square floor plan as well as the orthogonal positioning of the building to Albrecht Straße give the impression of repeating the geometry that exists in the next-door building, Martin-Gropius-Bau. And further, if the visitor was to compare the geometries of spatial organizations between the two buildings, one consisting of nine squares with the central one allotted to the courtyard, the other organized along the central axis with the sequence of entrance stairs, front vestibule, inner vestibule, court, and another set of stairs, it definitely gives the impression that the documentation center building is a slightly smaller version of the latter in terms of its geometry.

The contrast between the documentation center and the former Aviation Ministry building, an enormous structure built by the Third Reich and still standing across Niederkirchnerstraße, whose formal vocabulary is inescapably of National Socialist architecture, seems to be a missed opportunity. There is no question about the material contrast, and there is no disagreement as to what stylistic camp each belongs to – classicism and modernism. And in this comparison, there is no geometric similarity, unlike between the documentation center and Martin-Gropius-Bau. And yet, the rigidity of the floor plan and the stern treatment of the vertical and horizontal lines which exist in Wilms's design, are not so dissimilar to the "stripped off" classicism seen in Ernst Sagebiel's design.

Munich

As seen above, at Munich, the goal of establishing a contrast to the existing pieces of National Socialist architecture nearby was expressed in the competition program. The architects responded to the idea by a contrast of the overall form, which is enforced by the differences in the choice of color, building material, and window design.

The form contrast is created between the classicism, stern as it may be, of National Socialist architecture nearby, especially that of the Führerbau and the Administration Building, and the much more abstract, modernistic form of the documentation center (Figure 5.15). The center building is a complete cube, not in approximation but in precise actuality, measuring 22.45 meters in width, depth, and height.[35] In addition, the forecourt, the paved space between the documentation center and the site of the Honor Temple, also is a complete square with the same dimensions. Furthermore, the floors, both interior and exterior, are regulated by the unit of smaller squares. The perfect geometry of the cube and square did not originate from the historical context. In fact, the Brown House's rectangular floor

118 Formal Characteristics

FIGURE 5.15 Documentation Center, Munich, and Führerbau. Contrast between the two buildings. Photo by author.

plan was longer in the east–west direction than in the north–south direction. And the competition program showed it by using it to determine the project's buildable area, only shifting the historical building's footprint five meters westward.[36] The choice of the cube was special, as the runners-up – the designs that received the second, third, and "special" prize as well as one of the two designs marked for "special purchase" – all based their buildings' footprints on the elongated shape. The contrast created by the cube as the choice for the overall form was acknowledged by the competition's jury:

> Selbstbewusst wird der Würfel mit ausgeprägter Höhenentwicklung in den städtebaulichen Raum situiert. Er steht in starkem Kontrast zur Umgebung. … Der Würfel markiert den Ort der Täter ohne auf das "Braune Haus" Bezug zu nehmen. Er stellt sich nicht in die Reihe der Führerbauten, überragt sie aber.[37]

> (The cube is confidently positioned in the urban space with pronounced height development. It is in stark contrast to the surroundings. … The cube marks the location of the perpetrators without referring to the "Brown House." He does not stand in the row of Führer's buildings, but towers above them.)

FIGURE 5.16 Documentation Center, Munich. Expansion joint. Discreet vertical line in white concrete at the corner of the cube.

What could be considered the architects' obsession with the perfect geometry continued into the construction document stage of the design process, in which they devised a number of solutions in order to make possible the perfect cube design of the documentation center. First, there is an expansion joint that runs vertically at each of the four corners in the exterior (Figure 5.16). But, in order to avoid having these lines break the flat surface of the cube, they are treated so discreetly that they are almost invisible to the visitors, unless they are determined to find them. Second, the parapet at the top of the cube does not have a metal cap, which would be a standard detail but would have created a visible rim at the top of the building. As a result, when viewed from street level, the building appears to have a right-angled concrete corner – the same type as the vertical corners. Consequently, the building's appearance as a geometrically perfect cube is enforced. In a similar manner, the traces of the panels used for casting the concrete are made almost invisible. This third design feature is also an intentional detail. Typically, architects working with poured-in-site concrete construction intentionally leave visible the lines between the panels or the holes left by the tie bars in order to avoid the monotony of a flat surface and to showcase the material nature of construction. In comparison, for the Munich center, the architects chose to conceal these lines and holes, effectively drawing the observer's attention to the cubic nature of the building as a whole. Fourth, the windows are placed within the thickness of the concrete, and

120 Formal Characteristics

the window frames are inset, without anything protruding from the surface of the cube except the windowsills that channel rainwater away from the cube's surface. This creates the impression that the cube was there first and the windows were cut into it afterward.

The material choice for the documentation center also reflects the intention of establishing a strong contrast. The material of the cube is white concrete.[38] It is not painted white, but rather the whiteness derives from the material itself, which is much more expensive than regular concrete. The white concrete is not only for the exterior but also the interior. Of course, in order for this to happen, and to make sure that the building is insulated so that the heating and cooling of the interior is energy efficient, a layer of insulation needed to be incorporated. That means that the building is constructed of a double concrete wall. Those areas that do not appear to the visitors or museum staff members are of different materials, such as concrete blocks and regular concrete.

The Munich center is a case in which both the organizer and the architect recognized the possibility of expressing the contemporary society's position against the National Socialist past by way of the formal contrast of architectural designs.

Creating a Viewing Point of the Historical from the New

In addition to physically isolating the historical from the new and providing a formal contrast between the two, a third design strategy to bring the formal characteristics of the historical building to the fore is to set up specific spots within the center from which the visitor can view particular aspects of the historical building. This strategy is found in all four documentation centers, in different manners and to different extents, depending on the available aspects and the conditions of the historical building, sometimes proving to be greatly effective and other times not so much.

Cologne

To present the historical building to the visitor as the most important exhibit of the center, Peter Kulka devised another, ingenious design strategy, that is, to create places from which the visitors would view the features of the original building. His idea was to create a sequence of openings in the existing interior walls that separate office spaces from each other, which are lined up along Elisenstraße. He then used these openings as the route for visitors to circulate the exhibition spaces.[39] In the original scheme presented in the 1993 document discussed above, the central corridor was eliminated by tearing down most of the two rows of interior walls. When this original scheme did not advance for financial reasons, a new idea was to keep almost all the interior walls as well as the central corridor between the two rows of offices. The new scheme, making use of the newly devised openings for the visitors' procession, strengthened the notion that the historical building is the primary exhibit of the documentation center. The preexisting doorways were closed and unavailable for visitor circulation, and, additionally, the preexisting central corridors were, for the most part, left bare, without any exhibition.

These newly devised openings were made immediately adjacent to the exterior wall, but in a staggering fashion so that the series of openings do not line up with each other (Figure 5.17). This is quite different from the typical openings in

FIGURE 5.17 Documentation Center, Cologne. New openings. In the walls for the visitor procession. Photo by author.

122 Formal Characteristics

museums or historical palaces that connect interior spaces in a linear sequence. The placement of these openings now had a new added benefit: To have the visitors near the exterior wall gives them an opportunity to view the historical doors and walls from afar within the interior before they get close to the exhibition panels on the walls, further emphasizing that the building is the primary exhibit. There is another reason, explained by Kulka, for staggering the sequenced openings in the walls. Instead of providing a view through the entire processional space from the beginning to the end of the procession, the staggered arrangement obstructs the view. And this creates the sense that the opening "could close again at any moment."[40] That is, although the opening is there to allow the visitor's passage, the wall is perceived as if the opening did not exist. This makes the whole interior space closer to the historical arrangement of the interior space. An additional design strategy for these new openings can be observed regarding their proportion. They are narrow and tall, open all the way to the underside of the beam, making a clear contrast to the preexisting doorways, which are comparatively wide and short.

This visual effect may have originated in a photograph shown at a contemporary exhibit about National Socialism, held at the Münchner Stadtmuseum from September 24, 1993, to January 9, 1994.[41] For this exhibition, American photographer Michael Howells was commissioned by Winfried Nerdinger to take photographs of National Socialist buildings.[42] Among them, one particular photograph is to be noted. Titled "Dachau, KZ-Gedenkstätte" (concentration camp memorial), and taken in 1992, the photograph shows two overlapping doorways, one in the foreground and the other in the middle ground, and looks into the space beyond, which is obscured by darkness.[43] The second doorway has a sign above the opening that says "Brausebad (shower bath)." Most likely, Kulka was aware of this photograph and the meaning behind it – that many people were killed in a gas chamber under the pretense that they were being taken to a shower room.

Nuremberg

At Nuremberg, the most important viewing point of the historical building is at the end of the "*Pfahl*," which overlooks the assembly hall, the main space of the planned Congress Hall. The building was never completed, and accordingly the assembly hall remained bare, without roof, floor, seating or any other finishes. It currently is used by the city of Nuremberg for the parking of service vehicles. But the bare space, surrounded by the tall brick walls, which are the inner side of the U-shaped block, definitely demonstrates the form and scale of what the assembly hall would have been when completed.

A number of Domenig's design strategies clearly indicate to the visitor the significance of this spot. First, the viewing deck clearly marks the end of the stake, whose role within the new design has been clear to the visitor from the very beginning of the encounter with the documentation center, including from outside of it. Second, the viewing deck is set in the exterior, which not only turns the activity of going to the viewing deck into something special but also makes the visitor's body belong to the same space that was planned for the assembly hall. This experiential sense is strengthened by the selection of material for the floor of the deck itself: It is made of metal grating, which makes visible the underneath of the deck and gives the sense of floating in the enormous volumetric space of the assembly hall. The exhibit design clearly contributed to these design strategies. While the historical drawing of the expected assembly hall already was exhibited back in the gallery space in the most appropriate spot in the narrative sequence, the same image is enlarged and presented again at this end of the stake. Those who have experienced the space of the assembly hall can once again engage in the viewing of this image, which allows viewers to treat the space in front of them as one of the exhibits of the center.

Thus far I have focused on how the documentation centers' design features provided viewing points from which to observe the historical perpetrator buildings' formal characteristics. What about when there are no historical buildings within the project site, as is the case with Munich? Architectural design can assist in integrating historical, perpetrator buildings in the neighborhood into the center's exhibit. And the Munich design succeeds in this regard. In particular, the carefully designed size and location of the windows allow not only the selected views out, in particular to the Führerbau, the northern Honor Temple, the Administration Building, and Königsplatz, but also treat these historical places as part of the center's exhibit.

Munich

At Munich, the building takes the form of a white cube, and, as discussed earlier, conventional detailing – caps on the roof's parapet, vertical lines of expansion joints along the four corners of the building, or traces of poured-in-place concrete construction – are either omitted or reduced to achieve the visual impression of a perfect geometrical cube, and this succeeds in contrasting the center from the National Socialist architecture and thereby distancing the contemporary Munich from National Socialist activities in the city's past. It is therefore more striking that a series of windows break the surfaces of the cube. These windows are two stories tall and correspond to different floor levels: those at the northwest corner to the fourth and third floors; those at the southeast corner to the second and third floors; and those at the southwest corner to the first and ground floors. Cuts in the floor at these windows create exhibition spaces that are two stories tall. And these two-story volumes are surrounded by a balcony overlooking the lower floor.

The placements of these two-story-tall windows are highly intentional. Each of these balconies looks out to important historical perpetrator buildings in the neighborhood. On the third floor, the balcony looks out to the Führerbau up close as well as to the Königsplatz at a distance; on the second, across the street to the Administration Building; and on the first, to the Honor Temple. And the viewer's attention is drawn to these buildings because the exhibition at each spot relates to the building or an event that took place in it. For example, the gallery space on the third floor, overlooked from the fourth-floor balcony, showcases four video screens on which historical films of events that took place at the Führerbau, Honor

124 Formal Characteristics

Temple, and Königsplatz during and after the National Socialist regime are shown. The visitors looking at these screens from the gallery on the third floor also face the windows through which the actual historical buildings that appear in the films are visible (Figure 5.18). Similarly, on the third and second floors, the exhibits correspond to the view out to the historical buildings.

It is important to note the arrangements of the exhibits in relation to the setup of the gallery in the upper part of the exhibition space. From the gallery, the visitor's

FIGURE 5.18 Documentation Center, Munich. View out to Führerbau. Photo by author.

body naturally faces the two-story void space, where the exhibits were placed, and the view of the historical buildings beyond the windows. And the content of the exhibit inside the center building corresponds to the historical building outside. This design strategy of making a direct relationship between the visitor's bodily orientation and an exhibit, set up effectively by the placement of the balcony, is already used in the entrance foyer, in which an introductory video is shown on the opposite wall over the balcony, overlooking the stairs going down to the library on the basement level. This setup can be taken as a preparation for the other spatial relationships to come inside the building.

Berlin

In Berlin, across Niederkirchnerstraße from the documentation center site is one of the most significant buildings used by the National Socialist perpetrators, the former Aviation Ministry, discussed earlier.[44] It is a large, imposing structure that bears prominent formal characteristics of National Socialist architecture. It is clear in Ursula Wilms's writing that the architect intended to provide a view from inside the center:

> Mit einem deutlichen Einschnitt öffnet sich diese Hülle an der Nordseite im Bereich des Haupteingangs und des anschließenden Foyers. Von hier sind die selbstsprechenden Zeugen der Geschichte unmittelbar sichtbar: die Berlier Mauer und der Gebäudekomplex des ehemaligen Reichsluftfahrministeri ums.[45]

> (With a clear cut, this shell opens on the north side in the area of the main entrance and the subsequent foyer. From here, the self-speaking witnesses of history are immediately visible: the Berlin Wall and the building complex of the former Reich Aviation Ministry.)

The question remains, however, as to whether the difference between the past and the present is clear to the viewer, without which a view to the historical structures by itself does not necessarily help the visitor reflect on the past. A view of the former Aviation Ministry building can be had just by walking along the street. If architectural design is to partake in assisting the visitor, it needs to have a stronger presence, like the formal juxtaposition in Kulka's proposal or Domenig's stake, or even like Minich's white concrete or absolutely perfect geometry of the cube.

In the four documentation center projects, one can find design strategies that take advantage of formal characteristics, which are effective in presenting the past and the present communities' critical stances against the past. To begin with, there are a number of ways to physically isolate the historical from the postwar additions or their own insertions. There also are design strategies to create a stark contrast between the historical and their own by way of style, geometry or building materials. Lastly, each center design provides, to a varying degree of success, a point

126 Formal Characteristics

within the building from which the visitors are invited to view the historical, which would be overlooked otherwise. The architects are often highly intentional about these design strategies.

Notes

1 Alexander Scobie, *Hitler's State Architecture: The Impact of Classical Antiquity* (University Park: Pennsylvania State University Press, 1990).
2 The northern Honor Temple is immediately west of the project site; however, it is in ruin, and is hidden by the overgrown vegetations.
3 Matthias Donath, *Architecture in Berlin 1933–1945: A Guide through Nazi Berlin* (Berlin: Lukas Verlag, 2006), 20–1.
4 Kulturverwaltung der Stadt Köln and Peter Kulka, "NS-Dokumentationszentrum Im EL-DE Haus Köln, Appellhofplaz 23–25," May 1993, Deutsches Architekturmuseum, Frankfurt.
5 Ibid.
6 Ibid., 37.
7 Köln and Kulka, "NS-Dokumentationszentrum."
8 Ibid., 37.
9 Köln and Kulka, "NS-Dokumentationszentrum."
10 Ibid., 37.
11 Ibid.
12 Press release, by Günther Domenig (October 31, 2001), Az-W.
13 Jürg Steiner, "Die sachliche Architektur der 'Provisorien'," *Topographie Des Terrors: Ausstellungen 1987–2017*, ed. Stiftung Topographie des Terrors, Berlin (Berlin: Stiftung Topographie des Terrors, Berlin, 2017), 58–64; 64.
14 Now the concrete on the surface marks the zigzag shaped air raid protection trench.
15 Now the above ground structure has been cleared, and the basement remains. Immediately to the north is the site of the Gestapo house prison. It now is a memorial, marked by the gravel surface, under which are the foundations of five cells preserved and protected by a layer of sand. See Erika Bucholtz et al., *Site Tour "Topography of Terror" History of the Site* (Berlin: Stiftung Topographie des Terrors, 2016).
16 Reinhard Rürup, ed., *Topography of Terror: Gestapo, SS and Reichssicherheitshauptamt on the "Prinz-Albrecht-Terrain": A Documentation*, trans. Angress, Werner T. (Berlin: W. Arenhövel, 1989), 217–23.
17 Ursula Wilms, "Die Konzeption des neuen Dokumentationszentrums 2006–2010," *Topographie Des Terrors: Ausstellungen 1987–2017*, ed. Stiftung Topographie des Terrors, Berlin (Berlin: Stiftung Topographie des Terrors, Berlin, 2017), 65–7, 65.
18 Ibid., 66.
19 Dieter Hoffmann-Axthelm Comment on the jury results, 2006.
20 Wilms, "Die Konzeption des neuen Dokumentationszentrums 2006–2010," 65.
21 Stefania Kuszlik, ed., "Neubau NS-Dokumentationszentrum in München Vom Realisierungswettbewerb Bis Zur Grundsteinlegung" (Landeshauptstadt München Baureferat Kulturreferat, March 2012), 8–9.
22 Köln and Kulka, "NS-Dokumentationszentrum."
23 Ibid., 35.
24 Ibid., 29.
25 Köln and Kulka, "NS-Dokumentationszentrum."
26 Ibid., 37.

Formal Characteristics **127**

27 Ibid., 27.

28 Köln and Kulka, "NS-Dokumentationszentrum."

29 Ibid., 25.

30 Press release, by Günther Domenig (October 31, 2001), Az-W.

31 On September 16, 1998 as a part of a colloquium the City of Nuremberg organized for the invited competitors Presentation script, by Günther Domenig (November 15, 2000), Az-W. Competition program, 14.

32 Others also acknowledged the new "surgical incision" in deconstructivist style contrasting against the monumentality of the National Socialist propaganda architecture. See, for example: pamphlet "*Dokumentationszentrum Reichsparteitagsgelände*," by the Nuremberg City Museums (2001), the section titled "*Pfahl* aus Glas und Stahl" ("Spear of glass and steel"); news release "*Neues Dokumentationszentrum Reichsparteitagsgelände – eine nationale Aufgabe*," by the Nuremberg City Museums (November 15, 2000); and news release "*Neues Zeichen – Die Architektur des Dokumentationszentrum Reichsparteitagsgelände*," by the Nuremberg City Museums (November 15, 2000), Az-W.

33 The descent is characterized as a kind of a "lock from the past to the present," referring to the device that controls water flow in a canal News release, by the Public Relations Office, Nuremberg City Museums (November 15, 2000), Az-W.

34 News release, by the Public Relations Office, Nuremberg City Museums (November 15, 2000), Az-W.

35 Georg Scheel Wetzel Architekten, Site plan, and Roof detail section, both in the collection of the Documentation Center.

36 Stefania Kuszlik, ed., "Neubau NS-Dokumentationszentrum in München Vom Realisierungswettbewerb Bis Zur Grundsteinlegung" (Landeshauptstadt München Baureferat Kulturreferat, March 2012).

37 Stefania Kuszlik, ed., "Neubau NS-Dokumentationszentrum in München Vom Realisierungswettbewerb Bis Zur Grundsteinlegung," 16.

38 Specification document, at Georg Scheel Wetzel Architekten.

39 Interview, Gerd Fleischmann, June 18, 2019.

40 Kulka's statement was paraphrased by Werner Strodthoff in "Unverstellt: Das Kölner El-De-Haus als NS-Dokumentationszentrum," *Bauwelt* no. 37 (1997), 2099–101; 2099. The original German text is "als könne er sich jeden Moment wieder schließenum."

41 The exhibition catalog was edited by Winfried Nerdinger. Winfried Nerdinger, ed., *Bauen im Nationalsozialismus: Bayern 1933–1945* (München: Architekturmuseum der Technischen Universität München, 1993).

42 The photographer was Michael Howells, whose biography, although brief, is available in a book that showcases the University of New Mexico's photograph collection. His grandfather was one of the American soldiers who arrived first in Dachau toward the end of the war. Written by Eugenia Parry, the biography describes Howells's relationship to the Dachau concentration camp. See: Eugenia Parry, "Fool's Errand," in *Stories from the Camera: Reflections on the Photograph*, ed. Michele M Penhall (Albuquerque: University of New Mexico Press, 2015), 66–72.

43 The photograph is reproduced in the exhibition catalog, within the article written by Nerdinger. See: Winfried Nerdinger, "Bauen im Nationalsozialismus: Von der quantitativen Analyse zum Gesamtzusammenhang," in ed. Nerdinger, *Bauen im Nationalsozialismus: Bayern 1933–1945*, 8–17.

44 Matthias Donath, *Architecture in Berlin 1933–1945: A Guide through Nazi Berlin* (Berlin: Lukas Verlag, 2006), 18–19.

45 Ursula Wilms, "Die Konzeption des neuen Dokumentationszentrums 2006–2010," 65–6.

6

PHYSICAL TRACES

This chapter will focus on how the physical traces on a building that were left by human actions can be taken advantage of by the design that converts a historical place into a documentation center, thereby helping to present the past in a meaningful way. For the four documentation centers on National Socialism, which used to serve as places of National Socialist perpetrators, there are multiple layers of physical traces that can be of possible use to the architectural design. Classifying them by the agents that inflicted physical traces, they are: (1) the National Socialist regime during 1933–45, who constructed and/or used the building; (2) the Allied armies, who damaged and/or used the building during the war or postwar occupation; (3) the postwar German communities, who used, altered, or even destroyed the building; and (4) the architect, who converted the place into a documentation center. For each of the above four categories, I will look at the four documentation centers with regard to what physical traces were available, and how the architectural design took advantage of these physical traces to assist in meaningful presentations of the past.

We discussed, in Chapter 1, some postwar projects that incorporated the remains of historical buildings, each of which represented different design strategies: Dürer House in Nuremberg, Kaiser Wilhelm Memorial Church in Berlin, Alte Pinakothek in Munich, and Kolomba in Cologne. In all these cases, Allied bombing was the human action that left physical traces on the historical buildings. In the Nuremberg case, the postwar construction obscured the physical traces of bombing, reflecting the desire for normalization. In all other cases, the architectural design, newly applied by Egon Eiermann, Hans Döllgast, and Peter Zumthor respectively, made the scars clearly visible and even emphasized them, presenting the community's reflection upon the destructive forces of the war, and possibly an atonement for one's own nation causing such a war. In contrast, the four documentation centers faced additional challenges. To begin with, the ruins in general often exude a certain sense of awe or revelation, which is not appropriate to the historical buildings associated with National Socialist crimes. Additionally, focus on the Allied bombings and the resulting destruction would not immediately demonstrate the admission of the society's guilt but instead could allow self-victimization. Instead, at the documentation centers that stand on *Täterorte*, the present community's critical stance against their own National Socialist past had to be demonstrated.

Physical Traces by National Socialist Actions

By showcasing the physical traces of National Socialist actions, either in the construction or the use of the building, the architectural design could help bring the past to the present. The Cologne and Nuremberg centers highlight different aspects of such actions whose traces remain in the historical building.

Nuremberg

In Nuremberg, the building as a whole is the trace of National Socialist actions, with the incompleteness of the construction promoting the interpretation of the building as an action more than as a product. Architectural and local journalism commenting on Domenig's design mostly focused on the product aspect, discussing the formal and material contrast between the preexisting building and the new insertion created by the stake. However, one can observe at the site how the architect drew the visitor's attention to the action aspect of the historical building by his design strategies. And this aspect endows an actual visit with a much richer architectural experience.

The Congress Hall was still under construction at the end of the war, with the interior walls, floors, and ceilings still unfinished. After the war, the city government did consider taking down the National Socialist building, but could not, mostly for financial reasons. This, at least as a consequence, allowed for the idea of presenting the building in its raw state as a physical trace of the National Socialist actions. Keeping the building in an incomplete state eventually became an expression of the city's resolute commitment not to allow the fulfillment of the National Socialist intentions. Franz Sonnenberger, Director of Nuremberg's City Museums since 1994, looked back at the city's position at the time of the documentation center competition, speaking at an international symposium titled "Future of the Past: How Should the History of the Third Reich Be Transmitted in the 21st Century?" which Nuremberg City Museums organized and held on November 13 and 14, 1999, at the Deutsch-Amerikanischen Institut. Invited speakers represented various Holocaust-related museums including the U.S. Holocaust Memorial Museum, which had opened in 1993. The resolve and determination of those involved in the project to confront the past through the construction of

130 Physical Traces

the documentation center in the built relics of the National Socialist past is clear in his statement:

> The historical burden of the former Reich Party Congress site is perhaps a unique opportunity. Where else would there be a comparable possibility of throwing critical light on the façade of the Third Reich, thereby giving the lie to new myths and legends? Where else would it be possible to analyse the "motivation machinery" of National Socialism?[1]

On the occasion of the center's opening, Sonnenberger shared his reading of the unfinished interior wall of bare bricks as the banality behind the intended grandeur of National Socialist architecture.[2]

But it was the architect who, while accepting the city officials' charge to treat the unfinished building as a piece of the exhibit, understood more about the potential of physical traces. Domenig stated, "This task is exceptional. The exhibition … is a 'remembrance memorial' in the truest sense of the words 'negative contemporary history.'" And he resolved to create a center in which "There is nothing, however small … that does not demonstrate this frightening ideology." He kept the walls and ceilings as they had existed before him, stating that "The existing rooms, their walls and ceilings, are largely preserved in their raw concrete or brick surface structure."[3]

In particular, in the current exhibition spaces, the underside of the upper floor's concrete slab forms the ceiling, with sharp metals still protruding from the surface pointed down at the visitor. The bare brick interior walls have perpendicular protrusions here and there, which had been intended for the later construction of additional walls. And the treatment of the exhibition panels, discussed in Chapter 5, which are detached from the wall, keep both the panels and the wall the objects of the visitors' attention, preventing the historical building from receding into the background of the exhibit, and effectively showcasing the building as the trace of the deeds of the National Socialist regime.

Cologne

While at Nuremberg the historical building was available in its raw state as the physical trace of National Socialist actions, the situation was not so straightforward at Cologne. The treatment of the interior walls at the NS Documentation Center in the City of Cologne needs to be discussed from the point of view of promoting the conversion of an authentic historical site into a memory place. In particular, the surfaces of the walls and the floor were stained artificially by the design (Figure 6.1). After the war and before the building's conversion into a documentation center, the EL-DE House had been occupied by various functions of Cologne city government, whose use had accumulated as layers on the walls and floors. In line with the architect's intention to make the historical building the most important exhibit of the documentation center, as discussed in Chapter 5, Kulka and his collaborators began stripping layers, but it proved impossible to reveal the Gestapo layer without

FIGURE 6.1 Documentation Center, Cologne. Stained floor and walls. Photo by author.

destroying it. They ended up taking down layers all the way to the core materials. After the bare structure was revealed, they applied varnish of slightly varied color ranges to the walls. This was Kulka's idea.[4] A similar treatment was applied to the floor: it was made of bituminous concrete, with a variation of smooth and rough finishes, which created a visual resemblance to a floor that had been worn through a long time of usage. No documentations – plans or photographs – were available to show the interior conditions under the Gestapo occupation. It was not possible, therefore, to re-create or restore the interior to the state the building was in during the National Socialist regime. Therefore, the applied stains are merely a general semblance of aged surfaces that would have resulted through the passage of time.

The architect's inspiration to create irregular surfaces of the walls and floors must have come from the walls of the building's basement, which used to be a Gestapo prison. During the National Socialist era, those imprisoned had left inscriptions on the cells' walls, recording their suffering and leaving messages to their loved ones.[5] The basement rooms were used as filing and storage spaces after the war. In 1979, the City Council gave permission to convert the basement into a prison memorial, and at that time the wall inscriptions were uncovered by removing the whitewash coating from the walls' surfaces.[6] Today, these wall inscriptions are a significant part of the exhibits at this victims' place. And they also are effective in preparing the center visitors to pay attention to the conditions of the walls' surface at the perpetrators' place above ground.

132 Physical Traces

Another notable design strategy also was influenced by the wall inscriptions by the Gestapo's prisoners. While, in Chapter 5, the detachment of exhibition panels from the wall was discussed as a way to isolate the historical building and to treat the historical walls as an object of the exhibit rather than the background of the exhibited objects, in the Cologne center, one additional relationship is found between the wall and the exhibit.[7] Here, the exhibit is imbedded on the stained surface (Figure 6.1), which makes the textual exhibit literally a part of the historical fabric.

The irregularities on the walls' and floors' surfaces, newly created by the architectural design, on the documentation center's exhibition spaces upstairs bring about the sense of age, which the visitor may perceive in multiple ways. On the one hand, the stains on the walls and floors could suggest the crude and violent operations against humanity by the Gestapo during the National Socialist era. On the other hand, they could suggest the passage of time since the National Socialist era, allowing the visitors to distance themselves from the past and offering a space in which to reflect on the past deeds critically or for the current community to detach themselves from the evil actions of the past.

Berlin

While historical buildings no longer stand on the center's site in Berlin, there are a number of physical remnants visible. The visitor is aided by audioguide as well as informative sign posts when strolling through the grounds of the center. In addition to the excavated basement walls along Niederkirchnerstraße, there are a number of building foundations along Wilhelm Straße revealed exactly at the ground level (Figures 6.2 and 6.3). Additionally, the wartime trench's zig-zag shape is marked on the ground, so as the kitchen cellar and prison cells (Figures 6.4, 6.5, and 6.6). While the underground space as well as the structure used to hold the above-ground building remain visible, the prison cells have been covered and turned into a memorial for the victims, whose surface slightly sunken below the ground level.

Actions by the Allied Forces: Air Raids and Occupation

Like at the Belin center, at the Munich center site, too, the historical building the National Socialist government used does not remain, having been torn down after the war. In Munich, however, the center is successful in exhibiting, with the aid of films, the physical actions taken upon adjacent buildings by the American army. In particular, the vertical windows at the northwest corner allow the view out to the neighboring Führerbau and the northern Honor Temple. And at this spot the two-story volume gallery shows films of these two buildings from both during the Third Reich and the occupation by the Allied forces. As a result, the visitor is to watch "the blowing up of the 'Temples of Honors' and the repurposing of the 'Führer Building' as America House after 1945" in the film while seeing the current state

Physical Traces 133

FIGURE 6.2 Documentation Center, Berlin. Basement walls of the buildings along Niederkirchnerstraße. They serve both as an exhibit on their own and as the backdrop of temporary exhibit. Photo by author.

of the two buildings through the windows.[8] The remains of the Honor Temple and the scars from the bombing on the Führerbau are made more meaningful by the combination of the historical films and the center's architectural design. Another film shown at this spot explains the American occupying forces' taking down the

FIGURE 6.3 Documentation Center, Berlin. Segments of building foundations exposed on the ground surface, along Wilhelmstraße. Photo by author.

eagle emblem of National Socialism from the façade of the Führerbau and replacing it with their own eagle emblem. Although the façade of Führerbau, shown in the last film, cannot be seen through the windows, the visitors are likely prompted, after leaving the documentation center, to go just a few additional yards to verify the holes in the Führerbau where the emblem used to be.

FIGURE 6.4 Documentation Center, Berlin. Wartime trench. The location and the form marked on the ground. Photo by author.

Actions Taken by the Postwar German Communities

When it comes to the question of whether to incorporate the traces of the actions taken by the postwar German communities into the designs of documentation centers, the four centers present different circumstances in terms of the availability of such traces and the different positions toward the past of the architect.

FIGURE 6.5 Documentation Center, Berlin. Excavated kitchen celler. Photo by author.

Cologne

At the Cologne center, the architect's intention was to focus on the National Socialist past as the subject of the center and to exclude the traces of postwar actions as much as possible. As discussed in Chapter 2, the EL-DE House was returned to the owner after the war and was rented by the city to house a number of its administrative departments. With the intent to make the historical building the primary exhibit of the documentation center, the architect and his team chose to get rid of the traces of the actions of the postwar period and to restore the building to the time of the Gestapo occupation. The layers of the wall finishes applied during this time were stripped off. As discussed earlier, when the team realized it impossible to recover the very layer at the time of Gestapo occupation, it decided to strip all the layers to the structural core and to re-create the layer. As a result, the visitors to the Cologne center, as they enter the building, are immediately brought face to face with the time of the Third Reich, although it was recreated by the architectural design.

Another significant postwar action was the extension of the building. Kulka had fully intended to distinguish the original building from the postwar addition, especially since the formal characteristics themselves, both interior and exterior, do not allow the differentiation. The most important of the proposed design elements in this regard was the bridge over the boundary between the original and the postwar addition. It was not executed. As a result, it is difficult to identify the

FIGURE 6.6 Documentation Center, Berlin. Prison cells, covered and turned into a memorial for the victims. Photo by author.

postwar building at the site. The only notable design element that could draw the visitor's attention is the water drain pipe that runs from the roof to the ground (see Figure 5.3), at the boundary between the original and the postwar elevations. This feature, however, is only on the Elisenstraße side, and is not repeated on the main façade on the Appellhofplatz side. If Kulka's original proposals had been realized,

138 Physical Traces

and in particular, the distinction between the postwar additions and the original building had been indicated clearly by, for example, the bridge over the boundary or the diagonal floating special exhibition space in the addition that was intended to protrude out to the street front, the postwar actions would have been clearer (see Figures 5.1 and 5.2). As if to compensate, the exhibition makes clear the postwar history of the civic movement that worked to make the building available for public view by situating this segment of the exhibit in the very beginning of the visitors' procession.

Nuremberg

At Nuremberg, the documentation center occupies the northern orthogonal end block, only a portion of the building being constructed to become the Congress Hall. And that particular portion was not occupied, while some other places were put to use after the war, and some of these uses continue into the present. Rather than trying to hide these actions from the visitors, Domenig's design makes it possible for them to confront critically these treatments of the building by presenting them fairly prominently, if only at a few selected spots throughout the building. First, the space originally meant for the large assembly hall, which remained without a roof, is used as a parking lot. Second, the southern end block is used as a concert hall by Nürnberger Symphoniker. On the way from the viewing spot back to the entrance hall, visitors also can look over, from the "*Pfhal*," a courtyard within the northern orthogonal end block, which also is used as a parking lot. On some days, the visitors see some individuals in service uniforms working or taking a break there. These views remind the visitors of the postwar normalization of the building by adopting pragmatic purposes away from memory work. The understanding of the postwar phase of the building's history is promoted by the exhibit placed at the end of the sequence, immediately before the visitors confront these scenes at the end of and along the "*Pfhal*," which includes various ideas as well as practices for the usages of this building after the war, including a sports venue and a shopping center.

Berlin

In Berlin, various postwar actions left physical traces at the site, and this applies not only to the actions taken during the Third Reich but also after the war. These physical records represent the long and winding process German communities took before establishing the documentation center for the local population and an international audience. And to those who carefully comb the grounds of the center, these remains showcase the differing postwar positions and attitudes about memory work in general and about the treatment of the former site of National Socialist headquarters of perpetration in particular. These different attitudes are shown through the following: clearing the structures associated with the National Socialist past; building the wall that divided Berlin; using the site for totally unre-lated purposes and obliterating its past; drawing attention to the obliteration of the difficult past by unearthing the remains of those structures; and attempting to use the site for commemoration of the past. And the winding postwar history of this National Socialist perpetrator place is presented physically, in chronological order, by: the Berlin Wall; a stone block with its drill marks, used to commemorate the actions taken at the site by the Active Museum of Fascism and Resistance group; and remains of concrete exposed at the ground level from the construction of Peter Zumthor's winning design in the 1993 competition. The concrete is marked by a group of narrow vertical posts standing nearby. Each post carries a plate on top, stating "Wir haben beim Bau des Dokumentationszentrum mitgehelfen" ("I helped build the documentation center") Figures 6.7, 6.8, and 6.9).

The design of the documentation center per se, however, does little to present these physical traces. Instead, it combines all these phases of postwar history together with the time of the Third Reich. This is the result of the two design strategies discussed in the previous chapter. While successfully presenting the contemporary stance against the National Socialist past and the postwar failure to deal with that past by isolating the center from the terrain ("topography"), the two design strategies – to cover the terrain with "gebrochenem, grauem Natursteinschotter (broken, gray natural stone gravel)" and to visually lift the center building from the ground, do end up treating the varied pasts as one.[9]

Munich

At Munich, no significant actions by the German community are physically available for observation. The introductory film at the center's entrance foyer on the ground floor showcases the history of the building, including the demolition of the building damaged by the air raids after the war, and the excavation and removal of underground structures during the period leading to the design competition. However, none of these actions left physical traces to be seen at the center. And the narrative of the center's exhibit is focused not on the Brown House but rather on the National Socialism headquarter district, to which the Brown House belonged, and further on the city of Munich.

Actions Taken by the Execution of the Documentation Center

Nuremberg

At Nuremberg, Domenig inflicted physical traces upon the preexisting building, accomplishing much from the architectural design to demonstrate the current position against the National Socialist deeds. The most striking and pronounced aspect of design is the "*Pfahl*," or stake, of glass and steel, which cuts diagonally through the orthogonally organized massive preexisting building of stone, bricks, and concrete. Others acknowledged this design element as a "surgical incision." Visitors to the documentation center are presented the National Socialist past via the stark contrast in forms and materials to Domenig's new insertion, whose deconstructivist style

FIGURE 6.7 Documentation Center, Berlin. The Berlin Wall. It runs along Niederkirchnerstraße, the center site's north boundary. Photo by author.

contrasts against the monumentality of the National Socialist propaganda architecture of marble, bricks, and concrete based on right angles and bilateral symmetry.[10] But the clash of the two is not just about the form and the material choice. From afar, the sight of the end of the stake thrusting out of the massive polychrome marble building is a simple contrast that functions as an unequivocal marker of the center's entrance.

FIGURE 6.8 Documentation Center, Berlin. Commemoration of the Active Museum of Fascism and Resistance. Photo by author.

But Domenig's design places the visitors close to the physical conditions of the way the stake left traces of its incision on the National Socialist building. This happens in a number of strategic locations. First, upon entering, when the visitors climb up the steel steps, they pass through the opening made into the heavy wall of marble and brick before arriving at the entrance hall. Second, having climbed the main stairs from the entrance hall, which are of steel and glass and running parallel to the stake, visitors go through the opening, cut diagonally to the original brick wall but perpendicular to the stake, which leads to the room for an introductory video. Third, after going through a couple of orthogonal exhibit rooms, visitors arrive at the upper part of the stake, which forms a lookout to the front street on one side and to the entrance hall on the other. The floor here is of frosted glass, making clear the notion of incision. As the visitor comes close to the glass lookout, they also come close to the cut surface of the historical building fabric of marble and bricks. Fourth, after going through another set of exhibition rooms, visitors now cross a bridge over the space located on the central axis of the old orthogonal block, which was to become a secondary entrance to the Congress Hall and is the only space whose interior finish of polychrome marble was completed during the National Socialist era. Here, Domenig's steel bridge is reached through a newly-made opening in the brick walls. Because the bridge is narrow, being just wide enough to allow one person comfortably to occupy it, the visitor comes very close to the cut surfaces of these openings.

FIGURE 6.9 Documentation Center, Berlin. Remains and commemoration of Peter Zumthor's building. Concrete exposed on the ground surface and a group of posts with lists of names who were involved in the execution. Photo by author.

In addition to the above examples that are at the beginning of the visitors' procession through the center exhibit, throughout the building the existing fabric – both walls and floors – were cut and taken away where the new elements – the stake, stairs, and bridge – were inserted. Additionally, the preexisting walls and floors

Physical Traces **143**

also were cut, in order to open a window or to allow access from one exhibition space to another. There also are places where brick interior walls were cut, in order to make openings to set up a route through the exhibit spaces, or to place a study center above the entrance hall. A set of floor plans and sections, now at the Domenig Archive of the Architekturzentrum Wien, shows where the walls and floor slabs were to be cut.[11] This was a significantly challenging task, as described by Walter Anderle, Nuremberg's City Master Planner, at the building's opening ceremony: "The existing building materials – hard bricks and high-quality concrete – offered an unexpectedly great resistance to demolition work." "…the construction work was faced with the most difficult tasks. 2 m thick masonry work had to be cut through in different places. With diagonal penetrations, this increased to 5 m."[12] To execute what is specified in these drawings, a circular saw was used (Figure 6.10).

There are a number of design strategies that can be observed in Domenig's design, which made the cut a prominent feature. First, in all these instances, the visitors come close to the cut surfaces, and in many situations it is even natural for them to touch them. Second, the newly added design elements – stake, stairs, and bridge – are kept detached from the cut surface of the historical building fabric. Third, the sections of granite, bricks, and mortar were left devoid of any finish or even polish, leaving the circular traces of the saw clearly visible to the visitor. As a result, visitors are presented the physical scars that the documentation center inflicted upon the historical building from the moment they enter it (Figure 6.11). The physical traces as a result not only remind the visitors of the past, but also overtly present a critical stance against the National Socialist actions. In other words, the architectural design takes the historical building as the physical trace of the National Socialist actions, and in turn leaves the physical trace of countering the National Socialist past.

Cologne

At Cologne, as at Nuremberg, the design for the documentation center called for cutting into preexisting interior walls that separated offices, as discussed in Chapter 5, in order to create a sequence of openings for a new circulation path for the visitors. However, the design intention regarding the actions taken by the architectural design against the historical fabric of the preexisting National Socialist building is distinctly different between Nuremberg and Cologne designs. At Nuremberg, the act of cutting is an act of the contemporary society against that of the National Socialists. And to promote this understanding, the physical traces of the circular saw that cut into bricks and granites are left visible. At Cologne, once the decision was made to keep intact the interior walls that run parallel to the hallways, the architect (and the exhibition designer) intended to keep the preexisting corridors and doorways as a part of the exhibit, and not to use them for the purposes of circulation from one room to another. New openings were made in each preexisting wall that separated two adjacent rooms to be used specifically for the visitor procession. In going through the exhibits, the visitor does notice clearly that these openings

144 Physical Traces

FIGURE 6.10 Documentation Center, Nuremberg. The circular saw used to cut the preexisting brick and stone walls. Source: Dokumentationszentrum Reichsparteitagsgelände, no. 1159-25.

Physical Traces 145

FIGURE 6.11 Documentation Center, Nuremberg. Traces of the circular saw. They are visible in the gallery. Photo by the author.

are new. Several design features assist in this realization (see Figure 5.17). First, these openings are much taller than the preexisting doorways, which emphasizes that they are not original features of the historical building. Second, these openings are staggered from each other. When visitors face the first of the sequence of these openings on the route, they are presented with a series of glimpses of the exhibits

146 Physical Traces

from each of the subsequent rooms. Third, these openings are void of any frames, which is a treatment completely different from that of the historical doorways. Using these new openings, being aware that they are new, the visitors realize they do not move about in the same way as did the Gestapo officers, and this realization is important, in order to make the experience meaningful against the perpetrator operations. However, in terms of the physical actions of cutting the walls, their traces are not visible. The surfaces of the cut sections are finished clean and neutral. The actions of opening the walls are not taken as a critical force against the National Socialist actions.

Berlin

In considering the traces of actions by the architectural design applied to the site to convert the historical site to a documentation center, Berlin's Documentation Center takes a strategy completely opposite to that seen at Nuremberg. At Berlin the center leaves no physical traces of its actions against the historical remnants. And this is achieved by the new center building not physically touching either the remnants of the historical buildings or the historical ground.

First of all, the new building of the documentation center does not physically engage with the remnants of the historical buildings. The linear trench that exhibits the basement walls of the buildings that lined up along Prinz Albrecht Straße and the ones that are visible on the ground's surface, which are made available by signposts throughout the grounds for a self-conducted tour with an audio guide, are treated separate from the new building. The notion that the ground had once hidden the National Socialist perpetrators' past, but was excavated, clearly is expressed in the center's name – formerly called "terrain" of the "Prinz-Albrecht-Terrain" and later "topography" of the "Topography of Terror." The clear separation of the new building from this ground expresses both the sense of revealing the once-hidden past and that of the critical stance of the present community against National Socialism.

In addition to separating the new building from the physical remnants of the historical perpetrator buildings by the location, the new building is lifted from the ground, creating the appearance of not touching it. This especially is visible on the building's north and south sides, seen by those who face it from the main approach and those who are taking the site tour and have gone around to its south side (see Figure 5.8). At the corner of the building, in particular, its exterior panels do not go into the ground, stopping a few inches above it. This notion of the building not touching the ground is less clear at the bottom of the stairs, at which the support structure of the steps visibly goes into the ground. Some detail design could have created a stronger sense/appearance of the steps being supported from above rather than from below.

In comparison to the Nuremberg center, which clearly created the critical stance of the present community against the National Socialist regime by inflicting scars, the detachment strategy may be a more subtle presentation of the current stance.

This relationship, however, is expressed in a different way, as if it is unpleasant to touch something extremely undesirable. The relationship is appropriate especially since what is lifted away from the past that remains in the ground is that of the permanent and temporary exhibits, classrooms, and a small café, the spaces in which the visitors spend the majority of their time at the center.

Moreover, on the building's east and west sides, the new center exposes its basement, having the ground dug into that level. The visitors are discouraged, if not prohibited, from approaching the basement areas from the exterior ground level, as the stairs to the sunken space to the west have a chain across them, and the slope between the basement level and the ground on the east side is too steep to walk comfortably. More importantly, the ground, on both the east and west sides, is covered with large, cracked stones quite inappropriate for walking on, even to those who might think of attempting to do so. In fact, no one walks on the large area of the entire site covered with these stones. This relationship, while somewhat contrary to that of the building's appearance elsewhere of detachment from the ground, is appropriate for the use of the building's basement, which includes the library, the archives, the Foundation offices, and seminar rooms. All these functions are to get closer to the past.

Any buildings go through a number of layers of time, during which some human actions leave physical traces on the building, and architectural design can assist in selectively present a certain past while obscuring others. In case of perpetrator buildings, traces may be made by the National Socialist regime, the Allied armies, the postwar German communities, or the construction of a documentation center. The architect may leave the historical building whose construction was never completed in its raw state or re-create irregularities on the surfaces of the wall and floor resembling the accumulated use of the building over time. The architect may cut into the historical building, leaving the cut section unfinished, as a critical statement against the agent that created the historical building.

Notes

1 Franz Sonnenberger, "A City Confronts Its Past," *Die Zukunft der Vergangenheit: wie soll die Geschichte des Nationalsozialismus in Museen und Gedenkstätten im 21. Jahrhundert vermittelt werden? / The Future of the Past: How Should the History of the Third Reich Be Transmitted in the 21st century?*, ed. Franz Sonnenberger et al. (Nürnberg: Museen der Stadt Nürnberg, 2000), 54–5.

2 Franz Sonnenberger, News release, by the Public Relations Office, Nuremberg City Museums (November 15, 2000), Architekturzentrum Wien Dünther Domenig Archive.

3 Press release, by Günther Domenig (October 31, 2001), Az-W.

4 The author's interview with Gerd Fleischmann, June 18, 2019.

5 Manfred Huiskes and Alexandra Gal, eds., *Die Wandinschriften des Kölner Gestapo-Gefängnisses im EL-DE-Haus, 1943 – 1945, Mitteilungen aus dem Stadtarchiv von Köln 70* (Köln: Böhlau, 1983). See also: Werner Jung, *Wände, die sprechen: die Wandinschriften im Kölner Gestapogefängnis im EL-DE-Haus / Walls That Talk: The Wall Inscriptions in the Cologne Gestapo Prison in the EL-DE-House* (Köln: Emons, 2014).

148 Physical Traces

6 Barbara Becker-Jákli and NS-Dokumentationszentrum (Historisches Archiv der Stadt Köln), *Cologne during National Socialism: A Short Guide through the EL-DE House* (Köln: NS Documentation Centre of the City of Cologne: Emons, 2011), 18–20.

7 The author's interview with Gerd Fleischmann, June 18, 2019.

8 Winfried Nerdinger, *Erinnerung gegründet auf Wissen / Remembrance Based on Knowledge). Das NS-Dokumentationszentrum München / The Munich Documentation Centre for the History of National Socialism* (Berlin: Metropol-Verlag, 2018), 183.

9 Ursula Wilms, "Die Konzeption des neuen Dokumentationszentrums 2006–2010," *Topographie Des Terrors: Ausstellungen 1987–2017*, ed. Stiftung Topographie des Terrors (Berlin: Stiftung Topographie des Terrors, Berlin, 2017), 65–67, 65.

10 See, for example: pamphlet "Dokumentationszentrum Reichsparteitagsgelände," by the Nuremberg City Museums (2001), the section titled "*Pfahl* aus Glas und Stahl" ("Spear of glass and steel"); news release "Neues Dokumentationszentrum Reichsparteitagsgelände – eine nationale Aufgabe," by the Nuremberg City Museums (November 15, 2000); and news release "Neues Zeichen – Die Architektur des Dokumentationszentrum Reichsparteitagsgelände," by the Nuremberg City Museums (November 15, 2000), Az-W.

11 A set of drawings at the Domenig Archive show where the walls were to be cut. Walter Anderle, Nuremberg's City Master Planner, spoke about the difficulty: "The existing building materials – hard bricks and high-quality concrete – offered an unexpectedly great resistance to demolition work." "…the construction work was faced with the most difficult tasks. 2 m thick masonry work had to be cut through in different places. With diagonal penetrations, this increased to 5 m." Press release, by Walter Anderle (October 31, 2001), Az-W.

12 Press release, by Walter Anderle (October 31, 2001), Az-W.

7

DESIGNATION

This chapter expands the possibilities of buildings' presentation of the past by way of designation. At first glance, "to be designated" refers simply to being given "a specified status or name" as an institution of certain human activities by a society, and in the particular cases of the four documentation centers, to being identified as a research and educational institution on the history of National Socialism in general and on the events and activities during that era in a particular city. However, the four documentation centers' designation requires another layer in relation to the places' pasts. These centers need to be identified as the place in which National Socialist crimes were committed during the Third Reich. In order to take fullest advantage of it having been an authentic perpetrator place, the designation needs to include both the institutional identity of the present and the place's history. And the presentation of that designation needs to be effective to passersby as well as to visitors, that is, for both witting and unwitting audiences. In this chapter, we will examine how the pronouncement is achieved on the immediate front of the building, to the street, and further beyond. Granted, architects may not take the design of such pronouncements – signposts, poster cases, and so on – as a significant part of their contributions, or these tasks may not be included in their scope of work. And when it comes to the question of naming the institution, it often is the case that community leaders or stakeholders are in charge of that decision. However, by examining the variety of pronouncements and their effectiveness, this chapter tries to draw the attention of architects and their design collaborators to what they could do to enhance their design work in terms of presenting the buildings' and places' designations – both those of the present and the past – in meaningful ways. This could include designing a setting for such designations or incorporating a display into the overall architectural intentions.

150 Designation

How Designation Is Pronounced

Before we make specific observations about the ways designations are presented in the physical environment at the four centers, we will touch on two other ways to do so. First, the institution's designation may be presented to the public by way of publications, in print or online, by the institution or the city. The building's past also may be acknowledged by the registry of historical monuments. In whatever way the designation is to be pronounced, that of the National Socialist past presents a challenge especially when their environments are "normalized," that is, used for something unrelated to the difficult past. The challenge may even be acute when the buildings themselves are normalized. We will therefore expand our considerations to a wider range of perpetrator places beyond the four centers.

A nuanced balance is required between serving as an institution on the difficult past and being a part of people's everyday life. The same can be said about the means of designation, that is, the way the place's present institutional identity and tits history are pronounced to the street. On the one hand, clear presentation of that identity is helpful, both to visitors and passersby. Especially for the latter, the designation can be their first opportunity to acknowledge the place's National Socialist past and the center's role as a site of research and education. On the other hand, such an indication may not be welcome as a part of everyday life, especially for the places that have been normalized or for those that stand in an area that has been predominantly normalized.

To take Munich as an example, the documentation center now is part of what is officially designated as "Kunstareal München," or the area of arts, which has a size of about 500×500 meters, and which is located centrally in the city, only about 500 meters north of the Munich Central Rail Station and about the same distance away from Odeonsplatz adjacent to the Residenz.[1] The list of museums and colleges within the Kunstareal includes world-renowned institutions such as Alte Pinakothek, discussed in Chapter 1, and Glyptothek and the State Collection of Antiquities on Königsplatz. Shortly after the war, in late 1945, a group of victims of political persecution put forward a proposal to change the name of Königsplace to Platz der Opfer des Nationalsozialismus (Square of the Victims of National Socialism) and of Brienner Straße to Straße des Nationalsozialismus (Street of National Socialism), in order to cement the past in the designation. It was turned down based on the reasoning that negative references to the past were not appropriate.[2] The State Museum for Egyptian Art and the State University for Television and Film Munich are also on the list, housed in a building designed by Peter Böhm. The University relocated to the new building in 2012, and the Museum opened in 2013. It is important to note that the latter new building occupies the site of the chancellery building, whose construction had been started in 1938 but was unfinished at the end of the war with only the basement built.[3] The Führerbau and the Administration Building also are on the list of cultural institutions in the area, housing Hochschule für Musik und Theater München, and Museum für Abgüsse Klassischer Bildwerke and Zentralinstitut für Kunstgeschichte respectively.

Neither the official list provided by the Kunstareal nor each institution's website recognizes the National Socialist past of these places, but instead identifies them merely for their present functions.

The fear that a simple pronouncement of the building's National Socialist past could inadvertently be mistaken as support is real, as, even without such designation, places that the Party celebrated are taken as demonstrations of affirmation by neo-Nazi supporters, as was the case with Feldherrnhalle. This building goes back to the time of the Kingdom of Bavaria (1805–1918), having been commissioned in 1841 by King Ludwig I, and its name, Feldherrnhalle, or Field Marshalls' Hall, refers to its original purpose, to honor the Bavarian Army. The building was modeled after the Loggia in Piazza della Signoria, Florence, and, just like its model, is composed of three arched bays wide and one bay deep. It is located on Odeonsplatz, which was developed as the forecourt of the Residenz at the originating point of Brienner Straße, which connects the Residenz westward to Nymphenburg Palace. Its positioning in relation to the Residenz is the same as its model's relation to the Palazzo Signoria. The National Socialist Party adopted Feldherrnhalle as its important landmark commemorating the Beer Hall Putsch, of November 1923, the failed attempt of Hitler and the National Socialist Party to overthrow the German government. It was treated as one of the "sacred sites" of the Third Reich, and a memorial plaque, called the Mahnmal der Bewegung (memorial of the movement), designed by Paul Ludwig Troost, was added to the building's east side. Two honor guards were stationed on each side of the memorial, and it was mandatory for passersby to give the Nazi salute.[4]

After the war, Feldherrnhalle became a controversial site in relation to National Socialist memory. There were efforts to erase its association or to denounce National Socialism and its deeds, but some actions taken at the building were questionable in their intention and others in support of National Socialism. One instance evolved around a graffiti on the north-facing plinth of the building, reading: "Dachau-Velden-Buchenwald / Ich schäme mich daß ich ein Deutscher bin (I'm ashamed that I am a German)." A photograph, taken on May 20, 1945, was used by the U.S. army for its reeducation campaign, and was published all over the world with the headline reading "A German regrets!"[5] Soon afterward, another graffiti appeared on the east side. Listing Goethe, Diesel, Haydn, and Rob. Koch, it pronounced, "Ich bin stolz Deutscher zu sein (I am proud to be German)." Another event took place in June of the same year. Even before the American occupying forces' directive to destroy public National Socialist monuments, ordinary citizens of Munich destroyed the Mahnmal der Bewegung (memorial of movement), on the east side of the building.[6] It was a memorial for the Beer Hall Putsch of November, 1923, designed by Troost, carrying the names of Party members who died in the event. During the Third Reich, the memorial was guarded and the citizens passing by it were made to give the Hitler salute. On June 3 of the same year, local people spontaneously smashed the memorial plaque as an act of denazification.[7] On November 9 of the following year, people gathered in Odeonsplatz, and demanded the removal of the statues of the National Socialist criminals.[8] From the 1960s onward, the

152 Designation

Federal Border Police and the Bundeswehr used the site for military ceremonies, which now no longer are held there out of consideration of the possible associations to power and oppression.[9] On August 18, 1987, a neo-Nazi group used the site to hold a memorial ceremony for Rudolf Heß, Hitler's former Deputy, who had died the day before in Spandau Prison.[10] And this was only one of a number of occasions on which extreme right-wing circles tried to exploit the symbolic meaning of the building. At least as late as 2004, the site still was a subject of contention, with an extreme right-wing group trying to hold a gathering and Munich City Council preventing it.

Historical Registration

A related issue exists with regard to monument protection of built heritage associated with National Socialist perpetration, which poses a special set of challenges in Germany.[11] The registration as an historical monument is important from the point of view of making available and presenting, with a critical stance, the *Täterorte*, or the buildings and locations that were associated with the Third Reich's atrocities, because the first step for a critical presentation of historical places is acknowledgment, and such registration would do exactly that. However, when the historical building is taken as the representation of the past ideology, heritage protection, which really is a protection of the building and not the ideology, can be misconstrued as affirmation of the past. This misconstruing is the opposite side of the same coin that propels the demolition of an historical building that is associated with a difficult past, as seen in denazification.

While places that carry the National Socialist past are recognized in the historical registry, which provides information on the role of the building and the place during the era, when it comes to presenting such a past in the place where it physically happened, the challenge is even greater. Winfried Nerdinger pointed out that the Bavarian government had categorically rejected putting up memorial plaques on former National Socialist buildings owned by the State of Bavaria.[12] At Führerbau, mentioned above, the administration of the music school that occupies the building fears the possibility of discouraging international students if they are more forthright about the dark past of the building the institution occupies.

Physically Presenting the Designation

The way the building announces the designation to the street is an important but also a complex consideration for architectural design, especially given that many historical perpetrator buildings or places are normalized, and their pasts are year by year becoming obliterated. Those authentic perpetrator buildings or places that now serve as documentation centers on the National Socialist past carry the task not only of fulfilling the function of being documentation centers but also of standing in for that city's other places of perpetration which have been normalized and for the city as a whole as a place of perpetration. Designation also is important, for it benefits not only those intentional visitors who already have interests in the National Socialist past but also those for whom their unintentional encounter with the documentation centers possibly becomes an early step in reflection on the National Socialist past. To those in the latter group, the designation needs to communicate the content clearly and to pique their interest enough that they either return as intentional visitors in the future or at least are moved to learn more about the National Socialist past.

The questions on designation would include how the name associated with the institution is made visible or recognizable to the audience and how widely it is applied. Some institutions make it quite visible, absolutely overt, and others are subtler, in order, in some cases, to negotiate with other motivations, such as fitting into the neighborhood. An additional question would be how the name of the institution is used in a larger context than the immediate boundaries of the institution. In some cases, the name is taken up to characterize the surrounding area, making clear the community's support of the mission of the institution, and in other cases the name is confined to the institution's boundaries, thereby restricting the reach of its mission. I will observe the location of the signage at each documentation center site. Fundamentally, there are two types: The first is detached from the building, either in the sidewalk in front of the building or in the exterior space within the center's property. The second group of designation is on the building near its entrance.

In addition to the location, I will examine the ways in which the designation is presented, which is the second topic of this chapter. Typically, textual presentation gives the name of the institution, and additionally, the basic information for visiting, including the hours, fees, and the title of the permanent and temporary exhibitions. But additionally, images are provided, which may be drawn from the content of the exhibit. In addition to the information about the institution and the content of the exhibition in text and image, each center also draws the attention of visitors and passersby by way of various artifacts in different ways – stumble blocks (Cologne), building materials from the perpetrators' unfinished construction project (Nuremberg), remnants of significant historical artifacts from a different but related era (the Berlin Wall in Berlin), and a contemporary media installation that commemorates the victims of the Holocaust (Munich).

Name of the Institution Carrying the Past

But before looking at the locations and formats of designation, some consideration needs to be given to the question of the institution's nomenclature, and in particular whether the name reflects the place's history and whether it pronounces the current mission of the institution. Some names are more effective in accomplishing these goals than others, which is sometimes a reflection of memory politics and the community leaders' expectations or reservations toward the institution. The name "documentation center," as compared to "museum" or "memorial" is rather special

154 Designation

nomenclature in comparison to other institutions that also memorialize the history of the Third Reich. In the United States, the national institution dedicated to the Holocaust is the U.S. Holocaust Memorial Museum. In Germany, the Jewish Museum and the Memorial to the Murdered Jews of Europe are internationally well known. The name "documentation center" derives from the history of the institution having been a collection point for historical documents. In Cologne and Nuremberg, the centers had begun as depositories of documents concerning those who were persecuted by the National Socialist regime, under the auspices of their individual cities. And at this time, the institutions were not open to public, nor did they offer exhibits. Additionally, "documentation center" seems more appropriate in comparison to "museum," which conjures up the idea of "muse" and artistic accomplishments. The idea of "museum" could mean that what is being exhibited is celebrated, taken as something valuable. Even when we call an institution a "history museum," there is a positive, celebratory connotation to the history. This does not mesh well with an institution whose purpose is to examine critically the negative deeds committed in the past and what allowed them to occur, with the intention of never repeating that history. The sensitivity toward different types of pasts, and how to differentiate their commemoration accordingly, is apparent in the speech made by Michael Petzet, the then Conservator General of Bavaria, when, in 1987, Nuremberg's businessmen proposed to convert the former Congress Hall into a leisure center.[13] Petzet was writing to the city administration that the building was the "most important testimony of the gigantomania of National Socialism" and should be left unused. In this text, he identified the appropriate type of commemoration for the built heritage associated with the National Socialist past, namely, the *Mahnmal*, a critical statement about or a warning from the past, differentiating it from the *Denkmal*, a mere reminder, or *Ehrenmal*, which honors someone or something from the past.[14]

Especially for the former perpetrator place that has been converted into a documentation center, it would be ideal for the institution's name to depict not only the current purpose but also the place's history. However, it also needs to be understood that the acknowledgment and designation of these four buildings as places to present the National Socialist past is a result of the memory culture that gradually shifted in Cologne, Nuremberg, Berlin, and Munich, first within West Germany and afterward in unified Germany.[15] During that time, the citizens went through a number of ideological, political, and moral stances. Denial of the past and willful forgetfulness were prevalent during the 1950s and 1960s, causing the buildings' demolition or use for mundane purposes. Some people thought little of, or at least did not bring forth to public awareness, family members', acquaintances' or their own participation in the genocide either as perpetrators or bystanders. Additionally, portraying themselves as innocent victims could be a way to avoid confronting the difficult past, in which case people may have expounded that National Socialism had been imposed upon them, that they were the casualties of Allied bombing, or that they were suffering from the East–West conflict. The ideological war against the Eastern bloc stood against many efforts to confront the past. For example, the

Association of the Persecuted of the Nazi Regime was considered Communist-infiltrated and met police action when they held a memorial ceremony in 1953 at the former deportation station in Grunewald, two stops before Wannsee on the S-Bahn (Line 7). Many efforts to break the silence were, if not attacked, dismissed as East German propaganda. Few legal proceedings were conducted against National Socialist criminals by the government of the Federal Republic of Germany until the establishment of the Central Office of the State Judicial Authorities (Zentralstelle der Landesjustizverwaltungen) in Ludwigsburg in 1958, and many held positions in West German society.[16] While military resistance was commemorated, it was mainly to showcase West Germany's democratic values to observers abroad, and large parts of the population still regarded the resistance as treason. The fates of various buildings were determined by these attitudes. In 1956 the Gestapo head-quarters at Prinz-Albrecht Straße 8 in Berlin, still partially standing after the Allied forces' bombing, on the current site of the Topography of Terror Documentation Center, were imploded to the foundation.

Still, a few individuals were fighting to confront the difficult past. An exhibit titled "The Past Admonishes" was held in 1960 in West Berlin's Congress Hall, and afterward toured West Germany and abroad. At the opening of the exhibition, Professor Hans Reif, president of the International League of Human Rights, stated it was "such a cruel error when we once again allow those who bore great responsibility for what happened to escape criticism."[17] *The Yellow Star, Der gelbe Stern*, a collection of photographs of the Holocaust compiled from government and individual collections by journalist Gerhard Schoenberner (1931–2012), was first published in 1960.[18]

In this historical context, euphemism that obscures the National Socialist past of the place can be observed, to a varied degree, and the pasts other than that of the Third Reich, which have existed in the place, either before or after the National Socialist era, get included in the nomenclature. As a result, the focus of the mission of the documentation center can get clouded. Each institution's name refers to its past in a different way. Additionally, the most special nature of the four documentation centers, that is, standing on a historical authentic perpetrator place, is not always clear from the nomenclature. Of course, the institutional name is only one way to inform the past and the present of the place. Even if that information is not so clear from the name, the exhibitions certainly would fulfill the task. However, considering that the name constitutes people's first encounter with the institution, especially for those who are unfamiliar with it, such as international visitors, younger generations, and passersby, it is an important device for the fulfillment of the purpose of the documentation centers.

Cologne

The Cologne center's official name is "NS Documentation Center in the City of Cologne," and the center is referred to as the "EL-DE House." On the sidewalk of Appellhofplatz Street, near the center's entrance, stands a narrow and vertical flat

156 Designation

FIGURE 7.1 Documentation Center, Cologne. Sign post on sidewalk. Photo by author.

signpost, which is the first designation that anyone would encounter (Figure 7.1). The signpost prominently carries the name of the institution as "EL-DE-Haus" and the permanent exhibition's title "Köln im Nationalsozialismus" on both sides, and additionally, its south side provides basic visiting information and a brief history of the building, and the north side showcases the poster of the temporary exhibition. The part of the institutional name, "Documentation Center," is not included in this signpost, but it is on one of the plaques posted on the face of the building, immediately left of the center's entrance. It reads:

> Stadt Köln
> NS-DOKUMENTATIONSZENTRUM DER STADT KÖLN
> EL-DE-HAUS
> MUSEUM UND GEDENKSTÄTTE
> MUSEUM AND MEMORIAL

The prominence of the name "EL-DE House" is worth noting. This name also shows up on the building. The letters "EL-DE" in gold are on the glass over the entrance door to the center (Figure 7.2). These letters had existed during the Third Reich, and recreate the atmosphere, as do the pair of lamps adorning the entrance, "Leopold Dahmen" on a bronze plaque, and the crest on the building at the corner of the two streets. Although the building was referred to thus during and after the Third Reich, it does not, strictly speaking, identify the role of the building during that time. Instead, it refers to the building's history prior to it, in the sense that it refers to the owner whose intent was a residential and commercial property. While "NS" refers to National Socialism, it still does not spell out the purpose of the building during the Third Reich. Instead, such a name can an easily be taken as the subject matter of the institution.

FIGURE 7.2 Documentation Center, Cologne. Letters "EL DE" on the glass over the entrance door. Photo by author.

158 Designation

Images are often more powerful in capturing one's attention. In Cologne, images are used to showcase the temporary exhibit (Figure 7.3). One such location is the signpost on the sidewalk, and the second is one of the windows on the ground floor, where the poster of the temporary exhibit occupies the full frame of the window.

FIGURE 7.3 Documentation Center, Cologne. Poster of the temporary exhibit. Photo by author.

FIGURE 7.4 Documentation Center, Cologne. Stumbling stones. In front of the center entrance. Photo by author.

In addition to the textual and imagistic presentations, the institution's identification is bolstered by additional artifacts. In front of the entrance to the center, two items are notable to visitors and passersby. Stolpersteine, or stumbling stones, are concrete cubes, ten centimeters in size, with a brass plate on top (Figure 7.4). They are the creation of the artist Gunter Demnig and commemorate the persons who lived or worked in the place but became victims of the National Socialist aggression. In the sidewalk in front of the document center are four such "stones" that refer to a family of four individuals who lived in this location. A second artifact is a commemoration on the sidewalk, for the "1000 Roma and Sinti" who fell victim to the National Socialists' atrocity.

Nuremberg

For the Nuremberg center, the first part of its name, "Dokumentationszentrum" refers to the building's current purpose while the second part, "Reichsparteitagsgelände," recalls the time of the Third Reich, in which the larger, surrounding area was designated as the "Party Rally Grounds." In this sense, the Nuremberg center's name is the clearest of the four in terms of acknowledging both the present and the past. However, the reference to the role of the past is not specific to the building, which was meant to be the Congress Hall. The institutional name appears both on

160 Designation

the signpost on the sidewalk and on the surface of the building. And the signpost on the sidewalk is made of steel and glass, referencing the architectural design that converted the historical building into a documentation center (Figure 7.5).

Furthermore, at Nuremberg, additional posterboards clarify the history of the area and the content of the exhibit. In the space between the sidewalk and the

FIGURE 7.5 Documentation Center, Nuremberg. Sign post. The materials refer to the center design. Photo by author.

building's surface are a couple of panels, standing tilted from the ground, also referencing, in a different way from the glass-and-steel signpost, the design vocabulary of the documentation center (Figure 7.6). They show, in both text and image, a brief history of the area, with an area plan indicating National Socialist buildings. They help to contextualize the Congress Hall building during the Third Reich.

FIGURE 7.6 Documentation Center, Nuremberg. Exhibition panels. They explain the history of the area. Photo by author.

162 Designation

FIGURE 7.7 Documentation Center, Nuremberg. Large stone blocks. Remnants from the construction of the Congress Hall. Photo by author.

Another location for posterboards is on the surface of the building, immediately below the name of the building. Here, posters of temporary exhibits are displayed. With these two sets of information boards, Nuremberg's designation includes both the institution's role in the present and the place's history in the National Socialist era.

While at Cologne there were remnants from the past that recreated physically the role of the building in the past, at Nuremberg, large stones, piled in the space between the sidewalk and the building, refer back to Hitler's intention for the building (Figure 7.7). These stones are remains from the construction of the Congress Hall, and they also showcase the fact that the building was never completed during the Third Reich.

What is particularly notable with the Nuremberg center is the fact that the designation of the documentation center appears in a much larger context. In front of the center building is a stop for trams and busses (Figure 7.8). And the station is named "Doku-Zentrum." To compare, the subway station in front of the Cologne center takes the name of the street, "Appellhofplatz." A number of bus and tram lines serve the "Doku-Zentrum" stop, and the tram line no. 8, in particular, connects Hauptbahnhof, Nuremberg's central rail station, and Doku-Zentrum, terminating at the documentation center. And this means that at the Hauptbahnhof, the identification of the documentation center is visible in the public transport

FIGURE 7.8 Documentation Center, Nuremberg. Tram and bus stop in front of the center. Photo by author.

signs. These help make its existence widely known to those who are not otherwise aware of it. And this especially is noteworthy since the area of the former Reichsparteitagsgelände has been normalized to its pre-National Socialist era's purpose as a leisure park, and many people who come for that purpose are presented with the designation of the documentation center. This indicates how the documentation center works as a representative of perpetrator places in the city.

At Nuremberg, no fence surrounds the former Congress Hall property, and the name of the building is attached to its face in large letters; however, because of the sheer size of the building, these letters may not stand out to passersby. A vertical sign made of steel and glass and standing away from the building also bears the name, without any further explanation. The content of the documentation center is explained by another sign, which is made of two vertically standing plaques that explain the historical background of the area and the building.

Berlin

When it comes to the Berlin center's "Topography of Terror," while, of course "Terror" refers to that of the Third Reich, the phrase "Topography of Terror" comes from the postwar exhibition, held as a part of a larger event at the Martin-Gropius-Bau, next door to the documentation center's site. A new gallery was designed by

164 Designation

Jürg Steiner and was constructed over the excavated underground kitchen cellar, one of the structures added to the site by the National Socialist Party. Steiner's design was a steel post-and-beam structure. The visitors had entered Steiner's shelter and descended into the underground floor of the former kitchen cellar, where the exhibit was located. This particular exhibit was organized by Reinhard Rürup, an important figure in the development of the current documentation center, and was named "Topography of Terror." The exhibition was successful, extended longer than originally intended, and raised much interest in the community. When the foundation was established in 1992 to develop a building on the current site to exhibit the history of the National Socialism and the Third Reich, the foundation was named after this forerunning exhibit. Therefore the name refers to the postwar development toward the establishment of the documentation center. While the postwar history of the development is not at all insignificant, it does not, strictly speaking, address the role of the place during the National Socialist era.

In Berlin, the designation of the site is rather complicated because of the double role it plays. In particular, the entire length of the site's northern boundary, between Albrecht Straße and the center site, is one of two locations in which substantial portions of the Berlin Wall stand, and for this reason it is designated as the Monument to the Berlin Wall (Figure 7.9). In fact, coming to the center site from the Potzdamrplatz station, the first encounter is with the marking on the street of where the Berlin Wall stood, which transforms, at the center site, to the still-standing wall. Likewise, the first signpost the visitor encounters is within the site, not on the sidewalk, and is for the Berlin Wall. The two additional signposts stand close by but further into the site, showcasing the institutional name, visitor information, and the content of the temporary as well as permanent exhibit, but do not give an explanation of the history of the site (Figure 7.10). Therefore at this point two different historical times, that of the Third Reich and that of the Cold War period, coexist.

As for the contents of the two signposts at the site's entrance, while the identity of the present institution is spelled out, in terms of the name "Topographie des Terrors," location, visitor information, as well as the permanent and temporary exhibitions in posters, the role of the place during the Third Reich is not given (Figure 7.11). To compare, the signpost for the Monument to the Berlin Wall provides a brief history of the wall. The lack of information about the site's National Socialist past at the site's entrance is also different from the Cologne and the Nuremberg centers, at which a brief history of the place was given on the sidewalk. In Berlin, prior knowledge is expected from both the visitors and passersby in order for them to know the past of the site.

At Berlin, the name of the institution is in white on the glass pane at the entrance, which, depending on the location of the sun, can be fairly obscured (Figure 7.12).

There is another entrance to the center site, which is at its northeast corner, at the intersection of Albrecht Straße and Wilhelmstraße. The designation is even more scarce here, with only one signpost carrying the institutional name, address, and visiting information.

FIGURE 7.9 Documentation Center, Berlin. Sign post for the Berlin Wall memorial. Photo by author.

Munich

The name of the Munich center, "NS Dokumentationszentrum München," similar to that of the Cologne center, refers to National Socialism and its current function. However, as at Cologne, "National Socialism" could be understood as the subject of documentation and does not explicitly specify the purpose of the place during the Third Reich.

166 Designation

FIGURE 7.10 Documentation Center, Berlin. Sign post with basic visitor information. Photo by author.

In Munich, the signpost on the sidewalk in front of the documentation center carries a current map of the area in two different scales (Figure 7.13). Neither is specifically about the National Socialist past. The focus on this past is given on the signpost that stands in the middle of the forecourt of the documentation center, which requires the visitors to enter into the forecourt, and therefore is not legible

FIGURE 7.11 Documentation Center, Berlin. Sign post on the content of exhibitions. Photo by author.

by passersby (Figure 7.14). The information about the National Socialist past is brief but comprehensive, utilizing both text and image in the form of historical photographs as well as a map of the area. Once the visitor or passerby is motivated enough to come into the forecourt, the signpost fulfills the purpose of designation, addressing the present institution's purpose and the history of the place.

168 Designation

FIGURE 7.12 Documentation Center, Berlin. Institutional name on the building. Photo by author.

The face of the building of the Munich center carries two pieces of information (Figure 7.15). First, it spells out, in text, the name of the institution and its purpose: "NS-Dokumentationszentrum München / Lern- und Erinnerungsort zur Geschichte des Nationalsocialismus" (A place to learn and remember the history of National Socialism). This is on the white concrete, indicating the permanence of the designation. The second piece of information is on the glass and is the title of the temporary exhibit. This information is changed as the temporary exhibit changes.

In Munich, a contemporary art piece titled "Brienner 45" is installed between the sidewalk and the center's forecourt. It is a work of Benjamin and Emanuel Heisenberg, who won an invitational international art competition of 2012. The piece is made of a number of video screens, emerging from the ground slanted, sending a message about the reasons for the rise of National Socialism in Munich as well as its consequences (Figure 7.16). It gives an impression similar to that of a contemporary art museum. While certainly attractive to some audience or passersby, the art project's message is not so direct, and as a consequence, it could give an erroneous information about the center's exhibit, which is nothing close to the typical contemporary art gallery.

The forecourt of the Munich center was named "Max-Mannheimer-Platz." The sign has additional information:

FIGURE 7.13 Documentation Center, Munich. Sign post on the sidewalk. It provides information of area cultural institutions. Photo by author.

Max Mannheimer (1920–2016), Kaufmann, Künstler, Holocaust-Überlebender, Präsident der Lagergemeinschaft Dachau, Vizepräsident des Internationalen Dachau-Komitees, Mitinitiator des NS-Dokumentationszentrums

(Merchant, artist, Holocaust survivor, President of the Dachau camp community, Vice President of the International Dachau Committee, co-initiator of the Nazi Documentation Center)

FIGURE 7.14 Documentation Center, Munich. Sign post in the center forecourt. Photo by author.

This brief biography of Mannheimer covers and represents the history, from prior to, during, and after the National Socialist era to the establishment of the document center.

Pronouncement of the building's designation, both of the current institution and of the historical use, is an important part of the documentation center projects. The

FIGURE 7.15 Documentation Center, Munich. Institutional name and its exhibitions, on the surface of the building. Photo by author.

four centers each combine text, image, and three-dimensional objects, placed both on the surface of the building and detached from it. They are the first thing that the visitor or the passerby encounters of the center, and yet the information they carry is not always straightforward. At Cologne, "EL-DE" refers not the Gestapo but the original owner of the building. The Berlin Wall stands along the center's frontal

FIGURE 7.16 Documentation Center, Munich. Art installation, "Brienner 45." Photo by author.

street, which is outside the time span of the documentation center's coverage. And at Munich, the contemporary video installation emerges from the ground at the site's edge along the street, which could erroneously characterize the content of the documentation center as similar to a contemporary art museum.

Notes

1 "Kunstareal München," https://kunstareal.de/
2 Winfried Nerdinger, *Erinnerung gegründet auf Wissen / Remembrance Based on Knowledge, Das NS-Dokumentationszentrum München / The Munich Documentation Centre for the History of National Socialism* (Berlin: Metropol Verlag, 2018); 9–11, 13.
3 Ulrike Grammbitter, Klaus Bäumler, and Iris Lauterbach, *The NSDAP Centre in Munich* (Berlin and Munich: Deutscher Kunstverlag, 2015), 87, 96.
4 NS-Dokumentationszentrum München et al., *Munich and National Socialism: Catalogue of the Munich Documentation Centre for the History of National Socialism* (München: Beck, 2015), 201.
5 NS-Dokumentationszentrum München et al., *Munich and National Socialism*, 306–7.
6 Ibid., 308.
7 Ibid.
8 Ibid., 305.
9 Ibid., 380.

Designation **173**

10 Ibid., 355.

11 "Monument Protection in Germany | Historic England," accessed November 25, 2019, http://historicengland.org.uk/whats-new/debate/recent/town-and-country-planning-act-70th-anniversary/monument-protection-in-germany/.

12 Nerdinger, *Erinnerung gegründet auf Wissen / Remembrance Based on Knowledge*, 35.

13 Michael Petzet later became the President of the German National Committee of ICOMOS (1989–) and the President of ICOMOS International (1999 and 2008). See: "Michael Petzet, Advisor, Conservationist,""dOCUMENTA (13) – dOCUMENTA (13)," accessed May 25, 2017, http://d13.documenta.de/#participants/participants/michael-petzet/.

14 Sharon Macdonald, *Difficult Heritage: Negotiating the Nazi Past in Nuremberg and beyond* (New York: Routledge, 2009).

15 The history of memory culture and politics took a significantly different route in the former East Germany.

16 The Nuremberg Trials were conducted in 1945–46 by the Allied forces, and the subsequent Nuremberg Trials, 1946–49 by the U.S. forces.

17 The exhibition panels were blackened out as censorship because they held names of West Germany politicians with Nazi pasts.

18 Schoenberner was the founding Director of the House of the Wannsee Conference.

8

MEMENTO

In Chapter 5 through 7 I discussed a number of ways in which architectural design assisted a physical perpetrator building or place to present its dark past in meaningful ways. They were as follows: formal characteristics; physical traces that particular actions left on the building's fabric; and the presentation of the center's identity – historical or present – to the visitors and passersby. In addition to these, memento is another strategy, being a physical object – in our case a building or a place – from the past, which, when re-encountered, allows a person to recall that past. As discussed in Chapter 4, a memento by definition requires the person to have personally experienced the past being recalled; however, when it comes to Germany's National Socialist past, authentic places serving as mementos in the pure sense of the term is quite rare these days. This is simply because those who were alive between 1933 and 1945 are aging or already have passed away. Given these circumstances, it is worthy to turn these buildings into places of quasi-memento, especially for the younger generations and the international audience. We discussed the concept of quasi-memento in Chapter 4, but briefly, it is a physical object that, by either being actually from the past or having the semblance of such, gives a sense of the past to those who did not actually experience that past. And a number of specific design strategies are found in the four centers to help the historical building or the place effectively work as a quasi-memento to allow the visitors to gain memento-like experiences, that is, to put themselves in the shoes of those who actually experienced the past events. Some of these are accomplished by the exhibitions, but there are instances in which architectural designs do so on their own or by enhancing the exhibitions. This chapter will highlight some of the notable strategies. They are:

1. incorporation of oral history;
2. large-scale photographs that are as big as the architectural space allows;

3. incorporation of the spatial experiences that could have happened in the past into the current exhibition route; and
4. creation of new spatial experiences that put the visitor at unease.

Oral History

The most obvious strategy for staging a personal experience in visitors who have never had that experience on their own is to offer an oral history. Oral history itself is not a design of the physical environment, but when placed within a physical environment in which the past being recounted took place, oral history becomes even more powerful by giving listeners the opportunity to feel as if they themselves are experiencing that piece of history. Adding historical photographs helps make the experience more immediate by mutual reinforcement: They connect the current physical environment and the past events recounted in the interviews, while oral history makes historical photographs, which on their own could seem "objective" or remote, come alive for the visitor. This is helpful especially for creating a quasi-memento for those who were not in the building/place when the event was happening. A clear example of this is found at the Nuremberg center.

Nuremberg

The last stop on the visitors' route of the Nuremberg center is dedicated to oral history. Since 1985 there always had been an exhibit on the city's National Socialist history, titled "Faszination und Gewalt," held at the hall of the Zeppelin Grandstand.[1] Because of the lack of heating in the building, the exhibit was held only during the summer months, but it attracted many visitors. When the city decided to establish a permanent exhibition space in the former Congress Hall, a study was conducted, reviewing the existing exhibit and looking to new aspects. Gregor Schöllgen, Professor of Modern History at the University of Erlangen, served as the Speaker of the Scientific Advisory Board, which also included Reinhard Rürup from the Topography of Terror Foundation. In April 1998, four months before the competition for the Nuremberg center was first announced, Schöllgen shared in *Frankfurter Allgemeine Zeitung* his observation that there was strong community support for the idea of including oral history in the new exhibit, saying that "many witnesses agreed to talk about their experiences" of the National Socialist rallies.[2] In one of the videos in the exhibit, two elderly women recollect their experiences of a Party Rally day. As young friends, they competed with each other about how many times they managed to gain glimpses of the Führer. One of the two recollected:

> For me the Party Rallies were just about as important as Christmas. My friends and I had a kind of competition: Who could see the Führer the most times. In 1937 I saw him twelve times, and in 1938 thirteen times. ... My father had given us two painters' ladders and a long board and the uncles had carted the ladders and the board over to the southwest corner of the Town

176 Memento

> Hall. ... Then we set up our ladders and laid the board between them at the top and my two aunts and I stood on top of the board ...[3]

In another video, an elderly man stands in front of the ruined Zeppelin Grandstand and demonstrates a military salute, using his umbrella for a gun. Photographs and videos of the Party Rally day accompany the video exhibit, providing a sense of the physical environment to the recounting of the past and helping extend the visitors' imagination. The effect of making real is mutual. The photographs of the physical environment also are given a sense of reality by the oral history, and the personal experience is given the physical place by the photographs.

More can be done with oral history: While it is a powerful device to bring the visitors close to the personal experiences of the past in an intimate way, additional efforts can be made explicitly to create for visitors a connection between the physical environment and the experiences of people who encountered that place in the past. Wouldn't it be powerful if there was a personal statement spoken about how a person felt about walking in front of the National Socialist headquarters? Or about a large building complex being constructed in their city? This is not something I observed in any of the four centers.

Large-Scale Photographs

Large-scale photographs that fully occupy the architectural space help create the real sense of the place, turning that space into a quasi-memento. This is successfully done in the Cologne and Nuremberg centers.

At the Cologne center, after checking in at the ground-floor lobby, the visitor follows the processional route upstairs to the permanent exhibition area. The first exhibit one confronts on the second floor, even before leaving the stairwell, is a large-scale photograph of Appellhofplatz Street during the National Socialist period (Figure 8.1).[4] It has been enlarged to fill the entire height of the interior space, from the floor to the ceiling. In fact, in the view from the stairwell, just prior to entering the permanent exhibition gallery, the openings in the wall successfully frame the photograph, creating a sense that the space photographed expands even beyond the limits of the floor and ceiling, emphasizing the sense of being within the image. The selection of this particular photograph is most appropriate as the beginning of the documentation center exhibition sequence because it takes such great advantage of the actual physical place. The photograph looks down Appellhofplatz Street from south to north, with the EL-DE House on the left side of the street. The exhibit label identifying the photograph as having been taken during the National Socialist era takes the viewers back to that time in history and prepares the visitor to view the architectural spaces as if they were in the building during that past. The visitor may identify themselves as the figure in the photograph, who was at that moment passing the front of the EL-DE House. The sense of having been there is particularly strong to those visitors who remember passing under the two large lamps that create a kind of déjà vu from when they entered

FIGURE 8.1 Documentation Center, Cologne. Large photograph looking northward on Appellhofplatz. EL-DE House can be seen on left. Photo by author.

the center a few minutes earlier. Some observant visitors, again recalling what they saw before entering the building, also may notice that the building at the time of National Socialism was much narrower than the present one.

At Nuremberg, too, large-scale photographs are used in a number of crucial moments in the exhibit sequence and help turn the building into a quasi-memento.

178 Memento

One of the most striking instances of this is an image of Hitler ascending the steps at the 1934 Reich's Harvest Thanksgiving Festival, held annually in the hills of Bückeberg near Hamelin, 45 kilometers southwest of Hannover (Figure 8.2). In the image, he is leading the group of his top officials through a narrow opening created by two blocks of soldiers. Behind him, on the flat ground, are a mass of people whose end is not to be seen.

FIGURE 8.2 Documentation Center, Nuremberg. Large photograph of Hitler ascending steps. Photo by author.

Den Sakralcharakter, den die Riefenstahlschen Parteitagsfilme vermitteln, besaß in vielleicht noch stärkerem Maß das Erntedankfest, zu dem Hitler jedes Jahr nach Bückenburg in der Nähe von Hannover kam. Dort stand er dann auf der Kuppe eines weithin sichbaren Berges einem Moses gleich, um die Huldigungen der norddeutschen Landbevölkerung entgegenzunehmen, die etwa eine Million Teilnehmer betrug.[5]

(The sacred character conveyed by [Leni] Riefenstahl's party rally films was perhaps even more marked by the Thanksgiving Day, to which Hitler came every year to Bückenburg near Hanover. There he stood like a Moses on the top of a mountain that was visible from afar, in order to receive the homages of the northern German rural population, which was about one million participants.)

Although not taken in Nuremberg, the image easily can be transferred in the visitor's mind to Hitler, his party members, and the general public occupying the spaces in Nuremberg's Reichsparteitags Gelände, either Zeppelin Grandstand or the Congress Hall, if it had been completed. The black-and-white image confronts the viewer a number of gallery spaces before, starting about where they cross the bridge. The emergent figure of Hitler, which becomes gradually larger as the visitor progresses through the exhibit procession, almost gives the sensation that Hitler is in motion and approaching the visitor. It gives the real sense of the past happening. Some other exhibition techniques using large-scale photographs at Nuremberg that are effective in making the past experiences transferable include a set of cut-outs of National Socialist uniform-clad men standing in the middle of the exhibition space.

Creating the Sense of Bodily Experiences of the Past

One of the ways to take advantage of the authentic perpetrator buildings to present the past is to create the sense of bodily experiences of the past. Architectural design could assist in enabling this mechanism. The visitor possibly would be encouraged to imagine being a perpetrator who committed evil deeds from the very place. The Cologne and Nuremberg centers take advantage of the buildings still being standing. And in the case of the Munich center, where the historical building is no longer standing, the adjoining perpetrator building is engaged in this effort. Although alterations have been made to the building since then, in the case of Cologne, or the perpetrators never operated from the building still under construction, in the case of Nuremberg, or the spot at which the visitor stands did not exist in the past, in the case of Munich, architectural design could stage the physical environment in such a way so as to create the sense of bodily experiences as they could or would have happened in the past, thereby making the physical environment a quasi-memento.

180 Memento

Cologne

Because time had passed since the use of the building by the perpetrators, and the building had gone through some changes, it was not always possible to recreate the exact same physical conditions in the building or the place. This was true even with the EL-DE House in Cologne, where the original perpetrator building survived the war:

> The office rooms and aisles where the Gestapo had its offices have basically remained as they were at the time. However, there are no surviving layout plans of the house or views of the individual rooms from the time before 1945.[6]

While Peter Kulka's intention was to make the building the primary exhibit of the documentation center, as discussed in Chapters 5 and 6, the lack of documentation made it impossible to recreate the physical environment as it was in the past. Instead of bringing in furniture or adding operational objects such as maps or charts to the walls in the interior space, to recreate a possible semblance of the offices of the Gestapo during their operation, Kulka and his collaborators stripped the walls and the floors to the bare structure, as discussed in Chapter 5, and finished them with irregular patterns. However, as the spatial organizations were believed to have remained the same, the rooms and the corridors were kept as they were found. Additionally, some elements of the building systems such as electrical cords hung from the ceiling or radiator units along the walls, were kept as they were found, without knowing for certain they were as the Gestapo operatives had seen them. The effect was to recreate the sense of being in the past or of the time having past. After the center's opening, an architectural critic characterized them as "spatial dramaturgy" and commented on their effect on the visitor:

> Aus Türen, Fensterbänke, Heizkörper wurden der vom Architekten Peter Kulka und dem Bielefelder Kommunikations-Designer Gerd Fleischmann auf das eindringlichste entwickelten Raumdramaturgie und Ausstellungskonzeption als Spurenelemente integriert. Kalte Neonrohren an den Decken, offen liegende Leitungen, ein Asphalt-Estrich, der Feucht wirkt, e saber nicht ist und den Eintretenden prompt verunsichert – das sind Mittel, Besucher zu einer ehrlichen Wahrnehmungsbereitschaft auch den eigenen Empfindungen und Gedanken gegenuber zu bewegen.[7]

> (The doors, windowsills, and radiators were integrated as trace elements by the architect Peter Kulka and the Bielefeld-based communication designer Gerd Fleischmann into the most strikingly developed spatial dramaturgy and exhibition concept. Cold neon tubes on the ceilings, exposed cables, an asphalt screed that looks damp, but it is not, and promptly unsettles those entering – these are the means to induce visitors to be honest about their feelings and thoughts.)

At the entrance to the building, Kulka's subtle design strategy treats the two entry movements – one at the present, of entering the documentation center, and the other in the past, of entering the Gestapo headquarters – in one sequence. The typical experience of the visitors at any building's entry would be nothing special, but Kulka found an opportunity to turn the visitor into a sharp observer of past experience. At the entrance, the visitor has an experience of oscillating between the past and the present through their bodily experience. The architect has set up a screen of metal grille to divert the straight line of entry sequence. The visitor first crosses the threshold plane created by the façade of the building, moving from the street into the entry alcove, and taking a couple of steps upward. In the past, the entry sequence would have been to move straight forward, facing the guard stationed behind the glass window of the "porter's lodge," or the front booth at the entrance. The metal grilles obstruct this entry sequence (Figure 8.3), and redirect the visitor's procession to the new entry on the side. This redirecting has created the situation where the visitors stop at the metal grilles, at which moment they look upon the porter's lodge, before they go back to their original task of entering the building. Kulka commented: "Entrance and staircase on Appellhofplatz to the former porter's lodge are left in their original state."[8] By stopping the visitors' natural move into the building by blocking the straight directional path but allowing visitors to pay attention to the entrance that would have been taken by a Gestapo officer, this particular design has turned the building into a quasi-memento.

View Out: Cologne, Nuremberg, and Munich

One design strategy that creates the experience of quasi-memento common to the Cologne, Nuremberg, and Munich, and to a lesser extent Berlin, centers is to take advantage of the windows that frame a specific view, which recreates the views that the National Socialist perpetrators may or may not have had in the past. What is offered for the visitor's spatial experiences are varied in three different ways in the three centers.

At the Cologne center, the windowpanes facing the two frontal streets – Appellhofplatz and Elisenstraße – as well as the inner courtyard are for the most part frosted. This is because of Peter Kulka's intention to keep the visitors' attention focused on the interior space, both the building fabric and the exhibition, without distractions from the present, outside world. However, a few transparent panes of windows do allow glimpses outside. One of the most successful exceptions through the center building is the window facing the Court of Appeals building across Appellhofplatz Street. Because the rest of the window panes are frosted, when an exception is made, the visitors' attention naturally is drawn outside. Here, the visitor is invited to see the view across the street and to compare it with the historical photograph of the courthouse building, which is printed on a transparent sheet and pasted on the transparent pane. The exhibition's text explains how the court incriminated citizens during the Third Reich. The label states:

FIGURE 8.3 Documentation Center, Cologne. Entrance. Photo by author.

Das Justizgebäude Appellhofplatz war Sitz des Amtsgerichts, des Landgerichts und auch der Sondergerichte. Hier Wurden ca. 600 Verfahren wegen. Rassenschande durchgeführt. 1979 fand dort der Prozeß gegen Kurt Lischka statt, der 1940 Leiter der Kölner Gestapo im EL-DE-Haus war.[9]

(The court building Appellhofplatz was the seat of the district court, the state court and also the special courts. Here about 600 proceedings were carried out because of racial defilement. In 1979 there took place the case against Kurt Lischka, who in 1940 was head of the Cologne Gestapo in the EL-DE-House)

With this information, some visitors would activate their imagination and place themselves in the shoes of the Gestapo officers who were involved in such actions (Figure 8.4).

FIGURE 8.4 Documentation Center, Cologne. Limited view out. Looking over the Court of Appeals building. Photo by author.

184 Memento

Nuremberg

At Nuremberg, similarly, a transparent contact sheet of a historical photograph is pasted on a glass windowpane. It is located at the end of the stake. At this point, the visitors have gone through the gallery exhibits sequenced chronologically in the orthogonally arranged historical interior spaces and have just exited onto the stake at one end, opposite from the entrance. From here, the visitors are to begin the gradual descent through the "*Pfahl*" back to the entrance foyer. The tip of the stake at this end forms an exterior deck overlooking the vast courtyard. This is the first time the visitors confront the enormous scale of the space intended for the assembly hall, which would have become the main body of the Congress Hall, but which was never completed and left without a roof. After the architect Ludwig Ruff's death in 1934, his son and collaborator Franz Ruff struggled with the challenge of the wide span of the roof structure. He was still designing it even after Hitler's attention left the project because of his invasion of Poland in 1939 and the beginning of the war. The visitors see in front of them a vast courtyard, bounded by the U-shaped structure, in its raw brick construction, whose compartmentalized organization is repeated around the semicircle of the circumference, but which now is used as a parking lot for service vehicles. On the glass facing this courtyard is a historical photograph that shows an architectural model of the intended assembly hall (Figure 8.5). By gazing through the photograph while also taking in the reality of the unrealized gigantic space, the visitor gains a hypothetical sense of actually being in the completed assembly hall.

Munich

At Munich, the historical Brown House no longer was available. While there are no remnants of the building, not even a foundation, the architects still succeeded in providing a quasi-memento-like experience by taking advantage of the surrounding buildings to create a sense of being inside Brown House. As discussed in Chapter 5, the documentation center's windows are located at each corner of the cube at different floor levels, which gives a glimpse of the neighboring buildings. To the south, beyond trees and low bushes, is the Administration Building; to the west, the northern Honor Temple; and to the northwest, the Führerbau. They all were built by the regime. Additionally, to the west, Königsplatz, which was adopted by the Party as the rally grounds can be seen with its Propyläen at some distance. And, where these exterior views are available, the exhibit shows historical events that took place in those buildings or places.

The windows at the northwest corner are especially successful. The exhibit carefully orchestrates the films as well as still images of the events that took place at these buildings, and it is very easy to generate the sense of quasi-memento here. The galley space at this point opens up to a two-story volume, with the balcony on the fourth floor overlooking the gallery on the third floor. Historical footage is from during the Third Reich and under the Allied Forces administration after

FIGURE 8.5 Documentation Center, Nuremberg. View out to the unfinished assembly hall. A photograph of architectural model is on the glass. Photo by author.

the war, corresponding to the exhibits of each floor: The fourth-floor balcony is a part of the exhibit on the time period 1933–39 (Figure 8.6), and the third-floor gallery a part of that on after 1945. Especially striking is the possible comparison that the visitors can make between two significant events that took place at the same building, one before and the other after 1945. They include: the celebration of the "martyrs of the movement" juxtaposed with the American occupying forces blowing up both the Honor Temples; and the signing of the 1938 Munich Agreement in contrast to the setting up of America House, both at Führerbau. Just as in Nuremberg, where the historical photograph of the architectural model was presented in front of the glass facing the space intended for the assembly hall, here in Munich, too, the visitors are confronted with the present views of the Führerbau and Honor Temple to compare to the historical footage of these buildings, which thus succeed in becoming quasi-mementos (see Figure 5.18).

Furthermore, what makes these windows successful is their composition. At Munich, the windows are a collection of slender openings, 10 windows facing west and 7 facing north, each window measuring 69 centimeters wide with 20-centimeter-wide concrete in-between. On the one hand, the 20-centimeter-wide concrete "mullions" partially obstruct what is otherwise a straight view to the historical buildings, but on the other hand they are effective in drawing the conscious attention of the visitors to the exterior views (Figure 8.7).

FIGURE 8.6 Documentation Center, Munich. View from the gallery on 1933–39 to Führerbau. On the screen a footage from Munich Agreement is shown, with Neville Chamberlain ascending the main stairs of Führerbau. Photo by author.

Berlin

As discussed in Chapter 5, it was the intention of the architect Ursula Wilms to present the view of the former Aviation Ministry building, located across Niederkirchnerstraße, north of the center site (Figure 8.8). And the view could have created the sense of going back to the National Socialist era, working in the Reich's Main Office building and looking over Prinz-Albrecht-Straße. The visitor's actual experience is not necessarily as Wilms planned, however. And instead, the gallery's spatial setup promotes internally rather than externally focused type of visitor experiences. Upon entry to the center building, in the foyer, the visitor's attention is naturally drawn to the reception desk, with their back facing northward, the direction of the intended view. In the next step in the visitor's procession, they are shown a large area model, which takes up their interest. And at this time, their body typically faces east, and their focus on the model. There is no particular design device that would turn the visitor northward while they are in the foyer. When their body finally is rotated to the north, in the subsequent step, a wall standing in front of them obstructs the view out and instead provides large photographs, of a street view of Prinz-Albrecht-Straße and an aerial view of the center site and its neighbors in destruction after an air raid. And after this, the visitor leaves the north-facing boundary of the center building completely. If the wall had ended short of the

FIGURE 8.7 Documentation Center, Munich. View from the gallery on after 1945 to Führerbau. Photo by author.

corner, and the glass had rounded the northeast corner of the floor plan, then the view to the former Aviation Ministry building could have been achieved. Another design strategy could have been of setting up benches. In fact, there are a number of them along the east-facing glass wall, and the view to the former Aviation Ministry building is possible. Unfortunately, without sufficient space between the glass and

FIGURE 8.8 Documentation Center, Berlin. View of the former Aviation Ministry building. To be had if one were to turn around at the entrance lobby. In reality, the visitors tend to have their back toward this view. Photo by author.

bench, the visitors tend to sit looking inward rather than outward (Figure 8.9). A view to the Aviation Building would have given additional significance to these model and photographs, giving them the spatial and locational reality and helping them orient themselves in relation to the actual place they occupy. This is a missed opportunity in terms of providing a moment to go back in time and possibly to imagine themselves being either perpetrators or victims.

Creating an Experience of Unease

At Nuremberg, architectural design also worked to provide a spatial experience of unease. Strictly speaking, this experience is neither something that was held actually by a National Socialist perpetrator nor something that would have been held if the building had been completed. Instead, it is an experience that may be understood as an architectural interpretation of the past experience.

In the space near the end of the exhibit sequence, where the narrative is at the height of the horror of the war and the Holocaust, the strategy of detaching the new construction from the preexisting building is at work, turning the exhibit floor into a sort of a bridge, which is detached both from the floor and the walls of the Congress Hall. But what Domenig did in addition allows the architecture, the old

FIGURE 8.9 Documentation Center, Berlin. Benches along the east-facing glass wall. Seen in the background is the former Aviation Ministry building. Photo by author.

and the new together, to give a warning to the future. In the existing building, three-dimensional horizontal layering of bricks was observed, with bricks protruding and receding significantly from one layer to the other. The documents attached to the competition program in fact included a black-and-white photograph of this space (Figure 8.10). Taking a hint from this, Domenig took advantage of the experiential

FIGURE 8.10 The former Congress Hall, Nuremberg, interior. Photograph provided by the Nuremberg City Museums at the time of the competition, 1998, taken in 1997. Source: Dokumentationszentrum Reichsparteitagsgelände, no. 0275-02.

effect of this wall detail. The corner of the brick wall was pronounced, hinting that around the corner a space exists. With the alternate hiding and revealing, the corner of the brick wall also raises the visitors' curiosity into the space beyond. When the visitor reaches the corner, the exhibit shows a floor-to-ceiling photograph depicting the horrific and devastating scene of the war. The architecture makes a statement, using the strategies of physical traces as well as memento that the danger of repeating the same grave error is just around the corner (Figure 8.11). Domenig took advantage of the experiential effect of this wall detail. When the visitor reaches the corner, a full-scale photograph depicts a devastating scene of the war. Domenig allowed the architecture, the old and the new together, to give a warning for the future.

This technique of creating a spatial experience of unease is even more removed from the direct experience of the past in comparison with, for example, the letter font at the Wannsee rail station (Figure 8.12). It does not recreate the past physical environment, but instead attempts to create the sense of an experience similar to that of the past. Similar design strategies can be found at Daniel Libeskind's Jewish Museum and Peter Eisenman's Memorial for Murdered Jews of Europe, both in Berlin. In both cases, the buildings' solid elements – blocks, columns, or walls – are arranged in such a way to block the views of the visitor in the space, that is a void, who are passing through the openings between the masses, which created the sense

FIGURE 8.11 Documentation Center, Nuremberg. Large photograph hidden in the alcove. Photo by author.

of unease, for there is no knowing of what is around the corner. The experience is likened by a number of critics to that of those during the Third Reich, in which the immediate future was uncertain.

As the population with direct experiences with the Third Reich dwindles, quasi-memento offers the visitors an experience of having been there in the past.

FIGURE 8.12 Wannsee Station, Berlin. Use of font to create a sense of being in the National Socialist past. Photo by author.

Oral history and large photographs that fill the entire height of the gallery space are useful, creating the sense of physical spaces within the center building. Designs can also help orient the visitor's body in a specific way, to confront a significant space within the center building or a historical building in the neighborhood, which in turn recreate the bodily experiences that may have taken place in the past. Additionally, when the visitors' processional route is laid in relation to the historical building's spatial qualities, the visitors may experience of a sense of unease, which could be taken as resembling to that during the Third Reich.

Notes

1 Bernd Ogan and Wolfgang W Weiss, *Faszination und Gewalt: Nürnberg und der Nationalsozialismus: Eine Ausstellung* (Nürnberg: Pädagogisches Institut der Stadt Nürnberg, 1990). This is the original exhibition catalog. It should not be confused with another publication with the same title and by the same authors, but based on a symposium: Bernd Ogan and Wolfgang W Weiss, *Faszination und Gewalt: Zur Politischen Ästhetik des Nationalsozialismus* (Nürnberg: Tümmels, 1992).
2 Gregor Schöllgen, "Speichern: In Der Kulisse Des Führers," *Frankfurter Allgemeine Zeitung*, April 7, 1998, sec. no. 82, page 44, https://fazarchiv.faz.net/fazDocument/saveSingleDoc/FAZ__F19980407REICHSP100.

Memento **193**

3 Hans-Christian Täubrich et al., *Fascination and Terror: Documentation Centre Party Rally Grounds: The Exhibition* (Nürnberg: Museen der Stadt Nürnberg, 2001), 65.

4 Barbara Becker-Jákli and NS-Dokumentationszentrum (Historisches Archiv der Stadt Köln), *Cologne during National Socialism: A Short Guide through the EL-DE House* (Cologne: NS Documentation Centre of the City of Cologne: Emons, 2011), 70.

5 Bernd Ogan and Wolfgang W Weiss, *Faszination und Gewalt: Zur politischen Ästhetik des Nationalsozialismus* (Nürnberg: Tümmels, 1992), 185.

6 Becker-Jákli and NS-Dokumentationszentrum, *Cologne during National Socialism*, 74–5.

7 W. Strodthoff, "Das Kölner El-De-Haus Als NS-Dokumentationszentrum," *BAUWELT* 88, no. 37 (1997): 2099–101, 2099.

8 Peter Kulka, "NS-Dokumentationszentrum Im EL-DE-Haus, Koln, Appellhofplaz 23–25," May 1993, 35. Deutsches Architekturmuseum, Frankfurt.

9 NS-Dokumentationszentrum Köln, exhibition label.

CONCLUSION

This study has focused on four documentation centers on the history of National Socialism which were created by converting authentic perpetrator places. It has examined these four projects, considering them as a subset both of National Socialist *Täterorte* and of postwar rebuilding in Germany. In doing so, we have gained a way of appreciating how German communities, emerging from the war and the subsequent allied occupation, have arrived at the point where they not only acknowledge the authentic place of perpetration as such but also use it for the purpose of reflecting upon abominable atrocities fellow community members committed against fellow human beings. Their achievements – in the form of the documentation centers – are to the great benefit to their own and international audiences. And, as I hope I demonstrated, the architectural designs did play a role, not a small one at that, by assisting the historical places present their pasts in meaningful ways.

While the study has focused on the four architectural designs, and as a consequence the observations are on the design features specific to the four buildings, I expect its findings to be applicable to other projects in the future. And here, I do not mean just the adaptive reuse of National Socialist buildings. Rather, I hope this study's findings are relevant to projects that are located in authentic places, especially perpetrator ones, for which the presentation of the place's past is beneficial. I do not think it is an exaggeration to say that every society has, at one time or another, committed a crime against humanity. When faced with physical remains of a difficult past, we tend naturally to express our abhorrence by destroying them. However, that is not always the best strategy. Once they are gone, they are lost forever. For some cases, if not for all, we could devise a way to present those remnants in a manner that clearly states our critical stance. The four mechanisms I have presented – formal characteristics, physical traces, designation, and (quasi-) memento – would give some concrete suggestions in coming up with such strategies. That, I believe, would give us a more productive way to confront our own difficult pasts.

BIBLIOGRAPHY

General

Adam, Peter. *Art of the Third Reich*. New York: H.N. Abrams, 1992.

Adorno, Theodor W. *Critical Models: Interventions and Catchwords*. Translated by Henry W. Pickford. European Perspectives. New York: Columbia University Press, 1998.

Anders, Günther. "We, Sons of Eichmann: An Open Letter to Klaus Eichmann." Translated by Jordan Levinson. Accessed September 20, 2019. http://anticoncept.phpnet.us/eichmann.htm?i=1.

Arendt, Hannah. "Eichmann in Jerusalem. I-V" *The New Yorker*, February 16, February 23, March 2, March 9, and March 16, 1963. www.newyorker.com/magazine/1963/02/16/eichmann-in-jerusalem-i; www.newyorker.com/magazine/1963/02/23/ii-eichmann-in-jerusalem; www.newyorker.com/magazine/1963/03/02/iii-eichmann-in-jerusalem; www.newyorker.com/magazine/1963/03/09/eichmann-in-jerusalem-iv; www.newyorker.com/magazine/1963/03/16/v-eichmann-in-jerusalem.

———. "The Aftermath of Nazi Rule: Report from Germany." *Commentary*, no. 10 (1950): 342–53.

———, and Amos Elon. *Eichmann in Jerusalem: A Report on the Banality of Evil*. New York: Penguin Classics, 2006.

Arndt, Karl, Georg Friedrich Koch, Lars Olof Larsson, and Georg C. Meerwein, eds. *Albert Speer, Architektur: Arbeiten, 1933–1942*. Berlin: Propyläen, 1978.

Assmann, Aleida. *Shadows of Trauma: Memory and the Politics of Postwar Identity*. Translated by Sarah Clift. New York: Fordham University Press, 2016.

———, and John Czaplicka. "Collective Memory and Cultural Identity." *New German Critique*, no. 65 (1995): 125–33. https://doi.org/10.2307/488538.

Bloom, Paul. "The Root of All Cruelty?" *The New Yorker*, November 20, 2017. www.newyorker.com/magazine/2017/11/27/the-root-of-all-cruelty.

Braum, Michael, and Ursula Baus, eds. *Rekonstruktion in Deutschland: Positionen zu einem umstrittenen Thema*. Basel: Birkhäuser, 2009.

Carr, David. *Experience and History: Phenomenological Perspectives on the Historical World*. New York: Oxford University Press, 2014.

196 Bibliography

———. *Time, Narrative, and History: An Essay in the Philosophy of History*. Studies in Phenomenology and Existential Philosophy. Bloomington: Indiana University Press, 1986.

Casey, Edward S. *Getting Back into Place: Toward a Renewed Understanding of the Place-World*. 2nd ed. Studies in Continental Thought. Bloomington: Indiana University Press, 2009.

———. *Remembering: A Phenomenological Study*. 2nd ed. Studies in Continental Thought. Bloomington: Indiana University Press, 2000.

Cohen-Pfister, Laurel, and Dagmar Wienröder-Skinner. *Victims and Perpetrators, 1933–1945: (Re)Presenting the Past in Post-Unification Culture*. Berlin: W. de Gruyter, 2006.

Cowell, Alan. "Teaching Nazi Past to German Youth." *The New York Times*, June 9, 1995, sec. World. www.nytimes.com/1995/06/09/world/teaching-nazi-past-to-german-youth.html.

Crinson, Mark. *Urban Memory*. London: Routledge, 2005.

Cruz-Pierre, Azucena, and Donald A. Landes, eds. *Exploring the Work of Edward S. Casey: Giving Voice to Place, Memory, and Imagination*. London: Bloomsbury Academic, 2015.

Czaplicka, John, Blair A. Ruble, and Lauren Crabtree, eds. *Composing Urban History and the Constitution of Civic Identities*. Washington, DC: Baltimore: Woodrow Wilson Center Press; Johns Hopkins University Press, 2003.

Dalton, Derek. *Dark Tourism and Crime*, 2015.

Diefendorf, Jeffry M. *In the Wake of War: The Reconstruction of German Cities after World War II*. New York: Oxford University Press, 1993.

Domansky, Elisabeth. "'Kristallnach,' the Holocaust and German Unity: The Meaning of November 9 as an Anniversary in Germany." *History and Memory* 4, no. 1 (1992): 60–94.

Durth, Werner, and Winfried Nerdinger. *Architektur und Städtebau der 30er/40er Jahre*. Bonn: Deutsches Nationalkomitee für Denkmalschutz, 1992.

Eley, Geoffrey. "What Is Cultural History?" *New German Critique*, no. 65 (1995): 19–36. https://doi.org/10.2307/488530.

Featherstone, Mark. "Ruin Value." *Journal for Cultural Research* 9, no. 3 (2005): 301–20. https://doi.org/10.1080/14797580500179634.

Forster, Kurt W. *Monument/Memory*. New York: Published for the Institute for Architecture and Urban Studies by Rizzoli, 1982.

Forty, Adrian, and Susanne Küchler, eds. *The Art of Forgetting*. Materializing Culture. Oxford; New York: Berg, 1999.

Gadamer, Hans-Georg. *Truth and Method*. New York: Crossroad, 1989.

Ghirardo, Diane Yvonne. "Italian Architects and Fascist Politics: An Evaluation of the Rationalist's Role in Regime Building." *Journal of the Society of Architectural Historians* 39, no. 2 (1980): 109–27. https://doi.org/10.2307/989580.

Grinceri, Daniel. *Architecture as Cultural and Political Discourse: Case Studies of Conceptual Norms and Aesthetic Practices*. Routledge Research in Architecture. London: Routledge, Taylor & Francis Group, 2016.

Gross, David. *The Past in Ruins: Tradition and the Critique of Modernity*. Critical Perspectives on Modern Culture. Amherst: University of Massachusetts Press, 1992.

Halbwachs, Maurice. *On Collective Memory*. Translated by Lewis A. Coser. Chicago: University of Chicago Press, 1992.

Handa, Rumiko. *Allure of the Incomplete, Imperfect, and Impermanent: Designing and Appreciating Architecture as Nature*. New York: Routledge, 2015.

"Hannah Arendt's Failures of Imagination." *The New Yorker*. December 3, 2013. www.newyorker.com/books/page-turner/hannah-arendts-failures-of-imagination.

Heiden, Konrad. *The Führer*. Translated by Ralph Manheim and Richard Overy. New York: Skyhorse Publishing, 2012.

Herf, Jeffrey. *Divided Memory: The Nazi Past in the Two Germanys*. Cambridge, MA: Harvard University Press, 1997.

Hirst, Paul Q. *Space and Power: Politics, War and Architecture*. Cambridge: Polity, 2005.

Hitler, Adolf. *My Battle (Mein Kampf)*. Translated by E. T. S. Dugdale. Boston: Houghton Mifflin Co, 1933.

———, Norman Cameron, R. H. Stevens, H. R Trevor-Roper, and Gerhard L. Weinberg. *Hitler's Table Talk, 1941–1944: His Private Conversations*. New York: Enigma Books, 2008.

"Hitler as Architect." *Time*. Accessed March 3, 2019. http://content.time.com/time/magazine/article/0,9171,904369,00.html.

Hooper, Glenn, and John J. Lennon, ed. Dark Tourism: Practice and Interpretation. London: Routledge, 2017.

"How World War II Is Taught in Different European Countries – OneEurope." Accessed August 29, 2018. http://one-europe.net/how-wwii-is-taught-in-european-countries-part-1 and http://one-europe.net/how-wwii-is-taught-in-different-european-countries-part-2.

Huse, Norbert. *Denkmalpflege: deutsche Texte aus drei Jahrhunderten*. München: Beck, 2006.

———. *Unbequeme Baudenkmale: Entsorgen? Schützen? Pflegen?* München: C. H. Beck, 1997.

Huyssen, Andreas. "Nostalgia for Ruins." *Grey Room*, no. 23 (2006): 6–21.

———. *Present Pasts: Urban Palimpsests and the Politics of Memory*. Stanford, CA: Stanford University Press, 2003.

James-Chakraborty, Kathleen. *Modernism as Memory Building Identity in the Federal Republic of Germany*. Minneapolis: University of Minnesota Press, 2018.

Jordan, Jennifer A. *Structures of Memory: Understanding Urban Change in Berlin and Beyond*. Cultural Memory in the Present. Stanford, CA: Stanford University Press, 2006.

Karl-Hofer-Symposion, and Wolfgang Ruppert, eds. *"Deutschland, bleiche Mutter" oder eine neue Lust an der nationalen Identität?: Texte des Karl-Hofer-Symposions, 12.-17. 11. 1990*. Berlin: Hochschule der Künste, 1992.

Kelly, Michael R. "Review of Memory, History, Forgetting, by Paul Ricoeur, Kathleen Blamey, and David Pellauer." *The Review of Metaphysics* 59, no. 3 (2006): 675–7.

Koschorke, Albrecht. *On Hitler's Mein Kampf: The Poetics of National Socialism*. Translated by Erik Butler. Cambridge, MA: The MIT Press, 2017.

Koshar, Rudy. *From Monuments to Traces: Artifacts of German Memory, 1870–1990*. Weimar and Now. Berkeley: University of California Press, 2000. http://libproxy.unl.edu/login?url=http://search.ebscohost.com/login.aspx?direct=true&db=nlebk&AN=66386&site=ehost-live.

———. *Germany's Transient Pasts: Preservation and National Memory in the Twentieth Century*. Chapel Hill: University of North Carolina Press, 1998.

Krier, Léon. *Albert Speer Architect 1932–1942*. New York: Monacelli Press, 2013; A Bruxelles: Aux Archives d'architecture moderne, 1985.

Lennon, J. John. "Dark Tourism Sites: Visualization, Evidence and Visitation." *Worldwide Hospitality and Tourism Themes* 9, no. 2 (2017): 216–27. https://doi.org/10.1108/WHATT-09-2016-0042.

Lethen, Helmut. "Kracauer's Pendulum: Thoughts on German Cultural History." *New German Critique*, no. 65 (1995): 37–45. https://doi.org/10.2307/488531.

Levi, Primo. *Survival in Auschwitz*. New York: Touchstone Books, 1996.

Lowenthal, David. "Fabricating Heritage." *History & Memory* 10, no. 1 (March 30, 2011): 5–24.

———. "History and Memory." *The Public Historian* 19, no. 2 (1997): 30–9. https://doi.org/10.2307/3379138.

198 Bibliography

———. *Possessed by the Past: The Heritage Crusade and the Spoils of History.* London: The Free Press, 1997.

———. *The Past Is a Foreign Country.* Cambridge: Cambridge University Press, 1985.

Lüdtke, Alf. "'Coming to Terms with the Past': Illusions of Remembering, Ways of Forgetting Nazism in West Germany." *The Journal of Modern History* 65, no. 3 (1993): 542–72.

Maier, Charles S. *The Unmasterable Past: History, Holocaust, and German National Identity.* Cambridge, MA: Harvard University Press, 1997.

Mitscherlich, Alexander, and Margarete Mitscherlich. *The Inability to Mourn: Principles of Collective Behavior.* New York: Grove Press.

"Monument Protection in Germany | Historic England." Accessed November 25, 2019. http://historicengland.org.uk/whats-new/debate/recent/town-and-country-planning-act-70th-anniversary/monument-protection-in-germany/.

Nerdinger, Winfried. *Architektur – Macht – Erinnerung: Stellungnahmen 1984–2004.* Edited by Christoph Hölz and Regina Prinz. München: Prestel Verlag, 2004.

———, ed. *Bauen im Nationalsozialismus: Bayern 1933–1945.* München: Architekturmuseum der Technischen Universität München, 1993.

———. "Umgang mit den Spuren Der NS-Vergangenheit – Indizien Zu Einer Geschichte Der Verdrängung Und Zum Ende Der Trauerarbeit." In *"Deutschland, Bleiche Mutter" Order Eine Neue Lust an Der Nationalen Identität.* Edited by Wolfgang Ruppert. Berlin: Hochschule der Künste, 1992: 51–60.

———. "Umgang mit NS Architektur – Das Schlechte Beispiel München." *Werk Und Zeit,* no. 3 (1988): 22–6.

Neumann, Klaus. *Shifting Memories: The Nazi Past in the New Germany.* Ann Arbor: University of Michigan Press, 2000.

Nora, Pierre, and Lawrence D. Kritzman. *Realms of Memory: Conflicts and Divisions.* New York: Columbia University Press, 1996.

Oakman, Joan. "The Most Interesting Form of Lie." *Oppositions,* no. 24 (Spring 1981): 38–47.

Olick, Jeffrey K. "What Does It Mean to Normalize the Past?: Official Memory in German Politics since 1989." In *States of Memory.* Edited by Jeffrey K. Olick, Julia Adams, and George Steinmetz. Durham, NC: Duke University Press, 2003: 259–88. https://doi.org/10.1215/9780822384687-010.

Peirce, Charles S. (Charles Sanders). *Philosophical Writings of Peirce, Selected and with an Introduction by Justus Buchler.* New York: Dover Publications, 1955.

———. Nathan Houser, and Christian J. W. Kloesel. *The Essential Peirce: Selected Philosophical Writings.* Bloomington: Indiana University Press, 1992.

Penhall, Michele M. *Stories from the Camera: Reflections on the Photograph.* Albuquerque: University of New Mexico Press, 2015. http://public.eblib.com/choice/publicfullrecord.aspx?p=4436037.

Philpott, Colin. *Relics of the Reich: The Buildings the Nazis Left Behind.* Barnsley, South Yorkshire: Pen & Sword Military, 2016.

Ricoeur, Paul. *Memory, History, Forgetting.* Chicago: University of Chicago Press, 2004.

Riegl, Aloïs. "The Modern Cult of Monuments: Its Character and Origin." Translated by Kurt W. Forster and Diane Ghirardo. *Opposition* 25 (1982): 20–51.

Rosenfeld, Gavriel D. "The Architects' Debate: Architectural Discourse and the Memory of Nazism in the Federal Republic of Germany, 1977–1997." *History and Memory* 9, no. 1/2 (1997): 189–225.

———, and Paul B. Jaskot, eds. *Beyond Berlin: Twelve German Cities Confront the Nazi Past.* Social History, Popular Culture, and Politics in Germany. Ann Arbor: University of Michigan Press, 2008.

Bibliography   **199**

Ruppert, Wolfgang, Hochschule der Künste Berlin, and Karl-Hofer-Symposion. *"Deutschland, bleiche Mutter" oder eine neue Lust an der nationalen Identität?: Texte des Karl Hofer Symposions, 12. – 17.11.1990.* Berlin, 1992.

Rürup, Reinhard. *Der lange Schatten des Nationalsozialismus: Geschichte, Geschichtspolitik und Erinnerungskultur.* Göttingen: Wallstein Verlag, 2014.

Schmemann, Serge. "Working through the Past." *The New York Times*, April 22, 2015. www.nytimes.com/2015/04/23/opinion/working-through-the-past.html.

Schöllgen, Gregor. "Speichern: In Der Kulisse Des Führers." *Frankfurter Allgemeine Zeitung*, April 7, 1998, sec. no. 82, page 44. https://fazarchiv.faz.net/fazDocument/saveSingleDoc/FAZ__F19980407REICHSP100.

Scobie, Alexander. *Hitler's State Architecture: The Impact of Classical Antiquity.* Monographs on the Fine Arts 45. University Park: Published for College Art Association by the Pennsylvania State University Press, 1990.

Sebald, W. G. *On The Natural History of Destruction.* London: Notting Hill Editions, 2012.

Simine, Silke Arnold-de. "The Ruin as Memorial – The Memorial as Ruin." *Performance Research* 20, no. 3 (May 4, 2015): 94–102. https://doi.org/10.1080/13528165.2015.1049040.

Sonne, Wolfgang. "The City and the Act of Remembering." *Daidalos* 58 (1995): 90–101.

Speer, Albert. *Inside the Third Reich: Memoirs.* Translated by Richard Winston and Clara Winston. New York: The Macmillan Company, 1970.

Sudjic, Deyan. *The Edifice Complex: How the Rich and Powerful Shape the World.* London: Allen Lane, 2005.

Taylor, Robert R. *The Word in Stone: The Role of Architecture in the National Socialist Ideology.* Berkeley: University of California Press, 1974.

Theodor W. Adorno. "The Meaning of Working through the Past." In *Critical Models: Interventions and Catchwords*, 89–103. New York: Columbia University Press, 2005.

Thies, Jochen. *Hitler's Plans for Global Domination: Nazi Architecture and Ultimate War Aims.* New York: Berghahn Books, 2014.

Trachtenberg, Marvin. *Building-in-Time: From Giotto to Alberti and Modern Oblivion.* New Haven, CT: Yale University Press, 2010.

Virilio, Paul, and Musée des arts décoratifs (France). *Bunker Archeology.* Princeton, NJ: Princeton Architectural Press, 2008.

Wiesenthal, Simon, Harry J. Cargas, and Bonny V. Fetterman. *The Sunflower: On the Possibilities and Limits of Forgiveness.* 2nd. ed. New York: Schocken Books, 1997.

Wolin, Sheldon S. *The Presence of the Past: Essays on the State and the Constitution.* The Johns Hopkins Series in Constitutional Thought. Baltimore: Johns Hopkins University Press, 1989.

Wüstenberg, Jenny. *Civil Society and Memory in Postwar Germany.* Cambridge: Cambridge University Press, 2017.

Yates, Francis A. *The Art of Memory.* Chicago: University of Chicago Press, 1966.

Young, James E. *The Texture of Memory: Holocaust Memorials and Meaning.* New Haven, CT: Yale University Press, 1993.

———. *The Art of Memory: Holocaust Memorials in History.* New York: Prestel, 1994.

———. "Memory and Counter-Memory." *Harvard Design Magazine*, Constructions of Memory: On Monuments Old and New, no. 9 (Fall 1999). www.harvarddesignmagazine.org/issues/9/memory-and-counter-memory.

———. *At Memory's Edge: After-Images of the Holocaust in Contemporary Art and Architecture.* New Haven, CT: Yale University Press, 2000.

Zalampas, Sherree O. *Adolf Hitler: A Psychological Interpretation of His Views on Architecture Art and Music.* Bowling Green, OH: Bowling Green State University Popular Press, 1990.

200 Bibliography

Archives
Cologne

NS-Documentation Center of the City of Cologne Library.
Deutscher Architekturmuseum Frankfurt, Peter Kulka archive.

Carrington, Bettina, and Layla Dawson. "Peter Zumthor Fuses a Historical Palimpsest with
Modernism at Kolumba, Art Museum of the Archdiocese of Cologne, Lending the Space
a New Kind of Spiritual Overtone." *Architectural Record* 196, no. 1 (January 2008): 78–87.
Deutsches Architekturmuseum, ed. *Architektur Jahrbuch*. München: Prestel, 1992.
Duka, Dominik. *Kolumba*. Prague: Krystal Publishers, 2011.
Kastner Pichler Architekten. "EL–DE–Haus." Accessed May 16, 2018. http://kastnerpichler.
de/portfolio/el–de–haus/.
Förster, Yorck. "Das Archiv Peter Kulka im DAM = The Peter Kulka Archives in the DAM."
*DAM-Jahrbuch / hrsg. vom Deutschen Architektur-Museum, Frankfurt am Main ; im Auftr. des
Dezernats für Kultur und Freizeit, Amt für Wissenschaft und Kunst der Stadt Frankfurt am
Main.*, 2006, 178–81.
Förster, Yorck, Ingeborg Flagge, Peter Kulka, and Deutsches Architekturmuseum, eds. *Peter
Kulka – Minimalismus und Sinnlichkeit: [Katalog anläßlich der Ausstellung "Peter Kulka,
Minimalismus und Sinnlichkeit" im Deutschen Architektur Museum (DAM), Frankfurt am Main,
11. November 2005 bis 5. Februar 2006, und der anschließenden Wanderausstellung] = Peter
Kulka – Minimalism and Sensuality*. Stuttgart: Menges, 2005.
Haupt, Peter, Wolfgang Pehnt, and Kristin Feireiss. *Egon Eiermann: Die Kaiser-Wilhelm-
Gedächtnis-Kirche*. Berlin: Ernst, 1994.
Huiskes, Manfred, and Alexandra Gal, eds. *Die Wandinschriften des Kölner Gestapo-Gefängnisses
im EL-DE-Haus, 1943 – 1945*. Mitteilungen aus dem Stadtarchiv von Köln 70.
Köln: Böhlau, 1983.
Jaeger, F. "Kunstgalerie in Leipzig – Peter Kulka." *Deutsche Bauzeitung* 133, no. 1 (1999): 54–61.
Jager, Markus. "Gästehaus der Benediktinerabtei Königsmünster, Meschede: [Architekten:]
Peter Kulka mit Konstantin Pichler, Mitarbeit: Werner Gronmayer, Realisierung: 1999–
2000." *Architektur-Jahrbuch / hrsg. vom Deutschen Architektur-Museum, Frankfurt am Main;
hrsg. im Auftr. d. Dezernats für Kultur und Freizeit, Amt für Wissenschaft und Kunst der Stadt
Frankfurt am Main.*, 2001, 108–13.
Jung, Werner. *Wände, die sprechen: die Wandinschriften im Kölner Gestapogefängnis im EL-DE-
Haus = Walls that talk: the wall inscriptions in the Cologne Gestapo prison in the EL-DE-House*.
Köln: Emons, 2014.
Kaehler, G. "Benedictine after All? The Architecture of Peter Kulka." *ARCHIS*, no. 11
(1998): 62–73.
Kaufmann, Stefan. "NS-Dokumentationszentrum Köln: 700.000 Euro Für Erweiterung Des
NS-DOK." *Die Welt*, August 14, 2012. www.welt.de/regionales/koeln/article108619066/
700-000-Euro-fuer-Erweiterung-des-NS-DOK.html.
Kolumba (Körperschaft), and Römisch-Germanisches Museum. *Pas de deux*. Cologne:
Kolumba, 2018.
Kulka, Peter. *Bauten Und Projekte 1990–95*. Köln: König, 1996.
———. "NS-Dokumentationszentrum Im EL-DE-Haus, Koln, Appellhofplaz 23–25,"
May 1993.
———, Yorck Förster, and Ingeborg Flagge. *Peter Kulka: Minimalismus und Sinnlichkeit =
Minimalism and sensuality*. Stuttgart: Edition Axel Menges, 2006.
———, Werner Strodthoff, and Kirsten Schewe. *Peter Kulka: Bauten und Projekte, 1990–95*.
Köln: W. König, 1996.

Kulturverwaltung der Stadt Köln, and Peter Kulka. "NS-Dokumentationszentrum Im EL-DE Haus Köln," not dated. DAM.

Lauterbach, Iris, Julian Rosefeldt, and Piero Steinle, eds. *Bürokratie Und Kult: Das Parteizentrum Der NSDAP Am Königsplatz in München: Geschichte Und Rezeption*. Veröffentlichungen Des Zentralinstituts Für Kunstgeschichte, Bd 10. München: Deutscher Kunstverlag, 1995.

Leib, Hajo, and Karola Fings. *Empathie und Engagement: drei Jahrzehnte Kölner Zeitgeschichte: Verein EL-DE-Haus, Förderverein des NS-Dokumentationszentrums der Stadt Köln*. Köln: Verein EL-DE-Haus e.V., 2017.

Matzerath, Horst. *Köln in der Zeit des Nationalsozialismus 1933–1945*. Köln: Greven, 2009.

NS-Dokumentationszentrum, ed. *Cologne during National Socialism: A Short Guide through the EL-DE House*. Köln: NS Documentation Centre of the City of Cologne: Emons, 2011.

"NS-Dokumentationszentrum Köln – NSDOK." Accessed February 7, 2019. https://museenkoeln.de/ns-dokumentationszentrum/default.aspx?s=686.

Pehnt, Wolfgang. "Ein Haus Für Sinn Und Sinne: Diözesanmuseum Kolumba in Köln, Peter Zumthor." *Baumeister* 104, no. 11 (November 2007): 48–63.

———, and G. Böhm. *Gottfried Böhm*. Studio Paperback. Basel; Boston: Birkhäuser, 1999.

Penhall, Michele M. *Stories from the Camera: Reflections on the Photograph*. Albuquerque: University of New Mexico Press, 2015. http://public.eblib.com/choice/publicfullrecord. aspx?p=4436037.

Strodthoff, W. "Das Kölner El-De-Haus Als NS-Dokumentationszentrum." *BAUWELT* 88, no. 37 (1997): 2099–101.

Nuremberg

Architekturzentrum Wien, Günther Domenig archive.

Colwell-Chanthaphonh, Chip. "Fascination and Terror." Edited by William Logan, Keir Reeves, and Sharon Macdonald. *Current Anthropology* 51, no. 3 (2010): 445–6. https://doi.org/10.1086/652279.

"DOCUMENTA (13)." Accessed May 25, 2017. http://d13.documenta.de/#participants/participants/michael-petzet/.

Dornberg, John. "Nuremberg Rebuilt: City at the Crossroads." *The New York Times*, April 8, 1984, sec. Travel. www.nytimes.com/1984/04/08/travel/nuremberg-rebuilt-city-at-the-crossroads.html.

Eichhorn, Ernst, Wolfgang Schramm, and Otto P. Görl. *3 x Nürnberg: Eine Bilderfolge aus unserem Jahrhundert*. Nürnberg: Verlag A. Hofmann, 2004.

Erlanger, Steven. "Nuremberg Journal; The Architect Who Speared His Own Nazi Demon." *The New York Times*, November 8, 2001. www.nytimes.com/2001/11/08/world/nuremberg-journal-the-architect-who-speared-his-own-nazi-demon.html.

Glaser, Hermann. "The Majority Could Have Stayed away without the Risk of Repression." In *The German Public and the Persecution of the Jews, 1933–1945*. Edited by Jörg Wollenberg and Rado Pribić. Atlantic Highlands, NJ: Humanities Press, 1996: 15–21.

Handa, Rumiko. "Presenting the Extremely Difficult Past: Günther Domenig's Documentation Center of the National Socialist Party Rally Grounds, Nuremberg, Germany." *Montreal Architectural Review* 4 (December 31, 2017). http://mar.mcgill.ca/article/view/32.

Headlam, Cecil. *The Story of Nuremberg*. 4th ed. London: J.M. Dent & Co, 1904. http://hdl.handle.net/2027/hvd.hn88tw.

202 Bibliography

Macdonald, Sharon. *Difficult Heritage: Negotiating the Nazi Past in Nuremberg and Beyond.* New York: Routledge, 2009.

Mende, Matthias, Henry Meyric Hughes, and Museen. *The Dürer House Nuremberg.* Nürnberg: Museen der Stadt Nürnberg, 1973.

Museen. "Dokumentationszentrum Reichsparteitagsgelände." Museen der Stadt Nürnberg. Accessed February 7, 2019. https://museen.nuernberg.de/dokuzentrum/.

"Nuremberg Rebuilt – City At The Crossroads." *New York Times.* Accessed July 27, 2017. www.nytimes.com/1984/04/08/travel/nuremberg-rebuilt-city-at-the-crossroads.html?pagewanted=all.

Nuremberg (Germany), and Albrecht Dürer Haus Stiftung. *The Dürer House in Nuremberg: The Home of Albrecht Dürer. Albrecht Dürer. The History of the Dürer House. Extracts from Dürer's Family Chronicle and Reminiscences. A Chronological Outline of Dürer's Life and Work.* Nuremberg: Albrecht Dürer Haus Stiftung, 1961.

Ogan, Bernd, and Wolfgang W Weiss. *Faszination und Gewalt: Nürnberg Und Der Nationalsozialismus: Eine Ausstellung.* Nürnberg: Pädagogisches Institut der Stadt Nürnberg, 1990.

———. *Faszination und Gewalt: Zur politischen Ästhetik des Nationalsozialismus.* Nürnberg: Tümmels, 1992.

Schmidt, Alexander, Bernd Windsheimer, Clemens Wachter, and Thomas Heyden. *Geländebegehung: das Reichsparteitagsgelände in Nürnberg.* Nürnberg: Sandberg Verlag, 2005.

———, Martina Christmeier, and Museen der Stadt Nürnberg. *Das Gelände: Dokumentation, Perspektiven, Diskussion, 1945–2015: Ausstellungskatalog des Dokumentationszentrums Reichsparteitagsgelände.* Petersberg: Michael Imhof Verlag, 2015.

Sonnenberger, Franz. "A City Confronts Its Past: Nuremberg's Documentation Centre on the Reich Party Congress Site; 1999." *Museum International* 51, no. 3 (July 1999): 53–7.

———, Eckart Dietzfelbinger, and Nuremberg Municipal Museums. *Faszination und Gewalt, das Reichsparteitagesgelände in Nürnberg = Fascination and Terror, The Nazi Party Rally Grounds in Nuremberg.* Nürnberg: Museen der Stadt Nürnberg, 1996.

———, Museen., Nürnberg. Internationales Symposium Die Zukunft der Vergangenheit – Wie Soll NS-Geschichte in Museen und Gedenkstätten im 21. Jahrhundert Vermittelt Werden? 1999, and Deutsch-Amerikanisches Institut., eds. *Die Zukunft der Vergangenheit: wie soll die Geschichte des Nationalsozialismus in Museen und Gedenkstätten im 21. Jahrhundert vermittelt werden?: Internationales Symposium am 13. und 14. November 1999 im Deutsch-Amerikanischen Institut / Amerika Haus in Nürnberg; [das … abgehaltene Internationale Symposium "Die Zukunft der Vergangenheit – Wie soll NS-Geschichte in Museen und Gedenkstätten im 21. Jahrhundert vermittelt werden?" …] = The Future of the Past: How Should the History of the Third Reich Be Transmitted in the 21st Century?* Nürnberg: Museen der Stadt Nürnberg, 2000.

Täubrich, Hans-Christian, ed. *Die Kongresshalle Nürnberg: Architektur Und Geschichte.* Schriftenreihe Der Museen Der Stadt Nürnberg / Museen Der Stadt Nürnberg. Petersberg: Michael Imhof Verlag, 2014.

Täubrich, Hans-Christian, ed. *Fascination and Terror: Documentation Centre Party Rally Grounds: The Exhibition.* Nürnberg: Museen der Stadt Nürnberg, 2006.

Berlin

Topography of Terror Foundation Library.

Heinle, Wischer und Partner.

Bibliography 203

Ballhausen, Nils. "Dokumentationszentrum Der Stiftung Topographie Des Terrors." *Bauwelt* 101, no. 16 (April 23, 2010): 20–7.

Barthel, Eckhardt. "Statement Zur Podiumsdiskussion Beim Öffentlichen Symposium Der Stiftung Topographie Des Terrors Am 9. Juli 2004." In *Historischer Ort Und Historische Dokumentation: Bauen Für Die "Topographie Des Terrors"*, 2004. www.topographie. de/veranstaltungen/veranstaltung/nc/1/nid/historischer-ort-und-historische-dokumentation-bauen-fuer-die-topographie-des-terrors/y/2004/m/07/d/09/z/1/?type=98.

Broder, Henryk M. "Holocaust Memorial: Over the Führerbunker, Berlin." *Spiegel Online*, May 10, 2005, sec. Culture. www.spiegel.de/kultur/gesellschaft/holocaust-mahnmal-ueber-dem-fuehrerbunker-berlin-a-355267.html.

Bucholtz, Erika, Philipp Dittrich, Angela L Kauls, Stiftung Topographie des Terrors, Germany, and Bundesamt für Bauwesen und Raumordnung. *Realisierungswettbewerb Topographie des Terrors, Berlin: 309 Entwürfe – Katalog zur Ausstellung der Wettbewerbsarbeiten.* Berlin: Bundesamt für Bauwesen und Raumordnung: Stiftung Topographie des Terrors, 2006.

Bucholtz, Erika, Andreas Nachama, Stiftung Topographie des Terrors, and Stiftung Topographie des Terrors – Internationales Dokumentations- und Begegnungszentrum. *Site Tour "Topography of Terror" History of the Site.* Berlin: Stiftung Topographie des Terrors, 2016.

Czaplicka, John. "History, Aesthetics, and Contemporary Commemorative Practice in Berlin." *New German Critique*, no. 65 (1995): 155–87. https://doi.org/10.2307/488540.

Donath, Matthias. *Architecture in Berlin 1933–1945: A Guide through Nazi Berlin.* Berlin: Lukas Verlag, 2006.

Fock, Gisela. "Die Kaiser-Wilhelm-Gedächtniskirche von Egon Eiermann." 1995.

Gerlach, Erwin. *Berlin: Kaiser Wilhelm Memorial Church.* Regensburg: Schnell & Steiner, 1998.

Helmer, Stephen D. *Hitler's Berlin: The Speer Plans for Reshaping the Central City.* Architecture and Urban Design, no. 14. Ann Arbor, Mich: UMI Research Press, 1985.

Hofer, Franz D. "Memorial Sites and the Affective Dynamics of Historical Experience In Berlin And Tokyo," A Dissertation Presented to the Faculty of the Graduate School of Cornell University In Partial Fulfillment of the Requirements for the Degree of Doctor of Philosophy, 2012.

Hoffman-Axthelm, Dieter, Andreas Nachama, and Nils Ballhausen. "Ein Treffen Im 'Sprechzimmer Der Geschichte.'" *Bauwelt* 101, no. 16 (April 23, 2010): 12–19.

———. "Architektur Als Gedächtnis: Über Die Möglichkeiten, Abwesendes Abzubilden." *Werk, Bauen & Wohnen* 76, no. 1/2 (1989): 28–31.

———. "Die Topographen Sind Am Ziel, Der Ort Geht Unter: Zur Entscheidung Eines Weiteren Wettbewerbs Zur 'Topographie Des Terrors' in Berlin." *Bauwelt* 97, no. 9 (February 24, 2006): 14–31.

———. "Zur Zeit: Notizen: Topographie Des Terrors." *Ästhetik Und Kommunikation*, no. 126 (2004): 4–5.

Ladd, Brian. *The Ghosts of Berlin: Confronting German History in the Urban Landscape.* Chicago: University of Chicago Press, 1997.

Lehrer, Steven. *The Reich Chancellery and Führerbunker Complex: An Illustrated History of the Seat of the Nazi Regime.* Jefferson, NC: McFarland & Co, 2006.

Leoni, Claudio. "Peter Zumthor's 'Topography of Terror.'" *Arq: Architectural Research Quarterly* 18, no. 2 (June 2014): 110–22.

Nachama, Andreas. "Topographie Des Terrors: Wittbewerb Für Ein Dokumentationsgebäude." *Bau Und Raum: Jahrbuch, Bundesamt Für Bauwesen Und Raumordnung*, 2006, 118–29.

204 Bibliography

———. *Topography of Terror Gestapo, SS and Reich Security Main Office on Wilhelm-and Prinz-Albrecht-Strasse*. Berlin: Stiftung Topographie des Terrors, 2010.

Realisierungswettbewerb Topographie des Terrors.Berlin: 309 Entwürfe – Katalog zur Ausstellung der Wettbewerbsarbeiten. Berlin: Stiftung Topographie d. Terrors, 2006.

Rürup, Reinhard, ed. *Topography of Terror: Gestapo, SS and Reichssicherheitshauptamt on the "Prinz-Albrecht-Terrain": A Documentation*. Trans. Werner T. Angress. Berlin: W. Arenhövel, 1989.

Schultz, Eberhard. "Kontrapunkt des Kurfürstendamms: Kaiser-Wilhelm-Gedächtniskirche, Berlin." In *Deutsche Architektur Nach 1945: Vierzig Jahre Moderne in Der Bundesrepublik*. Edited by Schreiber, Mathias and Peter M. Bode. Stuttgart: Deutsche Verlags-Anstalt, 1986: 53–5.

Scobie, Alexander. *Hitler's State Architecture: The Impact of Classical Antiquity*. Monographs on the Fine Arts 45. University Park: Published for College Art Association by the Pennsylvania State University Press, 1990.

Steiner, Jürg, and Nils Ballhausen. "'Mein Vorbild War Das Farnsworth House von Mies van Der Rohe': Gesrpäch Mit Jürg Steiner." *Bauwelt* 101, no. 16 (April 23, 2010): 28–31.

Stiftung Kaiser-Wilhelm-Gedächtniskirche. *Kaiser-Wilhelm-Gedächtnis-Kirche: Zukunftsperspektiven Für Ein Nationales Denkmal*. Berlin: Stiftung Kaiser-Wilhelm- Gedächtniskirche, 2017.

Stiftung Topographie des Terrors, Berlin, ed. *Topographie Des Terrors: Ausstellungen 1987–2017*. Berlin: Stiftung Topographie des Terrors, Berlin, 2017.

———. Bericht April 2003 bis März 2006. Berlin: Stiftung Topographie des Terrors, 2006.

———. Bericht April 2006 bis Mai 2010. Berlin: Stiftung Topographie des Terrors, 2010.

Till, Karen E. *The New Berlin: Memory, Politics, Place*. Minneapolis: University of Minnesota Press, 2005.

Volkmann, Barbara. *Diskussion zum Umgang mit dem "Gestapo-Gelände": Dokumentation ; [Diskussionsbeiträge anläßlich des Hearings zum Umgang mit dem "Gestapo-Gelände" am 27. Februar 1986 in der Akademie der Künste*. Berlin, 1986.

Winters, Peter Jochen, Florian Bolk, and Robert Bryce. *Topography of Terror Documentation Centre Berlin*. Berlin: Stadtwandel-Verl., 2012.

Zumthor, Peter. *Stabwerk: internationales Besucher- und Dokumentationszentrum "Topographie des Terrors," Berlin: Ausstellung 6. Dezember 1995-4. Februar 1996*. Berlin: Aedes Galerie und Architekturforum, 1995.

Munich

NS Documentation Center Munich.
Georg Scheel Wetzel Architekten.

Adam, Hubertus. *NS-Dokumentationszentrum München: Georg – Scheel – Wetzel Architekten; Lern- Und Erinnerungsort Zur Geschichte Des Nationalsozialismus*. Altenburg: Druckerei zu Altenburg, 2015.

Altenbuchner, Klaus, and Angelika Baumann, eds. *Ein NS-Dokumentationszentrum für München: ein Symposium in zwei Teilen, 5. bis 7. 12. 2002, 16. bis 17. 1. 2003: Tagungsband*. München: Kulturreferat der Landeshauptstadt München: Bayerische Landeszentrale für politische Bildungsarbeit, 2003.

Donath, Matthias. *Architektur in München: 1933–1945: ein Stadtführer*. Berlin: Lukas-Verl., 2007.

Dresler, Adolf. *Das Braune Haus und die Verwaltungsgebäude der Reichsleitung der NSDAP.* München: F. Eher Nachf, 1939. http://books.google.com/books?id=V7pcPZFf_3sC.

Eisen, Markus, Mirjana Grdanjski, Hans Günter Hockerts, Marita Krauss, Peter Longerich, Winfried Nerdinger, and NS-Dokumentationszentrum München. *NS-Dokumentationszentrum München: Munich Documentation Centre for the History of National Socialism; brief guide to the exhibit.* München: NS-Dokumentationszentrum, 2015.

Grammbitter, Ulrike, Klaus Bäumler, and Iris Lauterbach. *The NSDAP Centre in Munich.* Berlin [u.a.]: Dt. Kunstverl., 2015.

Nerdinger, Winfried, Christoph Hölz, and Regina Prinz. *Architekur macht erinnerung Stellungnahmen 1984 bis 2004.* München: Prestel, 2004.

————, and Metropol-Verlag. *Erinnerung gegründet auf Wissen/Remembrance Based on Knowledge Das NS-Dokumentationszentrum München/The Munich Documentation Centre for the History of National Socialism.* Berlin: Metropol Verlag, 2018.

————. 建築・権力・記憶: ナチズムとその周辺 [*Kenchiku・Kenryoku・Kioku: Nachizumu to Sono Shuhen*]. Translated by 海老澤模奈人 [Ebisawa Monato]. 東京 [Tokyo]: 鹿島出版会 [Kashima Shuppan-kai], 2009.

NS-Dokumentationszentrum München, Hans Günter Hockerts, Marita Krauss, Peter Longerich, and Winfried Nerdinger. *Munich and National Socialism: Catalogue of the Munich Documentation Centre for the History of National Socialism.* München: Beck, 2015.

Rosenfeld, Gavriel D. *Munich and Memory: Architecture, Monuments, and the Legacy of the Third Reich.* 1st edition. Berkeley: University of California Press, 2000.

Zentralinstitut für Kunstgeschichte. *Das Parteizentrum Der NSDAP in München.* Berlin: Dt. Kunstverl., 2009.

Buildings and Memorials in the United States

Chotiner, Isaac. "How Should We Remember the Confederacy?" *Slate*, May 9, 2017. www.slate.com/articles/news_and_politics/interrogation/2017/05/should_new_orleans_remove_its_civil_war_monuments_historian_david_blight.html.

Danto, Arthur C. "Vietnam Veterans Memorial." *The Nation* 241, no. 5 (August 31, 1985): 152–5.

Freed, James Ingo, and Janet Adams Strong. *An Architect's Journey: Designing the United States Holocaust Memorial Museum.* Cranford, NJ: Piloti Press, 2012.

Kytle, Ethan J. and Blain Roberts. "Take Down the Confederate Flags, but Not the Monuments." *The Atlantic*, June 25, 2015. www.theatlantic.com/politics/archive/2015/06/-confederate monuments-flags-south-carolina/396836/

Linenthal, Edward Tabor. *Preserving Memory the Struggle to Create America's Holocaust Museum.* New York: Columbia University Press, 2001.

Moomaw, Graham. "Mayor Jones on Confederate Statues: 'Rather than Tearing down, We Should Be Building Up.'" *Richmond Times-Dispatch*, June 27, 2015. www.richmond.com/news/local/city-of-richmond/mayor-jones-on-confederate-statues-rather-than-tearing-down-we/article_ac2e3115-d073-5e56-83b3-55dca3784e4c.html.

Manassas, VA Patch. "Richmond's Monument Avenue: Should Confederate Statues Remain?" ICYMI, May 24, 2017. https://patch.com/virginia/manassas/richmonds-monument-avenue-should-confederate-statues-remain.

Newsome, Melba. "Removing Monuments That Glorify the Confederacy Is More Complicated than You Think." NBC News, April 25, 2017. www.nbcnews.com/news/nbcblk/are-removing-confederate-monuments-erasing-history-n750526.

206 Bibliography

Remnick, Noah. "Yale Grapples with Ties to Slavery in Debate Over a College's Name." *The New York Times*, September 11, 2015, sec. N.Y. / Region. www.nytimes.com/2015/09/12/nyregion/yale-in-debate-over-calhoun-college-grapples-with-ties-to-slavery.html.

Shapiro, Gary. "Opinion | The Meaning of Our Confederate 'Monuments.'" *The New York Times*, May 15, 2017, sec. Opinion. www.nytimes.com/2017/05/15/opinion/the-meaning-of-our-confederate-monuments.html.

The National Trust for Historic Preservation (Stephanie Meeks, President and CEO). "Statement on Confederate Memorials: Confronting Difficult History | National Trust for Historic Preservation." June 19, 2017. https://savingplaces.org/press-center/media-resources/national-trust-statement-on-confederate-memorials.

"Universities and Slavery: Bound by History | Radcliffe Institute for Advanced Study at Harvard University." Accessed August 4, 2017. www.radcliffe.harvard.edu/event/2017-universities-and-slavery-conference.

Upton, Dell. "Confederate Monuments and Civic Values in the Wake of Charlottesville." September 13, 2017. www.sah.org/publications-and-research/sah-blog/sah-blog/2017/09/13/confederate-monuments-and-civic-values-in-the-wake-of-charlottesville.

INDEX

1953 Uprising 21, 87

Active Museum Association, or Verein
    Aktives Museum 56, 139
Administration Building, or Verwaltungsbau
    der NSDAP, Munich 12–7, 42, 59–62, 84,
    88, 94, 107, 117–8, 123, 150, 184
Adorno, Theodor W. 23
Aedes Architekturforum, Berlin 74
Alte Pinakothek, Munich 11, 28, 31–2, 86,
    108, 128, 150
Alte Wache, Cologne 43, 93
Altes Museum, Berlin 72
America House, or Amerika Haus, Munich
    16, 132, 185
Anderle, Walter 143
Anhalter Bahnhof, Berlin 28, 55
Architekturzentrum Wien 143
Arendt, Hannah 12
Association of the Persecuted of the Nazi
    Regime, or Vereinigung der Verfolgten
    des Naziregimes 44, 155
authenticity 1, 3, 5, 11, 22, 39, 74, 86, 90.
    116, 130, 149, 152, 155, 174, 179, 194
Autodrom, Berlin 56
Aviation Ministry building, or
    Reichsluftfahrtministerium, Berlin
    11–2, 19–21, 42, 54, 84, 87, 93, 105, 117,
    125, 186–8

Barthel, Eckhardt 73
Bavarian State Library, Munich 15
Bavarian State Ministry of Food,
    Agriculture and Forests, Munich 84

Bergen Belsen concentration camp 3
Berlin History Workshop 56
Berlin Wall 55, 87, 104–5, 125, 139, 153,
    164, 171
Böhm, Gottfried 33–4
Böhm, Peter 150
Brown House, Munich 2, 39, 59–64, 94,
    107, 117–8, 139, 184
Büro Georg Scheel Wetzel
    Architekten 2, 63

Casey, Edward 77, 80, 88
Central Art Collection Point, Munich 15
Chancellery building, Berlin 19, 54–5, 69,
    72, 86–7
Chamberlain, Neville 13, 186
Chipperfield, David 33
classicism 45, 69, 72, 84, 93, 117
Colosseum, Rome 45, 70
Congress Hall, Nuremberg 12, 19, 45–50,
    69, 100–1, 113–5, 122, 129, 138, 141,
    154, 155, 159–63, 175, 179, 184, 188
Court of Appeals, or Appellationsgerichthof,
    Cologne 41, 43, 93, 112, 181

Dahmen, Georg 44
Dahmen, Leopold 42–3, 157
Daladier, Eduard 13
deconstructivist style 114, 139
denazification 6, 10–2, 14, 17–8, 22, 35, 49,
    151, 152
Denkmal 50, 154
Der Angriff, newspaper 54–5, 104
Der Stümer, newspaper 89

208 Index

designation 58, 81, 83–4, 86–8, 149–72
Deutscher Werkbund 42
Deutsches Architekturmuseum,
 Frankfurt 95
documentation center, Berlin 2, 4, 19, 21,
 52–8, 103–7, 116–7, 125–6, 132–5,
 138–9, 146, 163–5, 185–8
documentation center, Cologne 1, 4, 12,
 40–5, 94–100, 109–12, 120–2, 130–2,
 136–8, 143–6, 155–9, 176–7, 180–1
documentation center, Munich 2, 4,
 58–64, 107–8, 117–20, 123–5, 139,
 165–71, 184–5
documentation center, Nuremberg 2, 4, 12,
 13, 18. 19, 45–52, 100–3, 112–6, 122–3,
 129–30, 138, 139–43, 159–63, 175–6,
 177, 184, 188–91
Döllgast, Hans 31, 128
Domenig, Günther 2, 50, 69, 100–2, 112–6,
 122–5, 129–30, 138, 139–43, 188–90
Donath, Matthias 46
Dürer House, Nuremberg 24–8, 48, 128
Dürer, Albrecht 24

Ehrenmal 50, 154
Eichmann, Adolf 12
Eiermann, Egon 30–1, 128
Eisenman, Peter 2, 57, 89–90, 190
EL-DE House, Cologne 12, 42–4, 93,
 94–100, 112, 130, 136, 155–7, 171,
 176, 180–3
Erberich, Hans 42
Europahaus 52
everyday life 1, 39, 150

Falser, Michael S. 10, 23, 25, 28
Farnsworth House 105
Feldherrnhalle, Munich 87, 151
figurative representation 85
Fischer, Karl von 58–9
Fleischmann, Gerd 45, 180
forgetfulness 3, 23, 43, 48, 154
formal characteristics 7, 19, 81, 83, 84–5,
 92–4, 104, 107–8, 120–3, 125, 136,
 174, 194
Frascari, Marco 82
Frauen Kirche, Nuremberg 48
Frauentorturm, Nuremberg 48
Freed, James Ingo 2
Frese and Kleindienst 50
Führerbau, Munich 11–2, 12–7, 42, 59, 62,
 84–5, 88, 93–4, 107, 117–8, 123, 132–4,
 150–2, 184–5
Führerbunker, Berlin 86–7

Gablonsky, Fritz 85
Gadamer, Hans Georg 7, 81–4
Georg Scheel Wetzel Architekten 2, 63
German Building Exhibition,
 Nuremberg 49
German Empire 48
Gestapo, Secret State Police 1–2, 12, 39,
 42–5, 52–7, 62, 73, 93, 94, 104, 111,
 130–2, 136, 146, 155, 171, 180–1, 182–3
Gigon, Annette and Mike Guyer 33
Glaser, Hermann 12, 47
Glyptothek. Munich 59, 150
Goethe House, Frankfurt 25, 31
Goodacre, Glenna 85
Grassi, Giorgio 56
Grinceri, Daniel 69–70
Gropius, Martin 53
Gropius, Walter 53

Hallmann, Heinz W. 2, 58
Hauptbahnhof, Nuremberg 48, 162
Hauptmarkt, Nuremberg 48
Haus der Kunst, Munich, former Haus der
 Deutschen Kunst 84, 88
Heinle, Wischer und Partner 2, 58
hermeneutics 7, 81–3
Historical Archive of the City of
 Cologne 44
Hitler, Adolf 2, 6, 13, 45–8, 54, 58–9, 68–73,
 77, 86–7, 151–2, 162, 178–9, 184
Hochschule für Musik und Theater,
 Munich 16, 150, 152
Hoffmann-Axthelm, Dieter 72–7, 105
Holocaust, television series 44
Holocaust denial 22
Holy Roman Empire 48, 70
Hölzinger, Johannes 50
Honor Temple(s), or Ehrentempel, Munich
 11–2, 16–8, 59, 63, 88, 94, 107, 117, 123,
 132–3, 184–5
Hotel Prinz Albrecht, originally Hotel
 Römerbad, Berlin 53, 55, 103–4
Hotel Wartburg, Berlin 53

icon 81–4
index 81–4
interpretation 7, 11, 32, 81, 109, 129, 188

Jewish Museum, Berlin 2, 57–8, 85,
 154, 190

Kaiser Wilhelm Memorial Church, Berlin
 27, 28–31, 86, 108, 128
Klenze, Leo von 31, 58–9

Index 209

Kolumba, Cologne 11, 28, 32–4, 75, 86, 109
Königsplatz, originally Königslicher Platz,
  Munich 12, 16–7, 58–9, 62–3, 94, 107,
  123–4, 150, 184
Koschorke, Albrecht 71
Krier, Léon 72
Krier, Rob 72
Kulka, Peter 1–2, 45, 50, 94–7, 109–12,
  120–2, 125, 130–1, 136–7, 180–1

Libeskind, Daniel 85, 190
Lorenzkirche, Nuremberg 48

MacDonald, Sharon 24
Maedge, Sammy 44
Mahnmal 50, 154
Martin-Gropius-Bau, Berlin 55–6, 75,
  117, 163
Matzerath, Horst 44
Mauthalle, Nuremberg 24
Max-Mannheimer-Platz 168
Mein Kampf 69, 71
memento 7–8, 81–4, 88–9, 174–6, 190
Memorial to the Murdered Jews of Europe,
  Berlin 2, 57–8, 89, 154, 190
Métivier, Johann Baptist 59
Mies van der Rohe, Ludwig 105
modernism 117
Mühlen, Norbert 25
Munich Agreement 13, 185
Munich City Museum 63
Museum für Abgüsse Klassischer Bildwerke,
  Munich 150
Museum of Applied Arts, Berlin 53
Mussolini, Benito 13, 70–2, 87

Nachama, Andreas 57, 75–6
Napoleon I and III 71
National Gallery, Washington, D.C. 83, 85
National Socialist German Workers'
  Party, or NSDAP Nationalsozialistische
  Deutche Arbeiterpartei 12, 59
Nazi Party Rally Grounds, Nuremberg 18,
  45, 48, 50, 71, 93, 100, 159
neo-Nazis 3, 22, 50, 151, 152
Nerdinger, Winfried 3–5, 32, 62–4, 77,
  122, 152
Neue Staatsgalerie, Stuttgart 72
Norisring, Nuremberg 18, 48
normalization 6, 10, 11–2, 16, 17, 22, 39, 43,
  128, 138
Nuremberg Castle, Nuremberg 24, 48, 70–1
Nuremberg City Museums 52, 116, 129
Nuremberg Laws 46

Nuremberg Trials 18, 46, 52
Nürnberger Nachrichten, newspaper 24
Nürnberger Symphoniker, Nuremberg 49,
  93, 100, 138

Oakman, Joan 72
Odeonsplatz, Munich 58, 84, 87, 150–1
Opferorte, victims' places 3, 43
Ostia station, Rome 70

Palais Barlow, Munich 13, 59, 93
Palazzo Venezia, Rome 72
Peirce, Charles Sanders 7, 81–4
Petzet, Michael 50, 154
Pfahl, stake or spear 50–2, 100–1, 112, 114,
  122–3, 138, 139–43, 184
physical trace(s) 7, 81, 83, 85–6, 88, 128–47,
  174, 190, 194
Piazza della Signoria, Florence 151
Pichler, Konstantin 1, 45
Pickford, Henry W 90
Platz der Opfer des Nationalsozialismus,
  Munich 62, 150
Platz des Volksaufstandes von 1953, at
  Aviation Ministry, Berlin 21
postmodernism 72
Prinz Albrecht Palais, originally Palais
  Vernezobre, Berlin 53, 55, 104
Propyläen, Munich 12, 59, 184

quasi-memento 8, 88–9, 174–81,
  184–5, 191
Quirinale Palace, Rome 70

Rathaus, Nuremberg 48
Reichsgerichte, Imperial Courts of Law 70
Reichsministerium für Volksaufklärung,
  or Reich Ministry of Popular
  Enlightenment and Propaganda, now
  Federal Ministry of Labor and Social
  Affairs, Berlin 93
Reichsparteitage, Nazi Party Rallies
  46, 48, 70
Reichsparteitagsgelände, Nazi Party Rally
  Grounds, Nuremberg 45, 71, 159, 163
Reichstag, Imperial Diet 48, 70
Reif, Hans 155
representation 7, 81, 85–6, 92, 152
Residenz, Munich 12, 58, 150–1
restoration 10, 23, 24–5, 28, 31–2.
Rock im Park, Nuremberg 18, 48
Rosenfeld, Gavriel 23, 72
Rossi, Aldo 72
Royal Museum of Ethnology, Berlin 53

210 Index

RSHA, or Reich Security Main Office 2, 53–6, 73, 103
Ruff, Franz 45, 184
Ruff, Ludwig 45, 184
Rürup, Reinhard 56, 164, 175

SA, Sturmabteilung, Brownshirts 52
Sagebiel, Ernst 19, 42, 117
Saussure, Ferdinand de 82
Schinkel, Karl Friedrich 53, 72, 104
Schoenberner, Gerhard 155
Schöllgen, Gregor 175
School of Industrial Arts and Crafts, Berlin 53, 55, 103
Schwechten, Franz 28
Sckell, Friedrich Ludwig von 58
Scobie, Alex 70
SD, Sicherheitsdienst (Security Service) 54–5, 73, 104
SDS, Sozialistische Deutsche Studentenbund (Socialist German Student Union) 44
self-victimization 3, 23, 24
semiotics 7, 81–2
Serenadenhof, Nuremberg 49
shelter for Roman archaeological site, Chur 75, 107
Siedler, Eduard Jobst 54
Soldiers' Field, at Zeppelin Field, Nuremberg 18
Sonnenberger, Franz 52, 129–30
Speer, Albert 19, 45, 49, 54–5, 69, 72, 86
SS, Schutzstaffel (Protection Squadron) 2, 39, 53–6, 73, 104
St. Sebald, Nuremberg 48
Staab, Volker 50
Staatliche Antikensammlungen, Munich 59
Steiner, Jürg 53, 56, 75, 164
Stirling, James 72
Streep, Meryl 44
Streicher, Julius 46, 48

symbol 68–70, 72, 73, 76–7, 81–4, 85, 86, 152

Täterorte, perpetrators' places 3, 6, 11–2, 22, 34–5, 39. 68, 129, 152, 194
Thies, Jochen 69, 72
Topography of Terror Foundation 57–8, 74–6, 175
Troost, Paul Ludwig 12–3, 42, 45, 59, 69, 151

United States Holocaust Memorial Museum, Washington, D.C. 52, 57, 129, 154

vegetations 17, 59–60, 62, 94
Vergangenheitsbewältigung, coping with or dealing with the past 3, 10, 23, 34, 73, 94
Victoria and Albert Museum, London 85–6
Vietnam Women's Memorial, Washington, D.C. 85

Wallner, Gerhard 2, 102
Wannsee 89, 155, 190
Weimar 48, 70
Wenzel, Jürgen and Nikolaus Lang 56
Westdeutscher Beobachter, newspaper 42
Wilms, Ursula 2, 58, 105, 117, 125, 186
Wittelbachers Palais, Munich 62
Wojak, Irmtrud 64

Zentralinstitut für Kunstgeschichte, Munich 150
Zeppelin Grandstand, or Zeppelintribüne, Nuremberg 11–2, 17–9, 49–50, 84, 175–6, 179
Zeppelin, Ferdinand Graf von 48
Zeughaus, Cologne 43, 93
Ziebland, Georg Friedrich 59
Zumthor, Peter 7, 32–4, 57–8, 68, 72, 73–6, 104, 107, 109, 128, 139